"Resisting shortsighted stereotypes, Emily Hunter McGowin invites readers into an expansive and beautiful vision of the Christian family. Unafraid of facing imperfection, pointing readers toward the richness found in vulnerability and community, this book keeps it real. McGowin's image of 'apprenticeship to love' offers an especially rich way for any family to imagine—or reimagine—their life together. She invites all readers, precisely in the midst of their own family's particular circumstances, to a way to ask, How will Jesus by his Spirit teach us to love today?"

**Holly Taylor Coolman,** assistant professor of theology at Providence College

"Like having coffee with a wise and gracious friend, but also like contemplating well-crafted art, *Households of Faith* is both approachable and profound. Emily Hunter McGowin embodies her vocation as a pastor-theologian, and in this writing, the reader is invited behind the curtain into the nuts and bolts of her calling. She suffers neither foolishness nor pretense; she gifts her reader the respect of frank speech, which makes you want to purge yourself of the false daydream into which you've been lulled concerning the purpose of families, and press forward instead into the coming kingdom. Neither does she guilt-trip the reader. Her successes spark ideas; her failures remind you that you are not alone and that it is possible to grow in your apprenticeship to love. Her expertise and her passion shine through on each page, providing insightful life hacks, revelations for difficult theological conundrums, and the confidence that the triune God works graciously and mightily through families."

**Amy Peeler,** Kenneth T. Wessner Chair of Biblical Studies at Wheaton College and author of *Women and the Gender of God*

"What does it mean to be a family in today's world? Emily Hunter McGowin asks this question, inspiring the reader to grasp a holistic vision for what family can be in light of God's kingdom. This is an essential question—one that both stimulated and challenged me to grapple with how family life is influenced and shaped by our culture, history, and sentimental yearnings. Both thoughtful and practical, McGowin invites readers to understand the complex world that families exist within and encourages them to live as apprentices to God's love in the daily chaos of our everyday life."

**Mimi L. Larson,** executive director of the Center for Faith and Children and assistant professor of educational ministries at Trinity Evangelical Divinity School

"A warm and loving space to consider the purposes and complexities of family. Setting aside the all-too-familiar trope of the 'ideal' Christian family, Emily Hunter McGowin instead invites us to explore the embodied reality of family life. Family is hard, and we need companions along the way to help us process our past experiences with God and with one another, frame our present, and cultivate hope for the future. With *Households of Faith*, McGowin has given us one such companion that is theologically rich and truly practical."

**Amy Brown Hughes,** associate professor of theology at Gordon College

"Emily Hunter McGowin weaves church history, biblical wisdom, and current-day applications into a highly readable and deeply knowledgeable work. *Households of Faith* will challenge and inspire readers within the context of their own family life as well as within life as part of the larger church family."

**Karen Swallow Prior,** author of *The Evangelical Imagination*

"The Christian family needs to be further radicalized; that is, returned to its life-giving roots and stripped of parasitic accretions. Emily Hunter McGowin does that work, reminding the Christian of what family really is, and in doing so offering a great gift to the people of God. By linking the Christian family tightly to the church, the church to the kingdom of God, and the kingdom to its King Jesus, McGowin narrates a beautiful golden chain that provides the Christian with both vision and practice that leads to Christlikeness. I can think of no better gift to the Christian family than a voice that relentlessly points to the kingdom. Emily McGowin has offered such a voice!"

**Malcolm Foley,** special advisor to the president for equity and campus engagement at Baylor University and author of *The Anti-Greed Gospel*

"Finally, a book that actually looks for the blueprint for families from the words of Jesus! Emily McGowin does not pretend to put forward answers or formulas for the Christian family, but she relies on the verb *practice* as a way of discovering what family means in God's kingdom. For those who desire to practice family as Christians, this book should be your guide."

**Jessica Hooten Wilson,** Fletcher Jones Chair of Great Books at Pepperdine University and author of *The Scandal of Holiness*

Emily Hunter McGowin

# Households
# of Faith

**Practicing Family in
the Kingdom of God**

ivp

An imprint of InterVarsity Press
Downers Grove, Illinois

InterVarsity Press
P.O. Box 1400 | Downers Grove, IL 60515-1426
ivpress.com | email@ivpress.com

©2025 by Emily Hunter McGowin

InterVarsity Press® is the publishing division of InterVarsity Christian Fellowship/USA®. For more information, visit intervarsity.org.

While any stories in this book are true, some names and identifying information may have been changed to protect the privacy of individuals.

The publisher cannot verify the accuracy or functionality of website URLs used in this book beyond the date of publication.

Cover design: David Fassett
Interior design: Daniel van Loon
Images: © marumaru / iStock / Getty Images Plus; © CSA Images via Getty Images;
        © mikroman6 / Moment via Getty Images; © Westend61 via Getty Images

ISBN 978-1-5140-0006-9 (print) | ISBN 978-1-5140-0007-6 (digital)

Printed in the United States of America ∞

**Library of Congress Cataloging-in-Publication Data**
Names: McGowin, Emily Hunter, 1983- author.
Title: Households of faith : practicing family in the kingdom of God / Emily Hunter McGowin.
Description: Downers Grove, IL : IVP, [2025] | Includes bibliographical references and index.
Identifiers: LCCN 2024032133 (print) | LCCN 2024032134 (ebook) | ISBN 9781514000069 (print) | ISBN 9781514000076 (digital)
Subjects: LCSH: Families–Religious aspects–Christianity. | Households–Religious aspects–Christianity. | Christian life. | BISAC: RELIGION / Christian Living / Family & Relationships | FAMILY & RELATIONSHIPS / Alternative Family
Classification: LCC BT707.7 .M35 2025 (print) | LCC BT707.7 (ebook) | DDC 248.4–dc23/eng/20240814
LC record available at https://lccn.loc.gov/2024032133
LC ebook record available at https://lccn.loc.gov/2024032134

32  31  30  29  28  27  26  25  |  13  12  11  10  9  8  7  6  5  4  3  2  1

For my children, William, Emmelia, and Althea,

with gratitude for all we've learned together about

practicing family in God's kingdom.

# Contents

# Introduction

**I don't have** family figured out.

This may not be the wisest way to begin, but I think it's important to manage expectations from the start. I am a theologian, priest, and professor, as well as a daughter, sister, wife, and parent. I have done a lot of thinking about families (almost a decade of research and writing), and spent many years living in families (first my family of origin and then the one I created with my husband, Ronnie). Still, I feel like I'm making it up as I go on a regular basis.

So, please don't assume I write this book as one who has found The Answer for how to be a healthy, gospel-oriented, Jesus-loving, kingdom-rooted Christian family in the twenty-first century. Instead, I write as a fellow laborer in the field, a colearner in the gospel, someone trying to figure out what life in God's kingdom means for households as they face the challenges and opportunities of the contemporary world.

Because Ronnie and I both come from homes marked by abusive relations, alcoholism, and chronic instability, we had to forge a new path when we got married. Many times, we discussed the fact that we didn't have models. We didn't know how to do this mutually loving, mutually self-giving, mutually supportive marriage thing. We didn't know how to parent without codependency, fear, and violence. Our mothers did the very best they could—and we are grateful for their endurance and examples. But they could only teach so much on their own. So, Ronnie and I set out to make our own way, trusting that God would lead us and accompany us.

We have been practicing family together for over twenty years now. We have three children in their adolescent and teen years, and one elderly cat. We make our home in the western suburbs of Chicago where I work at a Christian liberal arts college. Ronnie pastors a small Anglican congregation that we serve with another priest, while also managing our household and children. We have lived in five states and served churches in the Southern Baptist, Methodist, Episcopal, and Anglican traditions. I have studied in Baptist and Catholic institutions. Together we have endured the deaths of his brother and mother, the addictions of family members, the dissolution of friendships, a grueling PhD program, abusive church leadership, unemployment, medical emergencies, bankruptcy, and more. Of all the things we've done together, our family is the thing I am most proud of—not in an arrogant way, but in a wonderstruck, I-can't-believe-we-managed-to-do-this way. We know well the gift this is, and we are grateful for the ways we've been enabled to stop patterns of dysfunction and abuse.

At the same time, we're also grappling daily with the realities of our sinful world and trying to figure out how to be a Christian family through it all. We love our home country, the United States, but we cannot deny its wicked foundation in White supremacy, settler colonialism, genocide, and race-based chattel slavery.[1] We have sought to tell the truth to our children from their earliest days, to help them be more loving and just neighbors and more faithful heralds of Jesus' good news. But they've had their hearts broken—and ours too—over the past several years watching so many self-professed Christians in the United States sell their souls to Trumpism, Covid denial, election denial, White nationalism, abuse cover-ups, and more. Learning how to be disciples as a family in this moment has been the most challenging task of our lives.

I don't say all this to claim any special kind of authority. In fact, one of the biggest hurdles of this cultural moment is the growing realization that the people many of us trusted to have The Answer do not have it. In fact, it's clear from the fruit of their lives and ministries that they never did. While we twisted ourselves into knots and jumped through hoops trying to conform to the blueprints we were given for gender roles, singleness, marriage, and parenting, the leaders we looked to for guidance were exposed, one after the other, as colossally and catastrophically wrong. The Western church has undergone a true apocalypse—literally, an unveiling—in the past few decades. And White Christians especially have finally begun to wake up to the ways in which their understanding of the gospel has been twisted and perverted by the besetting sins of the American empire.

I write this book as a disciple of Jesus who is very much still *on the way*. This volume is what I have to offer the people of God at this time in this place given all that I've experienced and learned so far. Whatever you find here that is true, good, and beautiful, please take and use. Whatever is not, please set it aside and say a prayer for me.

## Christian Families in Between

Most of the households I know were completely overwhelmed by the challenges of the Covid-19 pandemic and its mishandling. Even so, despite the distress, the way our family and many others were forced to pivot and restructure life jolted us out of our ruts. Suddenly, it was possible to imagine another way of living. Things could be different from what they are.[2] And that was a powerful, albeit intimidating, realization.

Such disruptions in the status quo also forced us to seek out the trustworthy and settled things amid the quaking all around us. Through the cultural and political upheavals of the past century and a half, many Christians have looked to the "traditional family" as a source of stability. I understand the impulse. There has never been an idyllic past for families. But even just fifty years ago there was still a broad consensus in the West about many things: that lifetime monogamy is ideal, premarital sex is unwise, and two opposite-sex parents are important for childrearing. Today such expectations are openly contested and condemned by many as oppressive and wrong. When it feels like so much is changing so rapidly, it makes sense that people, especially Christians who are used to revering tradition, would reach for something stable.

It's also impossible to overstate the importance of our families to our lives. Family functions, for better or worse, as our foundation, our lodestone, our North Star. "No wonder," as Anglo-American author Rodney Clapp says, "we want to call it natural and believe it to be as final and invulnerable as the force of gravity."[3] Many things in the created order appear unchanging. The earth rotates and orbits the sun, causing patterns for days and seasons, as well as a glorious, revolving display of constellated stars. The earth's rivers run into the seas and the moon governs the ocean's tides. Gravity ensures that everything falls to the earth, from ripe southern pecans to discharged rocket boosters. All these things and more give creatures a sense of security—as they should. We know creation comes from a good God who made all things with a good purpose. The order we perceive in the world is surely for the good of all creatures. Why not the family too?

Yet, we also know creation is fallen, influenced top to bottom by evil, sin, and death. Our depraved condition extends to all human relationships, including the families we form. We are creatures of time, too, and as we move through time, both as individuals and communities, we accumulate a mix of things beneficial and poisonous. Such accretions—like proverbial moss growing on a rolling stone—make us who we are and influence the course of our lives. "History is not the past," African American author James Baldwin says. "It is the present. We carry our history with us. We are our history."[4] There is no ground, therefore, for nostalgia—a romantic, highly selective, longing for the past. Nor is there ground for the myth of constant progress, an idealism that says we are always and inevitably improving with the passage of time.

The truth is families have never been constant in the way many imagine. The paradigm for family (not to mention marriage and sex), which many Christians assume to be divinely designed is, in fact, a relatively recent development. The traditional family of Christian talk radio and conservative political platforms emerged in the nineteenth century among the White middle class of Western Europe and the United States, alongside industrial capitalism and Western imperial expansion. Despite the desire to hold on to something eternal and unchanging, many Christians today are seeking to preserve something that is highly contextual and changeable—and not even especially good for us.

Even though God in Christ has reconciled the world to himself, we remain today in "the time between the times" as attributed to American Episcopal priest Fleming Rutledge—already experiencing God's kingdom in part but awaiting its full consummation. We see occasional glimpses of God's redemption in our everyday lives, but also recognize that much yet remains to be redeemed. As a result, Christians above all must be cautious about what we look to for security, "for this world in its present form is passing away" (1 Cor 7:31). Transient things ought not be confused with eternal things, and historical things ought not take the place of transcendent ones. The biblical word for such mistaken trust is *idolatry*. Idols promise a guaranteed return in exchange for our worship. But they are liars, and their "blessings" are smoke and ash.

Because all Christians live in the tension between the already kingdom and the not-yet kingdom, so too do Christian families. There are ways in which we are able, by the Spirit's power, to experience the eternal kind of life Jesus offered his followers when we give ourselves to his way. It's something of a miracle that, through careful discernment and creative improvisation, we can witness moments of God's kingdom breaking into our humdrum lives.

At the same time, there are many ways we will not, even cannot, overcome the fallen forces, structures, and institutions in this present evil age. Our eager efforts, even with the best of intentions, can have unexpected and devastating consequences. Tragically, we can mess up some of the most important parts of our short lives.

If the kingdom of God is a seed growing secretly (Mk 4:26-29), then it makes sense that Christians often feel as though the gospel is failing to take root or produce anything at all. Even more so, then, Christian families seek to offer a witness to the gospel in a society stratified by racism and sexism, plagued by Mammon worship, soaked in violence, and organized by the will to dominate and exploit. Christian households straddling the already-not-yet divide in God's kingdom have a lot of work to do to discern and improvise faithfulness in such a setting. It will quite literally occupy our entire lives.

In the eagerness to find a way—*the way*—to be faithful amid a sinful society, many Christians have turned to sentimental visions of families past. But the good news of God's kingdom won't allow us to wrap ourselves in the warm blanket of maudlin idealism. First, because such visions are embedded in socioeconomic circumstances that elude most families today. But second, and perhaps more importantly, because the past is not where Christians live. Christ is Lord *today*. Now. And the kingdom of God is breaking in from the future to the present. One day the home of God will be with us in a new heaven and new earth (Rev 21:1). But until then, we are always facing forward, seeking to obey Christ in the present, while looking toward the horizon awaiting his glorious return.

The hard truth is this: there is no biblical blueprint for families. As much as we want one, as much as it might be easier if we had one, it's just not there. And when you look at human history, or even just church history, it turns out that the traditional family is not so traditional after all. In an unstable and rapidly changing world, Christians must look to truly eternal things for security: the triune God revealed in Jesus Christ and the kingdom he has inaugurated through his church. These form the basis for our stability; these form the paradigm through which we live in the world.

The family, therefore, draws its identity, purpose, and practice from the church. And the church draws its identity, purpose, and practice from the kingdom of God, which was proclaimed and inaugurated by Christ in the power of the Spirit. To put it another way, the family rightly understands itself in relation to the church, and the church rightly understands itself in relation to God's kingdom. So, both the church of Christ and the kingdom of God are necessary for Christian families to understand who they are and what they do.[5]

## Real Families in the Real World

There are no ideal families, and there are no families from nowhere. Families are made up of people with bodies. Such bodies bear the signs, seen and unseen, of age, gender, sexuality, racialization, class, disability, illness, and more. We are families shaped and powered by overlapping cultures, languages, and memories. And we are families living within spaces and places during epochs of time with specific histories. Whether we like it or not, these overlapping contexts have a significant impact on the lives of Christian households, including their ability to cope through trials and cultivate the kind of virtue essential to the Christian life.

Not only that, but the people who make up families have family histories of their own, along with the various experiences that their lives have given them. And Christian families take many forms beyond the oft-assumed nuclear family. Many kinds of Christian households exist, including single adults, single-parent families, couples with no children, divorced and remarried families with stepchildren, families headed by grandparents, and more. All these families with their complicated stories and challenges are the real-life households of God's people. The kingdom of God and the church of Christ serve as the framework within which embodied, encultured, and historical families live—and all of them need to be empowered to be faithful witnesses to the kingdom of God today.

The particulars of our histories and our present are precisely the things with which the Holy Spirit is working to make all things new.[6]

The way you were parented, for instance, significantly shapes how you care for children, whether yours or someone else's, many times in ways you aren't aware of. A childhood marked by parental abuse can lead to difficulty in forming intimate connections, which make forming a healthy family difficult. But the impact of a neighborhood or community on one's family can't be overlooked either. Think of the influence of something as simple as the zoning code on our daily lives, dictating where apartment complexes and gas stations can be built. Or the difference it makes for household members to be able to exercise flex time at work or work multiple days from home. Things like ready access to sidewalks, green space, and fresh food have a massive long-term effect on a family's health.

So much Christian talk about families deals in abstract ideals rather than embodied realities. Even framed within the church and the kingdom of God, Christian thinking about family must be rooted in real families living in the real world. Honoring this reality means naming and dealing with the many factors of our embodied contexts: jobs and schooling, recreation and chores, conflict and desire. These are not incidental things. They determine the vital nitty-gritty stuff with which our households must contend every day. Because this is where God's Spirit is at work—here and now in our lives as they actually exist.

Central to the good news of God's kingdom is that God has come among us in Jesus Christ, the Messiah of Israel. The transcendent Creator of the cosmos has come near in the flesh-and-blood person from Nazareth under the reign of the Roman Empire. Jesus had an ancestry of his own, going back hundreds of years among God's covenant people, Israel, and out of his people's stories and practices, at the table of Mary and Joseph, he learned and grew. Somehow God-in-the-flesh grew in wisdom and stature and favor with God and neighbor (Lk 2:52), and through his exemplary life, public crucifixion, and victorious resurrection, he initiated the new creation foretold by Israel's prophets. Gentiles, those outside the covenant people, have been welcomed in too. The sign of God's universal welcome is the Holy Spirit, sent by the Father and the Son to unite all of us to God and each other.

The incarnation means the love of the triune God extends to particulars, as my friend Beth Felker Jones says—fingers and toes, kitchens and dens, porches and playgrounds. And if God's love extends to such parts and places, then God's transforming presence is found there too. The crucial task of Christian families is to learn how to see and know God (discernment) and live in the already of God's kingdom (improvisation) amid the daily chaos of household life. I agree with Anglo-American Catholic theologian Holly Taylor Coolman that the point of the Christian family in whatever form it takes is *to be apprentices of love*.[7] As they learn how to love together, Christian families embody God's kingdom in preparation for new creation.

## Beyond Blueprints and Placebos

Even though Ronnie and I are what I jokingly call "professional holy people," sometimes we lose sight of the big picture while trying to keep up with our responsibilities. It's hard enough to feed our family, pay our bills, do our jobs, serve our church, maintain our friendships, and, somehow, get our kids prepared for adulthood, without also thinking about God's kingdom too. And we're doing all of this in an increasingly hurried and overstimulated world that is saturated with opinions. We live in the age of the expert, both the professionally affiliated and the self-proclaimed, and these experts have more and more outlets through which to spread their perspective on how things ought to be done. No matter the topic, whether it's dating, fitness, personal finance, friendship, breastfeeding, nutrition, or sleep, there's an expert, a book, a podcast, or a TikTok video for that. Since most of us are not conversant in the relevant literature, we are, in many ways, at the mercy of news media, friends, and family who broadcast or share the opinions of others. While access to all this information can be an empowering thing, it can also be overwhelming. At every turn, families are often asking: Are we doing this right? Depending on who you ask, you can get a very different answer. The constant questioning creates a lot of anxiety and fear, which it so happens, is essential for selling the myriad products and services on offer.

At the same time, there's no doubt that we live in perilous times. Human beings always have. Jesus himself said we should expect no less. Despite enormous progress in medicine and technology, humanity doesn't seem any closer to overcoming our penchant for mutual destruction. Speaking in the 1960s, Dr. Martin Luther King Jr. named our communal sin concretely as the three evils of society: racism, economic exploitation, and violence. While the rise of the internet, satellites, and smartphones have brought us many good things, there's no doubt the three evils continue in new ways into the present day. Choosing to live as Christian families within this environment, in whatever form our households take, isn't for the faint of heart. Yet, Jesus' calling "Follow me!" remains. We must do our best to discern what that means here and now.

With this book, I hope to speak a word to Christian families of all kinds that is neither a rigid, unattainable ideal nor an uncritical, feel-good placebo. I am not promoting a particular blueprint of family to which all Christians are expected to conform, nor am I trying to obliterate the notion of family as outmoded and useless. Instead, I am seeking a new paradigm for the family within the framework of the church and the kingdom of God, rooted in the Scriptures and the best of the church's traditions, that I hope will be empowering and encouraging as we learn to live as households of faith today. So, I invite you to join me in thinking carefully about difficult matters amid the lived complexity of your daily life. I know it's hard. But not only do I think we can do it—I really think we must do it.

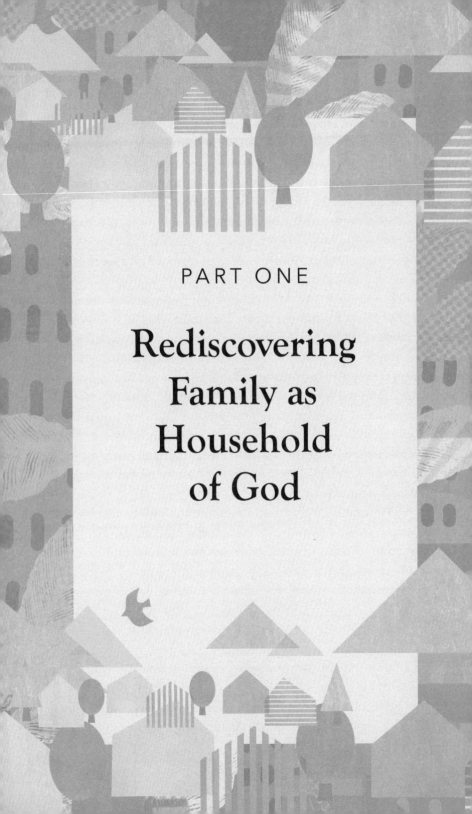

PART ONE

# Rediscovering Family as Household of God

# 1

# Searching for the Biblical Family

**I was twenty years old,** newly engaged to be married, and holding a thoughtful gift from my adoring fiancé. Why then was I crying? I had just finished the first few chapters of a book that claimed to explain what it really means to be a Christian wife, and for the first time in our two-year relationship, I was confronted with the prospect that I might not be able to conform to the wifely ideal my soon-to-be husband was expecting.

Nothing in our conversations thus far suggested we had different expectations. Yet this book offered a vision I found foreign and unfeasible. The author said I was to be entirely devoted to my husband's vocation, ready to drop everything to tend to his needs. The author said I was the God-ordained "keeper at home," someone whose focus was on the house and children, so that my husband's focus could be on his work. None of this made sense to me because I knew I was headed toward a future teaching theology, and I would be pursuing a PhD for that reason. How could I be the kind of wife this book was so confidently insisting I should be when my vocation seemed to work against it?

With some trepidation, I called my fiancé. I was wondering whether this conversation would be a turning point in our relationship. Would he be okay with me rejecting this wifely ideal? Or would he insist that this was the way it had to be?

Though I had been a student of theology for a few years, that anxiety-filled moment was my first time truly grappling with the family blueprint of my evangelical tradition. A *family blueprint* is what I call any idealized model of the family that people are expected to emulate. There are many such family blueprints on offer in the world. The one with which I was wrestling was and is an especially pervasive and powerful model among evangelicals today. My fiancé and I heard it taught from pulpits and in Sunday school classes, it was reinforced in books and conferences, and it was even symbolized in our wedding gifts (where casserole dish covers were engraved with my name, not his).

Like many of my friends, I assumed the biblical family had a well-defined, long-established shape dictated by divine principles drawn from Scripture. An unspoken part of our future "I do," then, was a mutual agreement to conform as much as possible to that "biblical" ideal. By properly imitating God's design, we thought we would not only bear witness to God's truth in Scripture, but also serve as a living sign of the gospel in the world. Also, we felt assured that this life would secure our family's overall happiness and success.

And what is God's design? The family blueprint I was given says that God created male and female to fulfill different roles. Adam and Eve are the archetypes for gender-based roles in marriage. Men tend and keep creation and women, their subordinate helpers, assist men in their work. Men work in the public sphere while women work in the private sphere. The result of sin entering the world is that women often try to usurp men's authority and men tend to be domineering over women. Through our redemption in Christ, though, human beings can conform to God's good purposes in marriage and family. The husband's loving headship over his wife symbolizes Christ's loving headship of the church, his bride, and the wife's loving submission to the husband symbolizes the church's loving submission to Christ (Eph 5:21-33).

In practice, the family blueprint I was taught said wives should take responsibility for the home and education of their children while husbands earn the household income and support their wives and children. Husbands are the "spiritual leaders" of the home. They exercise God-given authority over their wives and children, which they are supposed to express in self-sacrificing, Christlike love. Wives, on the other hand, are supposed to offer gracious submission to their husband's headship. Unusual circumstances might require both spouses to work outside the home, but that does not change the divine ideal. In fact, if wives submit graciously to their husband's leadership, then husbands will grow strong in their God-given role and children will flourish.

This family blueprint is derived from a particular way of telling the story of the Bible and it depends on a view of gender drawn from US culture and certain interpretations of Scripture. I have been interacting with this blueprint since I became a Christian in my teen years, but it wasn't until I saw it crystallized in a book written for me that I began to consider it might be wrong. Still, many Christians today are convinced the family blueprint I've described is not only the biblical family—the divinely ordained ideal for all—but also the traditional family, the form of family practiced for most of history.

## The Family and Families

We all have family blueprints in our background. Let's imagine a church in your neighborhood begins to promote a sermon series called "The Biblical Family." The church advertises the series through their website and marquee sign. They also send out glossy card stock mailers to every household within a two-mile radius listing the topics to be covered in these "practical and timely" messages. Now, take a moment and picture the images on their website and the mailer you pull out of your mailbox. What does the family in the picture look like? Who is in the picture? What are they doing? And what topics would be included in the series?

If you were born and raised in the United States and shaped by Anglo-American culture, as I was, more than likely the image of "the biblical family" that surfaces in your mind is that of a smiling husband and wife and a couple of kids living in a single-family home in the suburbs. Maybe there's a white picket fence and a dog too. Within such a vision of family, the sermons are likely to assume a middle-class standard of living, as well as a high degree of family independence. The sermon series, then, might include teaching on the roles and responsibilities of husbands, wives, and children, perhaps with special instruction on things like sex, parenting, and money management. Perhaps you've received preaching and teaching of this kind in your church before. It's very common!

For those not born in the United States, however, or for those who have grown up primarily in non-Western cultures, family is not so limited a sphere. Non-Western visions of family include what many call extended family: grandparents and great-grand-parents, aunts and uncles, cousins, godparents, and maybe even longtime neighbors and friends. Non-Western notions of family often assume a high level of interdependence and prioritize the well-being of the extended family over the interests of the individual. A sermon series within this vision of family might include concerns not addressed by those who imagine family in a narrower way. Perhaps it would include messages on honoring elders' wisdom, the value of tradition, caring for the next generation, and the submission of individual desires to family needs.

One such broader notion of family is portrayed in Disney's *Encanto*. While there is far more to the story than just the size and scope of the family Madrigal, the vision of a large extended Colombian family living and learning together under one roof captured the imagination of millions. Westerners, especially, are living in a time when social bonds appear to be loosening and communal trust is disintegrating, but *Encanto* portrays a close-knit, albeit imperfect, family caring for each other and seeking healing together. The appeal of such a story is not difficult to understand.

Acknowledging the differences between cultural notions of family, even just with respect to their size and scope, highlights the problem with any family talk. There's a difference between "The Family" as an abstract ideal and families as embodied, enculturated realities. There's a difference between the "Christian family" in theory and your family in practice—the complex, multi-faceted texture of your life together. Yet, many of us have come to consider as natural and God-given what was really created in the nineteenth century: one male wage-earner, one female homemaker, a consumerist household, gender-role specification, and small family units that largely fend for themselves.[1] But what constitutes family and what family life looks like has varied considerably throughout history along with Christian teaching on family.[2]

Not only have many Christians assumed a family form that is by no means universal, but they often ignore the fact that families through the ages have been deeply impacted by sin—both inside and outside families. One reason I think *Encanto* has been so powerful is the unflinching way it portrays both the traditions and the traumas our families pass down. Just because a particular family form evolved over time does not mean that form is divinely approved. By no means! Not only that, but countless families through the centuries have been catastrophically sinned against, subjected to unjust situations that broke family bonds and destabilized communities with consequences that persist into the present. Theorizing about families without reference to such failures in Christian history is a grave error.

Where I live in North America many ways of practicing family have emerged through the years, all of which, in varying degrees,

reflect the ravages of sin on the most intimate of human relationships. I'll just describe a few. The Pueblo peoples of the Southwest
had families in the seventeenth century in which kin loyalty, social
obligation, and property rights were determined by the mother's
bloodline, not the father's. Men moved into the homes of their
wives after marriage, and the wife's father and brothers were
vital to the children's upbringing—more so than the children's
biological father. Such matrilineal households proved puzzling
to Spanish Catholic missionaries when they arrived and sought
to "civilize" Pueblo families through evangelization.

The marriages of enslaved Black persons in the pre–Civil War
American South were often illegal, their families spanning multiple plantations. A couple's ability to reside together, let alone
with their children, depended on the whims of their enslavers
who had control over their lives and bodies. Enslaved women
were regularly raped to produce more children born into lifelong
slavery due to their mother's status, and enslaved husbands, if
they happened to be nearby, risked torture and death if they
dared protect their wives. Given hundreds of years' worth of
oppression and violence, the ongoing resilience of African
American marriages and families is remarkable.

Among slaveholding White southerners, on the other hand,
the eldest patriarch had total control over his household, which
would have included him and his wife, their children, their grandparents, enslaved people with their children, and sometimes the
families of their adult children. All these fell under the patriarch's
moral, legal, and financial jurisdiction. Though there was no
doubt affection among family members, southern White plantation families were held together by a combination of honor-
shame codes, coercion, and violence. This is not exactly what US
Christians mean when they invoke "the traditional family," yet it
was the norm for multiple generations.

Finally, White middle- and upper-class households in the
post–Civil War period took the form many romanticize today:

a wage-earning father and stay-at-home mother who presides over her children and manages the household. The sign of a man's financial success in the industrial period was his ability to have a "kept woman" not required to work beyond the home. Of course, poor families were never able to attain this ideal. Irish Catholic immigrants, for instance, sought unsuccessfully to create "proper" families, but poverty and competition for labor often prevented them from marrying, or forced both spouses into paid labor. The immigrant neighborhood and parish church became the household's primary means of support.[3] The "traditional" family of the Victorian period, then, was only traditional for a small segment of the population.

What do these historical snippets tell us? All families have a context that inevitably shapes its form and practices for good and ill, and all families are impacted by sin and injustice, both inside and outside the household. The variety of families through the ages warns us against idealizing our experience and perception of family—something we're all prone to do. Just because our family, or the families around us, have taken a particular shape, doesn't mean it represents a universal standard (The Family) that applies to all peoples everywhere. In fact, our tendency to romanticize families of the past too often overlooks heinous evils hidden behind our soft-focused ideals. Without an awareness of our cultural embeddedness, Christians who seek to live in the light of God's revelation are apt to read our idealization of the family into the pages of Scripture and read it back out again as divine design. Our interpretation of Scripture then becomes the "biblical family" to which all Christian families are called to conform. It's too easy to become like Spanish colonizers scattering and brutalizing Pueblo families in the name of God.

For too long, many Christians have promoted an idealized cultural construct as the only faithful way to practice Christian family, but this family paradigm emerged during the Victorian period. It was later commodified and sold as biblical through the medium of radio and television in the early twentieth century and then championed politically during the rise of the Religious Right in the 1970s and '80s. It's past time, therefore, that we take a critical look at what we've been offered all these years. Perhaps we'll see that Scripture doesn't say all that we've been told it says, and perhaps the so-called biblical family is more beholden to Western European history and culture than it is to the Bible. Indeed, the sermon series at the church down the street, as well as the podcasts and books it produces, may assume things about family that are neither good nor true.

## What Is the Biblical Family?

Ah, but one might object: all these historical forms of family failed to live up to God's design—sin and injustice prevented them from doing so—but that doesn't mean there isn't a design. Fair enough. Where then are we given the design for this "biblical family"?

The Bible, which is Spirit-inspired and trustworthy in all it teaches, tells a lot of stories about families. But telling stories about families is not the same as providing a model of family. The Bible provides wisdom and instruction about family relationships—husbands and wives, parents and children, fathers and sons, and more. But Spirit-inspired wisdom does not translate into a family ideal, nor are all trustworthy instructions directly transferable into the twenty-first century context.

This is not to say the Bible is not relevant—it is! "All Scripture is God-breathed and is useful for teaching, rebuking, correcting, and training in righteousness" (2 Tim 3:16). But what exactly is being taught, rebuked, and corrected is not unambiguous when we move from the world of the text to the world of today. As Anglo-American scholar John Walton has often said, "Scripture is written *for* us but not *to* us." To move from the text in the past to the world in the present requires good hermeneutics—the careful work of interpreting, explaining, and applying the words of Scripture to our contemporary moment. When we are careful with our herme-neutics, we realize the Bible includes much that could be rel-evant to a theology of families, but not all of it can be easily or neatly harmonized.

## Families in the Old Testament

Many Christians point to Genesis 1-2 for the divine design, which depicts the creation of man and woman and their vocation in the Garden of Eden. I will address Genesis in more depth later, but for now I'll simply point out there is no reference to prescribed roles in Genesis 1-2, nor is there any delineation of gender-based spheres. Instead, what is affirmed is that male and female share God's image, share human flesh, and share a vocation, and the first couple dwelled in Eden—a place from which they are exiled in the very next chapter, never to return. Whatever might be gleaned about the relationship between wives and husbands from Genesis 1-2, it is not a blueprint for families who now live as Eden's exiles.

In the rest of the Hebrew Bible, families are central to the over-arching story of God's covenant relationship with Israel. Jewish kinship was arranged by tribe, clan, and family. Tribe pertained mainly to territorial organization—that is, the land apportioned to the twelve tribes—but clan and family pertained most di-rectly to daily life. One married within one's clan and worked in households to care for the land, resources, and people on it. The strongest source of identity was the "father's house," made up of all the descendants of the living male ancestor, except for married daughters who left to join their husbands' families.

In such an extended family, fifty to a hundred people might live together in a cluster of homes with shared spaces for cooking and socializing. Interdependence was vital for the family's sur-vival, and the propagation of children was central. The cultivation of land and livestock, the maintenance of property and water rights, the establishment and strengthening of social ties, the preservation of a covenant relationship with God, the communication of faith, history, laws, and rituals—all this and more was bound up in one's progeny.[4] Children, then, were the flesh-and-blood sign of God's promise to bless and multiply his people. As a result, childlessness was viewed as a curse, a state to be pitied and avoided at all costs (Gen 30:1-22; 1 Sam 1; Deut 25:5-10). To be blessed with many children, especially sons, was God's blessing (Ps 127:3-5; 128:3-6), and one's descendants were how one's life endured after death (Gen 48:16; 2 Sam 18:18).

It's no surprise then that the story of Israel is in large part the story of Israel's families. None of Israel's notable families, however, could be credibly held up as examples. Take, for instance, the family of Sarah and Abraham, the matriarch and patriarch of Israel's faith. God forges a covenant with Abraham, leading him and his household out of Ur and into the land of Canaan. God promises he will bless and multiply Abraham's descendants so that they will outnumber the stars in the sky (Gen 12:1-9). Still, Abraham and Sarah's childlessness unto advanced age seems to present a serious barrier to God's promise. On two occasions Abraham's fear in foreign lands leads him to pretend Sarah is his sister to the point that she is taken into the harems of other men (Gen 12:10-20; 20:1-18). Though Sarah is rescued in both cases, these incidents further endanger the possibility of Abraham's promised heir.

Eventually, Abraham and Sarah take it upon themselves to make another way. Sarah gives her enslaved Egyptian woman, Hagar, to Abraham as a surrogate, and Hagar is forced to become a concubine in Abraham's family. Though God is faithful to Hagar, offering her protection and a promise to her and her descendants, she and Ishmael are eventually expelled at Sarah's insistence. In the end, despite their flaws and failures, Sarah conceives and bears a son, Isaac, through whom the rest of Abraham's descendants come.

We could also talk about Isaac's sons, Esau and Jacob, both of whom take multiple wives. As a result, they produce considerably more children than a single husband-wife union usually would. In the case of Jacob, we know the polygamous family yielded numerous conflicts and sibling rivalries, most famously between Joseph (the son of Rachel) and his brothers (the sons of Leah, Zilpah, and Bilhah). The whole book of Genesis relates story after story about the conflictual families descending from Sarah and Abraham, but they are decidedly not held up as examples to emulate. Instead, the focus of Genesis is God's covenant faithfulness to Abraham's descendants despite their innumerable failures. If you're looking for a family blueprint, you won't find it in the patriarchs.

The same could be said of the many other families whose stories are told in the Hebrew Bible. The stories of the kings, especially Saul, David, and Solomon, and their respective families feature prominently. God makes promises to them, too, even forming an eternal covenant with David that is eventually fulfilled in Jesus. But are the families of Saul, David, and Solomon paradigms to imitate? Definitely not. All engage in polygamy, and none are exemplary fathers (not even good-enough fathers!). Though David is described as "a man after God's own heart" (1 Sam 13:14; Acts 13:22), he makes grievous mistakes and causes terrible suffering for those under his power. And there's no denying that his family is deeply disordered (see, for example, 2 Sam 13). In their stories of rape, rebellion, and murder, David's children demonstrate the ineligibility of the Davidic family for idealization. There's no family blueprint here either.

The Law, Wisdom literature (like Proverbs and Job), and the Prophets offer teaching on family that stands in stark contrast to the disorder we see in the historical books. Rather than stories, these texts offer rules of governance, wise instruction, and exhortation to return to the Lord's ways. Children are exhorted to listen to and obey their parents so that their lives might be long and prosperous. Parents are encouraged to teach and discipline their children faithfully. Wives and husbands are warned away from behavior that creates disorder and undermines the household.

Perhaps most memorable is the exhortation of Deuteronomy 6:4-9:

> Hear, O Israel: The LORD our God, the LORD is one. Love the LORD your God with all your heart and with all your soul and with all your strength. These commandments that I give you today are to be on your hearts. Impress them on your children. Talk about them when you sit at home and when you walk along the road, when you lie down and when you get up. Tie them as symbols on your hands and bind them on your foreheads. Write them on the doorframes of your houses and on your gates.

Later in the same passage, the lawgiver says: "In the future, when your son asks you, 'What is the meaning of the stipulations, decrees and laws the LORD our God has commanded you?' tell him: 'We were slaves of Pharaoh in Egypt, but the LORD brought us out of Egypt with a mighty hand'" (Deut 6:20-21). In other words, it is the responsibility of parents to teach their children God's story and the covenant obligations of God's people. To do so, God's law is to be part of the structure of daily life: discussed at home, on the road, lying down, getting up, and more. The expectation is that faithfulness to the Lord will be passed on within families, from older generations to younger.

Even so, none of the instructions found in the Law, Wisdom literature, or the Prophets provide a clear *structure* of family to which God's people are expected to conform. How to live within their families? Yes. What form the family must take? No. Rather, the Hebrew Bible assumes the form of family that was most common in their historical and cultural context—one that is patriarchal, patrilocal, and patrilineal—and offers wisdom about how to live faithfully within it.[5] Thus, the emphasis of the Hebrew Bible is decidedly on the family's *function* rather than its form.

## Families in the New Testament

Compared to the Old Testament, the New Testament spends little time on families as such. The first-century context that forms the background to the Gospels and Epistles was influenced by both Greco-Roman culture and Jewish practice. In the Greco-Roman world, the family was a hierarchically arranged social institution. Practically speaking, it was organized mainly for the benefit of male elders and social elites. One's access to material and social goods—everything from food to education to marriage partners—depended entirely on conformity to prescribed roles, which were dictated by one's class and gender. The behavior of family members was governed by an honor-shame system where male honor depended on the protection and enforcement of women's modesty and chastity. Within this family system, one's identity was primarily familial and only secondarily individual.[6]

The Gospels tell stories about Jesus' birth into a family. Mary and Joseph submit to the Law's requirements for their son (Lk 2:22-38) and flee the country to protect him from Herod's murderous rage (Mt 2:13-23). Luke's Gospel contains the only story we have of Jesus as an adolescent. In it, he confounds his parents by remaining behind in Jerusalem with the teachers in the temple (Lk 2:41-52). Once an adult, Jesus exalts children as exemplary recipients of the God's kingdom and models for discipleship (Mt 18:1-5; 19:13-15; 21:14-16; Mk 9:33-37; 10:13-16; Lk 18:15-17). But families are more ambiguous in Jesus' teaching. Jesus never dissolves biological kinship or its obligations, but he certainly reorders biological kinship under the higher and more important calling of loyalty to him and his kingdom. Jesus never puts forward an ideal to which he expects families to conform. On the contrary, his example and teaching are destabilizing to those who want to shore up a family form, including prescribed gender-based roles.

The Acts of the Apostles speaks of households being converted, but again offers little direction to families as such. The sermons of the apostles don't speak to how families ought to conduct themselves apart from Peter's assurance that the promise of God is "for you and your children and for all who are far off" (Acts 2:39). Still, the families that appear in Acts are revelatory of the cultural expression of family in first-century Palestine.

For example, in Acts 10 Peter is summoned to the home of Cornelius, a Roman centurion. Cornelius "and all his family were devout and God-fearing," and he requests Peter's visit at the behest of an angelic message (Acts 10:2). Upon arriving at Cornelius's home, Peter announces the good news of Jesus Christ, his life, death, and resurrection (Acts 10:34-43), and while Peter is still preaching, the Holy Spirit descends on the gathered listeners (Acts 10:44). Based on their reception of the Spirit, Cornelius and his household, along with relatives and friends in attendance, are baptized (Acts 10:24, 48).

Later, on the outskirts of the city of Philippi, the apostle Paul and Silas meet Lydia, a dealer in purple cloth from Thyatira (Acts 16:11-14). As they speak with her, "the LORD opened her heart to respond to Paul's message" (Acts 16:14), and she comes to faith in Christ. As a result, "she and the members of her household were baptized," and Lydia welcomes Paul and Silas into her home (Acts 16:15).

While staying in Philippi, Paul and Silas are wrongly imprisoned on the pretense of disturbing the peace and advocating unlawful customs (Acts 16:20-21), but they are miraculously delivered from bondage by an earthquake. When the terrified jailer realizes what has happened, a dramatic conversion takes place:

> Then [the jailer] brought them outside and said, "Sirs, what must I do to be saved?" They answered, "Believe on the Lord Jesus, and you will be saved, you and your household." They spoke the word of the Lord to him and to all who were in his house. At the same hour of the night he took them and washed their wounds; then he and his entire family were baptized without delay. (Acts 16:30-33 NRSV)

In each of these stories, Gentiles and their households come to faith in Christ, and the families of Cornelius, Lydia, and the Philippian jailer did not look like the Western nuclear family today. Rather, their household (*domus*) would have included the head of house (usually the oldest male relative or *paterfamilias*) and spouse (if there was one), any children, stepchildren, or adopted children, aged parents (if they were still alive), enslaved persons with their children, and possibly some free persons working in the family business. They also would've had family gods, which were expected to be served by all in the household. So, when the religious allegiance of the head of house changed, the religious allegiance of the entire household changed. The shift in religious commitment resulted in the entire family receiving baptism, the sign of their collective repentance and God's promise to include them in the new covenant community.

Only once we get to Paul's epistles do we encounter the first passages that read like a family blueprint—and this is certainly how they've been interpreted by many. After all, the epistles to the Ephesians and Colossians contain a section often called "the household codes," and the pastoral epistles include specific instructions regarding the families of overseers.[7] But such instructions are tempered by Paul's clear preference for celibacy (1 Cor 7:7-8). If unmarried or widowed Christians find celibacy too great a burden, he says they are free to marry (1 Cor 7:9), yet he affirms the single state is best for unhindered service in God's kingdom (1 Cor 7:32-35). In fact, Paul says each person should remain in the state in which they were called because "this world in its present form is passing away" (1 Cor 7:31).

Based on the imminent return of Christ, Paul says singleness is preferable and significant alterations to one's social status, occupation, and living conditions are unnecessary. This means that even in the case of slavery, which assuredly goes against the neighbor love and one-body-reconciliation to which Christ calls us, Paul does not insist on abolition or outright manumission.

Rather, he teaches how enslaved persons can live for the Lord amid their present condition, and how enslavers ought to treat slaves in view of the gospel.

What does all this mean for passages of Paul's writings that talk about families? Just as in the case of slavery, Paul's instructions for husbands, wives, and children do not entail an endorsement of his audience's family structure or their gender-based roles. Rather, Paul assumes the existence of the *paterfamilias* and then counsels believers how to live within it under Christ's present lordship and imminent return. Paul's instructions to husbands, wives, children, and slaves pertain not to a divine, universal design, either for families or for slavery, but rather how to live faithfully in allegiance to Christ within one's current state. In other words, Paul was not answering the question: What is the proper structure for the Christian family or household? Rather, Paul was answering the question: How should Christians live in their current social situations in light of Christ's current lordship and soon return? Even in the so-called household codes, Paul isn't offering a family blueprint.

Discerning the so-called biblical family is much harder than it appears. Much Christian teaching today assumes a family model that is not clearly outlined in Scripture. Read on its own terms (for us but not to us), the Bible does not offer a paradigm of the family for its readers to emulate. Instead, it assumes the existence of families in various forms and settings, and offers stories, wisdom, ethics, and theology for understanding and living within those families today.

## Discerning and Improvising Family

Let me be clear: I am not saying there isn't a transcendent, divine purpose for families. I think there is! But for now, let's take a deep breath and loosen our grip on the language of "biblical family" or "traditional family." Most of the time, what we mean by those terms is not something the Bible teaches but a set of contextually constructed norms. Such norms emerged over time through a variety of political, social, and economic circumstances, but they have been turned into universal "biblical" ideals, which are then used to regulate people and behavior.

Besides, what makes us think that the goal of the Christian life is to mimic scripturally sourced models? Yes, Paul invites his churches to imitate him as he imitates Christ (1 Cor 4:16; 11:1), and Jesus commands us explicitly to follow him and learn from him (Mt 11:28-30), but the Bible does not provide neat and tidy blueprints or roadmaps, whether for families or friendships or work or government. (If it did, perhaps Christians wouldn't spend so much time fighting over the details of how God wants us to live!) The nature of Christian discipleship defies such an approach. One thing shared by the people the church calls "saints" is their ability to live faithfully and creatively within their circumstances in light of God's revelation and church teaching.

So, the goal of Christian discipleship is *not* conformity to a divine blueprint. Rather, the goal of Christian discipleship is to obey Jesus' command to "Follow me!" by imitating him in the Spirit's power with God's people in our current setting. In short, we must discern and improvise. To *discern* is to figure out what time it is and how we ought to live given what time it is. Canadian-American philosopher James K. A. Smith says it this way: "Discernment in the midst of history is our central burden: listening for the beat, feeling for the tempo so we can keep time with the Spirit."[8] To *improvise* is to produce something from whatever is available to us in the moment. Jesus is the ultimate exemplar for our lives, of course, but the pattern he gives us will inevitably be repeated differently in our unique situations. And we can only improvise faithfully as we are filled with the Spirit of Christ.[9] Both discernment and improvisation require effort, intentionality, and practice, and both are essential to following Jesus as individuals and families today.

After my disorienting encounter with "Christian wifehood," I finally got Ronnie on the phone to discuss things. He was surprised by my tears. As he listened patiently, out tumbled all my concerns about the book, about me, and about our future marriage. I ended through sobs: "I just don't think I can be this kind of wife. I'm worried you're marrying the wrong person!" His response was gentle but decisive: "Honey, I bought that book because I thought it would be encouraging to you. Obviously, I didn't read it, and it's not. If it's not workable, if it seems wrong for us, then trash it. We'll just make it up as we go along."

His words turned out to be prophetic. We have been discerning and improvising ever since. We had to discern and improvise when we discovered two months into the first semester of my PhD program that I was expecting a second child. After weeks of prayer, soul searching, and tears, we decided the best thing would be for Ronnie to take a part-time position to make caring for our children his full-time job. He was imitating Christ by emptying himself, taking on the form of servant in unselfish love for me and my dream (Phil 2:7). Did this conform to the family blueprint we were told to follow? Definitely not. But it was the wisest, healthiest decision for our family—and we have no regrets.

We had to discern and improvise again when we moved our family to Denver after my teaching contract ended and my PhD was nearing completion. I couldn't find work teaching in higher education, but Ronnie was invited to help plant a church. So, I took a full-time job in the private sector, putting my research skills to work in commercial property development while writing and applying for academic jobs on the side. For the first time we were a single-income family, and I was the sole breadwinner. Ronnie helped found a church and took care of our school-age children while I worked outside the home. Now it was my turn to deny myself to make sure our family was provided for while Ronnie pursued his dream. Did this conform to the family blueprint we were taught? Again, definitely not. But there's no doubt it was the right thing for us at that time.

Then, like so many other families, we had to discern and improvise again in the spring of 2020 when our state implemented a stay-at-home order amid the Covid-19 pandemic. Ronnie was serving as interim pastor to a small, mainly elderly church, and I was in my second year of teaching theology at Wheaton College. Suddenly, we had a month, which turned into three months, which turned into a full year, of working from home while the kids did school from home. There was no blueprint for how to do that. So, through trial and error, we worked together to assemble a schedule and assign duties that would allow each of us to do our work and maintain our sanity. It wasn't perfect, by any means, but we managed to get through that difficult year and a half with our sense of humor and mutual affection intact.

For over twenty years, Ronnie and I have been doing our best to follow Jesus by imitating him in the Spirit's power with God's people in our current setting. I don't want to suggest our way of doing things is the best way or the only way—and that's precisely the point. I realize that compared to the family blueprint many of us were brought up with, discernment and improvisation may sound alarmingly loosey-goosey. But gospel-fueled discernment and improvisation are what most healthy Christian families have been doing through the centuries without even recognizing it, and discernment and improvisation are what God's people have been doing with various degrees of success and failure since the church's earliest days.

# 2

# Beginning with Jesus

**Why does so much popular Christian** teaching on family start with the first few chapters of Genesis? It's an odd choice. What takes place in Genesis 1–2 is decidedly before the time when sin enters the world and irreparably changes human relationships. We now live after what Christians call the fall. Even if we wanted to return to that idyllic prefall state in the garden, we simply cannot, and Genesis 3, which describes the consequences of Adam and Eve's sin, is not something we're trying to emulate. Yes, we hold fast to God's promise in the face of human failure, but there is no going back to Eden, and neither Jesus nor his apostles ever suggest that such is the goal. We can only move forward in God's redemptive story through Christ by the Spirit, which culminates not in a return to Eden but in the coming of a new Jerusalem in a new creation.

As we ponder the meaning and purpose of Christian families, therefore, I want to suggest a radical reframing. "For Christians, the primary creation account is not Genesis," Rodney Clapp says, "but the first chapter of the Gospel of John." Indeed. John's first verse tells us, "In the beginning was the Word, and the Word was with God, and the Word was God." Furthermore, "All things came into being through him," and mind-blowingly, "the Word became flesh and lived among us" (Jn 1:3, 14 NRSV). So it is Jesus, the author and perfecter of our faith, with whom we must begin (Heb 12:2). Of course, we don't discard Genesis 1–2; rather we learn to read it in light of him. In this chapter, I want to re-introduce us to the Jewish man Jesus from Nazareth and what he had to say about family.

## Jesus from Nazareth

Jesus was the oldest son of Jewish peasants living in a rural area of first-century Palestine under the oppressive rule of the Roman Empire. He existed in quiet obscurity for the first thirty or so years of his life before beginning an itinerant ministry of preaching and healing. At that time, he was in his early thirties, unmarried, and childless—and he remained so throughout his life.

Though a few households regularly hosted Jesus and his disciples, he did not keep a home of his own (Mt 8:20). Rather, he left his family home, including his mother and siblings, and traveled throughout Galilee, Jerusalem, and the surrounding regions. He was almost certainly trained in Joseph's trade and did some kind of manual labor before his public ministry began, but Jesus' most notable work consisted of preaching, teaching, and healing wherever the Spirit led him. This peripatetic lifestyle means Jesus did not undertake paid employment for his bread but was supported through the donations of others, notably a group of prosperous women disciples (Lk 8:3).

Jesus was nurtured deeply by his family, chiefly Mary and Joseph, though extended family and friends played a part as well. He was prepared for his mission through his family's care and instruction. They did such a good job, in fact, that when he reached age twelve, he knew already that his proper place was in his Father's house discussing the things of God with Jewish leadership (Lk 2:41-50).

Yet, once he reached adulthood Jesus did not participate in married family life, something highly unusual in first-century

Jewish culture. In fact, Jesus shows us a full human life does not require marriage, children, a private home, or a regular source of income. The one who reveals what it means to be human did not possess any of the often-assumed markers of successful, mature adulthood. Truly, Jesus lacked almost all the things modern people tend to think are fundamental to the good life: romantic love, sex, children, private property, profitable investments, and a fruitful career. The one exception, it seems, is friends. Jesus had a close group of good but flawed friends. Instead of the modern norm, Jesus demonstrates that a God-honoring and fulfilling human life can consist simply in knowing and doing the will of God with friends.

From the start, Jesus' person challenges our assumptions about what constitutes the good life. We shouldn't be surprised, then, when the challenges continue in his teaching.

## Not Safe and Fun for the Whole Family

What does Jesus have to say about families? While he says we should care for our family members (Mt 15:4-6; Mk 7:9-13) and he cares for his mother from the cross (Jn 19:25-27), his teaching is not what we'd expect. In fact, Jesus seems to assume that family bonds are detrimental to, even incompatible with being his disciple. In some cases, he tells his followers to repudiate and abandon their families, promising that his message will divide households (Mt 10:21, 34-36; Mk 14:12; Lk 12:51-53). Jesus says repeatedly that loyalty to him and his kingdom supersedes all other loyalties, including to one's parents, siblings, spouse, and children. In fact, one's love for Jesus, he says, should be so strong that one's love for family looks like hatred by comparison (Lk 14:25-35). What kind of rabbi teaches his followers to love their enemies but hate their mother, father, spouse, and children?

For first-century Jews and Romans, the call to subordinate family ties for the sake of exclusive allegiance to a traveling rabbi was shocking to say the least. In these overlapping cultures, family identity was of primary importance. One's individual identity and access to essential elements of life were dependent on performing family duties. While there were people who occasionally critiqued the system and sought to live outside it, they were glaring exceptions to the overwhelming rule.

So, when Jesus teaches that allegiance to him supersedes allegiance to kin, he is swimming upstream against a powerful current. Yet it's a theme of his ministry, and when given an opportunity to soften his requirements, he declines to do so. We can sense the enormity of the material and relational costs in Peter's exasperated words: "We have left everything to follow you! What then will there be for us?" (Mt 19:27). In response, Jesus doesn't backtrack, but promises abundant blessings in the life to come. He says those who have left houses, livelihood, or family for his sake "will receive a hundred times as much and will inherit eternal life" (Mt 19:29).

Still, Jesus doesn't ask for something he doesn't model. Unlike cult leaders who insist their followers to do all the sacrificing while they enjoy a life of ease, Jesus embodies what he teaches. Three of the Gospels record an astonishing but apparently exemplary interaction between Jesus and his own family (Mt 12:46-50; Mk 3:2-35; Lk 8:19-21). In Mark's telling, after choosing the twelve apostles, Jesus enters a house and "a crowd gathered." The crowd of interested people is so numerous, filling the residence, the courtyard, and the surrounding area, that he and his disciples are prevented from eating (Mk 3:20). Somehow Jesus' family gets word of the excitement he's causing and, "they went to take charge of him, for they said, 'He is out of his mind'" (Mk 3:21).

While Jesus is talking to teachers of the law who accuse him of being possessed by Beelzebul, his family arrives (Mk 3:22-30). Finding themselves stuck outside at the edge of the crowd, they send a messenger into the throng to fetch Jesus, saying, "Your mother and brothers are outside looking for you" (Mk 3:32). Jesus' response is stark: "'Who are my mother and my brothers?'

he asked. Then he looked at those seated in a circle around him and said, 'Here are my mother and my brothers! Whoever does God's will is my brother and sister and mother'" (Mk 3:33-35).

Jesus declines to be controlled by family loyalty. He knows he is where he is meant to be: Preaching the kingdom and teaching his disciples. Like the teachers of the law, his family does not understand who he is (yet) and even risk blaspheming the Holy Spirit by attributing to insanity what is, in fact, the power of God. So, he states explicitly what is implicit in his way of life: his first loyalty is to God's new family in God's kingdom.

Again, Jesus' revised idea of family allegiance doesn't entail wholesale rejection. He continues to care for his mother, who accompanies him to the end of his life and beyond, and his brothers become his disciples too. Jesus responds compassionately and offers healing to those interceding on behalf of family members (Mt 9:18-26; 15:21-28; Mk 9:14-28; Jn 4:46-53), but there's no doubt that he radically subordinates natural kinship to the community of disciples—the family of God—who are gathered around him. Under God's reign, Jesus says, true family consists in fellowship with those who know and do God's will.

Why would Jesus relativize natural kinship in this way? Jesus is not unaware of the significance of family for individuals and society. Families are crucial for everything from child development and the cultivation of virtue to political and economic stability. As the wisest and most intelligent man in history, surely Jesus knows how important families are! Yet, Jesus is also aware that his claims on the life of a disciple are absolute, and loyalty to him and his kingdom will often overturn the family's status quo.

The threat Jesus poses to family cannot be overstated. The first-century family in the Greco-Roman world was a source of collective identity, pride, and social cohesion. It commanded ultimate allegiance and devotion for the mutual well-being of family members. Protecting family honor was paramount and something pursued at almost all costs. (If this is hard to imagine today, think of New Jersey mob boss Tony Soprano and his very extended "family" in *The Sopranos*.)

The family was sacred for first-century Jews too, and because of its association with religion, it was easy to assume that whatever was "normal" for the family also had a divine stamp of approval. For example, even though the Hebrew Scriptures prioritize the care of widows, orphans, and foreigners, this practice was difficult to maintain in Greco-Roman culture where the pressure was great to look out for family interests before all others. The teachings of Jesus, then, seriously undermined first-century norms. "You cannot serve two masters," he insists. A life of mercy, compassion, and service to neighbor is incompatible with a life of total allegiance to one's own kin. Dedication to the cause of the poor and marginalized is incompatible with devotion to the unjust status quo.[1]

This is a very difficult teaching. What do your parents, aunts, uncles, and cousins expect of you? What do your siblings demand of you? What do your grandparents hope for your future? As urgent as such expectations feel to us, it was even more intense to Jesus' first followers. Yet, Jesus says none of such family expectations have a claim more binding on you than his own.

As a result, Jesus soberly warns about the conflict and division he is likely to cause, both within families and within one's very self:

Do not suppose that I have come to bring peace to the earth. I did not come to bring peace, but a sword. For I have come to turn
  "a man against his father,
    a daughter against her mother,
  a daughter-in-law against her mother-in-law—
    a man's enemies will be the members of his
      own household."
Anyone who loves their father or mother more than me is not worthy of me; anyone who loves their son or daughter

more than me is not worthy of me. Whoever does not take up their cross and follow me is not worthy of me. Whoever finds their life will lose it, and whoever loses their life for my sake will find it. (Mt 10:34-39)

As a mother myself, I can't help wondering how Mary felt hearing her son talk about his new family in God's kingdom. No one knew Jesus as Mary knew him: his dimples and gestures, his sleep habits and speech patterns. She had bandaged his childhood wounds, recited the Scriptures to him, and taught him his prayers. Yet, Jesus' words threaten the bonds of family affection, loyalty, and honor that she and Joseph did so much to sustain.

Jesus had already left home with his ragtag group of friends, returning only occasionally and often stirring up trouble when he did (Mk 6:1-6; Lk 4:16-30). What mother wants to hear her oldest son say repeatedly that his followers must love him more than their own parents or children? Perhaps most striking is when Jesus responds to a woman who calls out from the midst of a crowd: "Blessed is the mother who gave you birth and nursed you!" Instead of acknowledging Mary and praising her faithfulness, which she most certainly deserved, Jesus replies soberly: "Blessed rather are those who hear the word of God and obey it" (Lk 11:27-28). If Mary didn't know before that her son's kingdom was not like other kingdoms, she did then.

Again, Jesus doesn't completely obliterate family ties. He blesses the marriage of friends at Cana by performing his first sign at their wedding (Jn 2:1-11). Upon encountering a widow mourning the death of her only son, Jesus raises him and "[gives] him back to his mother" (Lk 7:15). He blesses the children brought to him by eager parents and caregivers (Mk 10:13-16). And Jesus' commitment to the well-being of family is poignantly demonstrated in his last interaction with his mother before his death. John's Gospel recounts the episode:

> Near the cross of Jesus stood his mother, his mother's sister,
> Mary the wife of Clopas, and Mary Magdalene. When Jesus
> saw his mother there, and the disciple whom he loved
> standing nearby, he said to her, "Woman, here is your son,"
> and to the disciple, "Here is your mother." From that time on,
> this disciple took her into his home. (Jn 19:25-27)

At the very least, this passage shows an eldest son ensuring
the ongoing care of his mother. But there's more going on here
too. Before he breathes his last, Jesus calls his mother "woman."
This impersonal form of address is so jarring to contemporary
readers that the NIV contains an explanatory footnote: "The
Greek for *Woman* does not denote any disrespect." In other
words, Jesus is not dissing his mom. That is good to know! So,
why does he call her "woman"? There are perfectly good alternatives such as "mother," or even her name, "Mary," or as my oldest
likes to call me these days, "Bruh." Jesus calls her "woman" because in that moment, as significant and cherished as she is, Mary
is not functioning as his mom, and the apostle John, as important
as he is, is not functioning as his friend and disciple. Instead, both
are playing a symbolic role in the story of salvation.

The Man slowly dying on the center cross is, as strange as it
sounds, re-creating the world, and this re-creation begins with
humanity. He is dying, John's Gospel says, on *the sixth day*—the
day humans were created way back "in the beginning." Hanging
there on that cross, Jesus recreates humanity through his own
body and blood—making something completely new. As the
epistle to the Ephesians says, "His purpose was to create in
himself one new humanity out of the two [Jews and Gentiles],
thus making peace, and in one body to reconcile both of them
to God through the cross" (Eph 2:15-16).

So, what's going on with symbolic Mary and symbolic John?
"In giving his mother to the disciple," Fleming Rutledge says,
"[Jesus] is causing a new relationship to come into existence that

did not exist before." "Woman, here is your son." "Here is your mother." The "woman" is given to "the disciple" and "the disciple" is given to the "woman." Jesus isn't simply securing his mother's safety and provision before he dies. Jesus is "setting aside the blood relationship in order to create a much wider family."[2] His is a family made in his body and blood, through the waters of baptism by the fire of the Spirit. He is creating an expansive, diverse-yet-unified family, where biological bonds are transcended in his body, the church.

Who, after all, would look on this bloodied, cursed, and crucified man and claim him as leader of a new human race? Well . . . we would. We *do*. And in so doing, we find ourselves joined by the Spirit to a new family. At the foot of the cross, all those who would look to Jesus for new creation also receive in one another new sisters and brothers, aunties and uncles, "brought near [to God and to each other] by the blood of Christ" (Eph 2:13). Disciples like Mary care for children not their own, and disciples like John become children of parents not their own. All family loyalties are reoriented around Jesus and his coming kingdom. As Jesus said from the beginning, "Whoever does God's will is my brother and sister and mother" (Mk 3:35).

We might continue to wonder, though, *why* Jesus demands such a radical change of life among his followers. Jesus is not unaware of how shifts in allegiance could disrupt and destabilize communities and even nations. Yet, he insists. Why?

The central reason is that the most fundamental reality of Jesus' life was not the world as it is—neighborhoods and temples, armies and empires—but the world as God is remaking it. In his daily life, the reality to which Jesus was most conscious, the lens through which he saw everything, was the good news of his Father's kingdom in the power of the Spirit.[3] Jesus knew the kingdom of God was being inaugurated in him. Jesus knew that in his death and resurrection he would create the church in his body and blood and begin making all things new. As a result, these were the fundamental preoccupations of his every waking hour, and the grid through which he acted within the world.

Viewed in this light, it makes sense that Jesus saw God's kingdom as a threat to family in its Jewish and Greco-Roman forms. "My kingdom is not of this world," he says to Pilate (Jn 18:36), and yet families, with their fierce kinship ties and generational accumulation of wealth and power, are often formidable instruments for maintaining this world in its pervasive injustice and brutality. Think of the influence of the many notorious families throughout history: the Medicis, the Tudors, the Kennedys, or the Trumps.

So, Jesus puts everything in its proper perspective with his person, his church, and his kingdom at the center. Of course, we are no longer in the first-century Mediterranean world, but Jesus' teaching on family remains deeply challenging today.

## Jesus and Genesis

Our theology and practice of family begins with Jesus' call "Follow me!" and the new family he creates in his own body. God's family in God's kingdom has primacy over natural kinship because loyalty to Jesus precedes all other loyalties. We must learn to see family within the context of the church and the kingdom—not vice versa. We begin with Jesus because the new creation into which we've been baptized begins with Jesus.

Still, the approach I've outlined doesn't mean Genesis 1-2 has nothing to teach us about family. Jesus himself, when asked about divorce, quotes from Genesis 1-2 (Mt 19:4-12; Mk 10:5-9). If Jesus finds insight in Genesis for God's intention for marriage and, by relation, the family, so should we. What, then, do we have to learn?

In Matthew's Gospel Jesus is approached by a group of Pharisees who intend to "test him." They ask him an interpretive question about the law with reference to divorce, something hotly debated at the time: "Is it lawful for a man to divorce his wife for any and every reason?" (Mt 19:3). In response, Jesus refers first to Genesis 1:27: "Haven't you read . . . that at the beginning the Creator 'made them male and female.'" He continues by quoting Genesis 2:24: "For this reason a man will leave his father and mother and be united to his wife, and the two will become one flesh" (Mt 19:5). Then he concludes with his own commentary: "So they are no longer two, but one flesh. Therefore, what God has joined together, let no one separate" (Mt 19:6).

The Pharisees object to Jesus' answer, pointing out that even Moses permits a man to give his wife a certificate of divorce and send her away (Mt 19:7). In response, Jesus doubles down: "Moses permitted you to divorce your wives because your hearts were hard. But it was not this way from the beginning" (Mt 19:8). *It was not this way from the beginning*. With these words Jesus acknowledges that God had an intention for marriage "from the beginning"—that there is a divine will for marriage to which Genesis points. Further, Jesus is saying that the Pharisees' question betrays God's intention for marriage. In their debates about when a man can divorce his wife, the Pharisees have entirely missed God's heart.

Some Christians find in the creation stories of Genesis 1-2 a divine model for gender and marriage. They find prescribed gender roles where, for example, men are made to create and conquer, while women are made to receive and nurture. They also find a prescribed, gender-based structure for marriage. Husbands are to be spiritual leaders and rule their households sacrificially, while wives are to be capable helpers and serve their husbands and children cheerfully. This interpretation of Genesis 1-2 is very popular in my setting, but we need to ask: Does this interpretation coincide with how *Jesus* interprets Genesis 1-2? No, I don't think it does.

Let's note that Jesus says nothing about what women and men ought to be and do. In fact, it is striking that through all four Gospels, in all the teaching recorded from Jesus' time with his disciples, Jesus never talks about gender roles or gives instructions based on notions of masculinity and femininity. None of his preaching, parables, or warnings require or endorse sex-based tasks or gender-based norms of behavior. You will never see Jesus tell a male disciple to "man up" or instruct a female disciple to "be more submissive." Jesus never instructs his disciples to be more manly or womanly, and you will never hear Jesus sneer at women as women or make jokes about men as men.[4]

On the contrary, against Jewish custom, Jesus welcomes women as his disciples, giving them a place alongside the men, and sending them out as the first to proclaim his resurrection (Mt 28:10; Lk 10:38-42; 24:9; Jn 20:17). What's more, Jesus repeatedly subverts the whole notion of human hierarchies on which the idea of gender roles is built. The most famous instance of this occurs when James and John (with their mom) are caught jockeying for prime position in Jesus' new kingdom. Naturally, the other disciples get a little huffy about their scheming. So, Jesus admonishes all of them: They should not behave as the Gentiles do, who seek to dominate one another. "Instead," Jesus says, "whoever wants to become great among you must be your servant, and whoever wants to be first must be slave of all" (Mk 10:43-44).

If that wasn't clear enough, Jesus tells his disciples and the crowds that they are now part of one family with one teacher and one Lord:

> But you are not to be called "Rabbi," for you have one Teacher, and you are all brothers. And do not call anyone on earth "father," for you have one Father, and he is in heaven. Nor are you to be called instructors, for you have one Instructor, the Messiah. The greatest among you will be your servant. For those who exalt themselves will be humbled, and those who humble themselves will be exalted. (Mt 23:8-12)

Given Jesus' vision of mutuality in God's kingdom, it's no surprise that he doesn't teach his disciples to emulate human hierarchies—gender-based or otherwise.

So, if Genesis 1–2 is not about hierarchy and gender roles, then how does Jesus' interpretation of Genesis 1–2 help us to understand Christian families today? When Jesus talks about Genesis 1–2 with the Pharisees, he does so to highlight the *joining* or *unity* of the spouses:

> "Haven't you read," he replied, "that at the beginning the Creator 'made them male and female,' and said, 'For this reason a man will leave his father and mother and be united to his wife, and the two will become one flesh'? So they are no longer two, but one flesh. Therefore what God has joined together, let no one separate." (Mt 19:4-6)

Recalling Genesis 1:27, Jesus acknowledges the essential unity of human beings as female and male. As the first creation story shows, humanity is made in God's image. Though they share with the animal world the blessing to "be fruitful and increase in number" (Gen 1:22, 28), they are also instructed to "subdue" the earth and exercise rule over "every living creature" (Gen 1:28).

So human beings, male and female together, represent God in the world, especially in their vocation to rule over the earth. There is no hierarchy required (unless we're talking about humankind having "rule," which is an important but separate conversation). Neither is there discussion of marriage. Rather, Genesis 1:26-27 is explaining to its readers why there are two "kinds" of humans, female and male, and what they are for. The answer? *God made them and blessed them to be God's image on the earth.*[5]

When Jesus moves from humanity as "male and female" (Gen 1:27) to "become one flesh" (Gen 2:24), he links the distinction between human beings as male and female to the "one flesh" unity of spouses. That is to say, the joining that takes place in marriage depends on the distinction between the sexes, who were created together as God's image. Marriage, then, is a one-flesh unity-in-difference that depicts vividly God's created purpose in human beings: representing God on the earth together.

Again, there is no hierarchy in this account. Neither gender roles nor cultural notions of masculinity and femininity are at play. To find either in Genesis 1:26-27, especially as Jesus interprets it, one must import it into the text. But smuggling cultural stereotypes into the Bible only to turn around and read them back out of the Bible is what good professors call bad hermeneutics.

But what about the creation story of Genesis 2 with Adam and Eve in the garden? In his interaction with the Pharisees, Jesus doesn't get into the nitty-gritty. He only references the narrator's commentary about marriage in practice, what KJV preachers memorably call "leaving and cleaving." Interestingly, he never mentions procreation as the reason, or even a reason, for marriage. Still, we can explore the implications of Genesis 2 considering what we've already gleaned from Jesus' teaching. In fact, in the second chapter of Genesis, the relational aspect of human nature is underlined even more.

Genesis 2:7 says, "Then the LORD God formed a man [adam] from the dust [adamah] of the ground and breathed into his nostrils the breath of life, and the man became a living being." God gives the first human a task: "The LORD God took the man and put him in the Garden of Eden to work it and take care of it" (Gen 2:15). One can imagine the many things a person might do to work and take care of a magnificent garden, but the Hebrew tells us there's more going on here than just gardening. The words translated "work" and "take care" (or "tend" and "keep") in Genesis 2:15 seem to intentionally parallel the service of the Levites in the temple (Num 3:8-9). The first human, therefore, is assigned the work of tending to and caring for sacred space: the garden amid the world God has made as God's dwelling place. Notice that it is precisely in the task of tending sacred space that God says it is not good for the man to be alone (Gen 2:18). In other words, it is not good for the man to do his priestly work alone.

Genesis 2:18, then, isn't about human loneliness (though loneliness isn't good for us either). Rather, it is about fulfilling the man's divinely given vocation. Instead of being alone, the man must have an *ezer kenegdo* (Gen 2:18): an "ally in a task" or "one who aids someone in accomplishing a duty." What is this ally-ship for but the task for which the man was created? Woman will be one who helps man to accomplish their mutual, God-given task: tending and keeping creation, God's sacred space.

Some Christians argue the word *ezer kenegdo* indicates subordinate status, but they are quite simply wrong.[6] The word *ezer* occurs twenty-one times in the Bible. It is used twice to describe the woman in Genesis 2, sixteen times to describe God, and three times to describe an army aiding in battle. In Exodus 18:4: "and the other was named Eliezer, for he said, 'My father's God was my helper; he saved me from the sword of Pharaoh.'" In Deuteronomy 33:26: "There is no one like the God of Jeshurun, who rides across the heavens to help you and on the clouds in his majesty." And Psalm 33:20 says, "We wait in hope for the LORD; he is our help and our shield." These are just a few examples, but the point is this: The word *ezer* is never used with the sense of subservience, especially since it is used most often to speak of God. Since *ezer* is almost always referring to something related to the military, it may be best to translate it as "ally" rather than "helper."

Even so, some proponents of hierarchal gender roles will claim that the way woman is formed from man indicates subordinate status. Again, I disagree. Genesis 2:21-22 says, "The LORD God caused the man to fall into a deep sleep; and while he was sleeping, he took one of the man's ribs and then closed up the place with flesh. Then the LORD God made a woman from the rib he had taken out of the man, and he brought her to the man."

First, we should note that the Hebrew word *sela* does not mean "rib," as many English translations suggest (Gen 2:21). In the rest of the Scriptures, the word *sela* never means "rib";

in every other case, it is translated "side."[7] The Septuagint (the Greek translation of the Old Testament) uses the Greek word *pleura,* which also means "side." So, Genesis is saying that the woman is constructed out of the man's side. The woman is by no means derivative of the man; she is *his side*, or one-half of a whole. The point of Genesis 2:22 is not to emphasize the *difference* between Adam and Eve (whether in terms of essence, function, or roles) but their *similarity*. Put simply, Adam and Eve are made of the same stuff. Eve is not an alien creature but his ontological equal.[8] She is Adam's side—his very own flesh and bone—the best ally possible for priestly work in God's presence.

This interpretation, which many other scholars support, makes more sense within the context of the ancient Near East, where it was culturally more common to see women as wholly different creatures from men who are destined to be subordinate to them. (Not just the ancient Near East, either, but in later Greek thought too.) The author of Genesis, then, is offering a countercultural narrative, one that affirms women's full humanity and God-ordained status side-by-side with men amid a patriarchal society.

Yet, proponents of some family blueprints might object again: Isn't the ultimate point of woman in Genesis 1–2 the procreation of children? Isn't procreation the woman's true reason for existence? For a third time, the answer is no.

In Genesis 2, there is no reference to any procreative purposes whatsoever until after she and the man eat from the tree of the knowledge of good and evil (Gen 3:16). Yes, Genesis 1:26-27 contains a reference to procreation. In context, though, man and woman are created simultaneously in the image of God and blessed *as a pair* just as the animals are blessed to "be fruitful and increase in number" and "fill the earth and subdue it" (Gen 1:28). But there is no sense in Genesis 1 that fruitfulness and multiplication are functions that women bear exclusively. Rather, they are responsibilities the human couple shares. In Genesis 2, the man and woman are tasked with caring for the place where

God's presence dwells, and it is precisely the priestly work of preserving sacred space that man is unable to accomplish without
woman. She is man's "ally of the same kind" (*ezer kenegdo*).[9]

The main point of Genesis 1-2, therefore, is to explain the
identity and purpose of humanity within God's creation. The mutuality of human beings, female and male, is part of the portrait
of humanity that Genesis offers, and it becomes the basis for a
Christian theology of the marriage relationship. We learn this by
reading Genesis 1-2 with Jesus Christ in light of God's revelation
in him.

## From Who Jesus Is to How We Ought to Live

Okay, so we begin with Jesus, but how do we move from his
person and teachings to the way we're supposed to live today?
And how do we move from the way things are to the way things
ought to be? Such movement is the work of theological ethics,
and it is not easy. Neither Jesus nor the Bible can answer in a
straightforward way all our questions about how to live in our
contemporary world: Everything from educational models to
political policy to business operations to medical technology—
not to mention the many personal decisions we are faced with
throughout our lives. All these and more are left to us to discern
and improvise as faithfully as we can in view of Jesus and the
Bible's explicit teaching. That is why Christians have been arguing
about such things (and much more) for over two millennia, with
the matters of family, singleness, marriage, sex, and childrearing
being especially contentious.

A methodology for theological ethics far exceeds the bounds
of this book, but I want to name at least one thing that is essential to the Christian's ability to discern and improvise faithfully. We must be actively engaged in a life of repentance and
faith, seeking to walk in the "narrow" way of Jesus under the
reign of God (Mt 7:14). To know the will of God and do it means
joining other Jesus followers in an embodied manifestation of

the kingdom in the here and now. We will not do this perfectly, of course. That is not possible. But the point is to pursue a way of life characterized by following, praying, worshiping, joining, bearing one another's burdens, and the like.

Without such a formative context, where the Spirit is free to call, convict, and compel us, we are liable to mishear and misunderstand the voice of God. In fact, the New Testament makes it clear that it is possible to live in ways that look pious on the outside but are, in fact, far from Jesus (Mt 7:21-23; 23:27-28). We can think we are doing the right thing but have actually been led astray by our damaged consciences (1 Tim 4:2). Unless we are responding in repentance and faith every day to the invitation of Jesus, even if it's only with a veritable mustard seed of both (Mt 17:20; Lk 17:6), we cannot hope to discern and improvise Christian faithfulness today.

# 3

# God's Kingdom and God's Family

**In 203 CE, a wealthy Roman mother** named Perpetua was killed in the Carthage arena while a stadium full of people looked on. She had been imprisoned for being a Christian but refused to renounce her faith to avoid a violent death. Her son was still an infant, and her family was horrified that she might choose to leave her child behind. Her father came to the prison and begged her to apostatize: "Daughter, have pity on my grey head. . . . Consider your brothers; consider your mother and your aunt; consider your son who cannot live without you. Give up your stubbornness before you destroy all of us." But Perpetua refused. Though she dearly loved her family and her son, her loyalty was now to Christ and his community of disciples. She had exchanged the norms of the Roman household for that of God's household. "I cannot be called anything else than what I am," Perpetua said, "a Christian."

During her imprisonment with several others, Perpetua kept a diary of her experiences and dreams, which she attributed to the Holy Spirit. Her visions offered assurance of victory over death to her companions, a group of new believers preparing to be baptized. Among the group was an enslaved woman, Felicitas, who was also a new mother. Her child, a girl, was born in prison. Yet, upon their condemnation to be killed by wild beasts, the group, including the two mothers, rejoiced at their good fortune. Perpetua reported that her body and mind submitted to the sentence with peace: "God saw to it that my child no longer needed my nursing. . . . After that I was no longer tortured by anxiety about my child or by pain in my breasts." She was prepared to die for her faith, entrusting her child to God's care.

Once in the arena, Perpetua, Felicitas, and their friends were attacked by wild animals and then set upon by gladiators with swords. They died of their wounds after kissing each other in a sign of peace.[1]

Perpetua, Felicitas, and their companions are to be admired for their faithfulness. But their story—and the stories of all martyrs—also raises questions about the bonds that unite people and the kind of life that fosters such courageous witness. What would make Perpetua and Felicitas leave behind their babies to die as martyrs? Why did their loyalty to fellow Christians outweigh their loyalty to blood relatives? We know the group were catechumens who spent considerable time together for prayer, fasting, and instruction as they prepared for entrance into the church. Somehow during that time, the fellowship of God's family became more powerful than the bonds of biology; the water of baptism became thicker than the blood of kinship.

Jesus' summons to follow him does not dissolve family bonds, nor does it justify neglect of one's kin. Yet, Jesus' gospel does call us into a new family. And what is the gospel? Put simply, the gospel is the power of God through which Israel's exalted Messiah, on the basis of his death, resurrection, and ascension, restores all of life to be subject to God's reign.[2] In response to the gospel, we are "born again" into a household rooted not in blood but in the Holy Spirit (Jn 3:3). To understand family rightly and to pursue family life faithfully, we must do so within the proper paradigm: the family of God, the church, and the kingdom Jesus inaugurated. "Family first," then, is not a Christian principle. Rather, loyalty to Jesus and his household comes first, forming the framework within which we practice loyalty to one's household and the broader community.

The Christian life is always lived in response to Christ's prior initiative in salvation: "Follow me!"[3] We were dead in our transgressions and sins (Eph 2:1), yet "while we were God's enemies, we were reconciled to him through the death of his Son" (Rom 5:10). In view of what God has done, we respond to Jesus' invitation through repentance and faith—turning from our former ways and loyalties to swear allegiance to Christ alone. We are received into Jesus' community of disciples through the waters of baptism and the fire of the Spirit. We are placed into a family rooted not in heredity, but in Christ's body and blood, and we are initiated into citizenship not of this world and its nations, but that of the kingdom of God. Only within this context can the family's purpose rightly emerge.

## The Kingdom of God

What is the kingdom of God? God's kingdom is the preoccupation of the Scriptures and the primary focus of Jesus' preaching and teaching. The Bible's portrayal of God's kingdom is complex and multilayered, but a summary will get us started.

God's kingdom is God's rule or kingship—that is, God's authority and dominion over all the earth. As the psalmist says, "The Lord has established his throne in heaven, and his kingdom rules over all" (Ps 103:19). God's rule is manifestly present now in many ways, but God's rule is also being opposed by created agents working against God: creatures, spirits, demons, and humankind. When we pray "Thy kingdom come," we are praying that God's sovereign rule would be recognized by everyone and manifested everywhere.

The manifest presence of God's universal rule is characterized by right worship of God and right relationship in God's world. The Old Testament calls this reality *shalom*, a just and harmonious state of flourishing for all under God. Thus, God's kingdom has what we might call vertical and horizontal expression. As Jesus summarized in the greatest commandment: loving God and loving one's neighbors as oneself (Mt 22:37-40).

In addition, God's kingdom is God's people, the subjects who recognize God as their king and give God their allegiance. God's people share in a present reality under the rule of the Holy Spirit, which is both spiritual and material (Rom 14:17). In this sense, the kingdom of God is *almost* the same as the church—the community of Jesus' disciples that are embodying God's rule in their life together. But the kingdom remains its own thing, too, because God's kingdom is portrayed as a future reality, an inheritance to be bestowed on God's people when Christ comes again in glory (Mt 25:34).

So, the church is not precisely the same as God's kingdom, yet the people of God are so closely associated with God's kingdom in the New Testament that it is sometimes difficult to tell them apart. God has "rescued us from the dominion of darkness and brought us into the kingdom of the Son he loves" and one day an "entrance" will be "richly provided for you . . . into the eternal kingdom of our Lord and Savior Jesus Christ" (Col 1:13; 2 Pet 1:11).

Finally, God's kingdom is the space of God's rule. In some cases, the Bible speaks of God's realm as already present now, and sometimes the Bible portrays God's realm as a future hope. Somehow both are true at the same time. The realm of God's kingship is already present now, able to be entered, experienced, and manifested today, and the realm of God's kingship is not yet fully present, awaiting a future consummation in the age to come. In that day, as the book of Revelation so beautifully portrays, the heavens and the earth will be remade, and God will come at last to dwell fully within God's world.[4]

Based on all the above, the gospel of the kingdom proclaims the good news that Jesus Christ, in fulfillment of Israel's hopes, has saved us from sin and its consequences through his death and resurrection, and filled us with his Spirit such that we are joined in one body, the church, which lives under God's rule now as we await the consummation of God's kingdom in the future.

## The Church, the Family, and the Kingdom

The already-not-yet nature of the kingdom of God makes for a tricky paradigm in which to imagine the church and the family—and yet it must be attempted. Because it is precisely God's kingdom that makes meaning of our present lives. We live together in the tension of God's kingdom inaugurated now in Christ and God's kingdom yet to come (Rev 21:1-5).

Both the church and the family straddle the already-not-yet. Both must discern, therefore, what faithfulness looks like within our current context—in places where the kingdom of God has come in power through Christ by the Spirit and places where the kingdom of darkness continues to fight against God's ways. Unlike the church, however, which anticipates a future union with Christ in the new heavens and new earth, Scripture suggests that human families as we currently experience them will come to an end. They have an expiration date of sorts once God is "all in all" (1 Cor 15:28). It's not entirely clear what this means, but I think that it certainly does *not* mean that the relationships that make us who we are will be obliterated. Rather, I suspect that our lives will cease to be structured by the priority of biological kinship.

In addition to the image of Christ's bride, the church in which Christ's disciples have been joined is called the "body of Christ" (1 Cor 10:16; 12:27; Eph 4:12). We are perhaps so used to this language that its oddity doesn't occur to us, but it is an unusual image for God's people, suggesting a level of connectedness and intimacy that surpasses even bridal language. With Christ as the head, the body makes the presence of Christ known to the world through its words and deeds. Through the body, Christ demonstrates his coming kingdom in the here and now.

One of the most important aspects of the body of Christ for Paul is that it is made up of Jews and Gentiles. Consider his words to the mainly Gentile church in Ephesus:

> Surely you have heard about the administration of God's grace that was given to me for you, that is, the mystery made known to me by revelation, as I have already written briefly. . . . This mystery is that through the gospel the Gentiles are heirs together with Israel, members together of one body, and sharers together in the promise in Christ Jesus. (Eph 3:2-3, 6)

Contemporary churches don't talk much about Jews and Gentiles today, but the joining of these former enemies into a reconciled community is a central preoccupation of the New Testament. For Paul, the union of such disparate peoples is so surprising that it had to be disclosed directly by God: a mystery once kept hidden but now revealed. Thus, we discover that *joining* is central to the gospel of the kingdom.[5]

Last, and most importantly for our purposes, Scripture characterizes the church as God's household. Considering the centrality of natural kinship in the Old Testament, the New Testament's use of familial language is striking. We've already seen that Jesus speaks of his "brother and sister and mother" as those who "do the will of God" (Mk 3:35). Clearly his reframing of family became central to the new community of his disciples. Not only is "brothers and sisters" the preferred language of the epistles for addressing the church, but also Paul speaks of his ministry in both paternal and maternal language:

- "For in Christ Jesus I became your father through the gospel." (1 Cor 4:15)

- "My dear children, for whom I am again in the pains of child-birth until Christ is formed in you!" (Gal 4:19)
- "Just as a nursing mother cares for her children, so we cared for you." (1 Thess 2:7-8)
- "For you know that we dealt with each of you as a father deals with his own children, encouraging, comforting and urging you to live lives worthy of God." (1 Thess 2:11-12)

Yes, Christians remain part of their natural families. Both Jesus and his apostles teach followers of the Way how to live in a Christlike manner within those natural and social ties. Fulfilling the ethical and social obligations of Christian faith would have been especially difficult for the vulnerable members of non-Christian households like children, women, and enslaved persons, none of whom had say-so over their bodies. But the fact remains that the New Testament understands loyalty to God's household to *precede* loyalty to individual households, and this is assuredly why the Jesus way was, at least at first, viewed as a threat to the moral and political order of the Greco-Roman world.

How are we united in God's new family? Through baptism. Paul explains it this way to the churches in Galatia:

> In Christ Jesus you are all children of God through faith, for all of you who were baptized into Christ have clothed your-selves with Christ. There is neither Jew nor Gentile, neither slave nor free, nor is there male and female, for you are all one in Christ Jesus. If you belong to Christ, then you are Abraham's seed, and heirs according to the promise. (Gal 3:26-29)

Though practiced in various ways, Christian baptism is a ritual washing that signifies many things at once: cleansing from sin, participation in Christ's death and resurrection, and entrance into new creation. Unlike circumcision, the mark of the old covenant, baptism is received by all: women and men, children and elderly,

Jews and Gentiles, single and married, free and enslaved. Both the New Testament and early church history testify that the rite of baptism gradually undermined the class systems and power dynamics that governed behavior in the Roman Empire. The baptism ritual enacted a divine joining of many different bodies into one body in one Spirit with one head, Jesus Christ, under one Father (Eph 4:4-6).[6] Not only are we as individuals freed from sin and death, transformed into new creatures, but we are also formed into a community of new creation. Social disparities based on gender, slavery, and class cannot ultimately withstand the weight of that divine joining.[7]

If baptism unites all believers, then Holy Communion or the Eucharist nourishes that one body with spiritual food. Gathered around the table of the Lord, we share in the signs of bread and wine, which Jesus gave us to eat and drink "in remembrance" of him (Lk 22:19). In the Eucharist, the church celebrates the memorial of our redemption, requests sanctification by the Spirit, and seeks to serve God and one another "in unity, constancy, and peace."[8]

Whatever one believes about the presence of Christ in the bread and wine, the Lord's Supper "proclaim[s] the Lord's death until he comes" (1 Cor 11:26). And why does that matter? Because the Lord's death accomplished our peace, as Paul says, "creat[ing] in himself one new humanity out of the two, thus making peace, and in one body to reconcile both of them to God through the cross, by which he put to death their hostility" (Eph 2:15-16). As a result, those who gather for the meal without attending to the well-being of all the church's members—the new humanity created in Christ's body—"eat and drink judgment on themselves" (1 Cor 11:29).

Once our family was visiting a church for the first time. Our two older children chose to remain with Ronnie and me for the main worship service while our youngest, then seven years old, went to children's worship downstairs. We were told by the volunteers as we dropped her off that the children would be brought up to participate in Communion in the second half of the service. This meant we did not have to come down to retrieve them as we were used to doing at our regular church. We found this arrangement very convenient and settled into the familiar rhythms of the liturgy.

The worry started, however, when the priest began the eucharistic prayers and the children had not yet arrived. We exchanged looks and surveyed the sanctuary wondering what was going on. None of the other parents looked concerned. Maybe we had misunderstood the volunteers. Were we supposed to go get them after all? Soon, though, the ushers were dismissing our row.

After we received Communion, Ronnie headed out to find the kids. As he went out the door, they were already arriving from downstairs, led by their teachers in a long, slightly disorderly line. Our youngest smiled and waved as she passed us, looking as though it was the most normal thing in the world. We watched as the children entered the sanctuary and happily went forward together to receive the Eucharist. One-by-one they kneeled and received and then left in their small entourage to return to children's worship.

Ronnie and I were baffled and not a little annoyed. We were so used to children receiving Communion with their families that we couldn't imagine being bypassed entirely while they received together. Even though our daughter was not a bit bothered by the experience, we were unsettled and expressed our frustration to each other. If we come back, we concluded, we'll have to decide whether we want things to happen that way again. Maybe we'll ask her to remain with us next time.

It wasn't until we relayed this experience to our single friend Maggie that we saw things in a different light. She wondered aloud why it wasn't appropriate for children to receive Communion with their class since, through our baptisms, the church is our first family. She knew we sought to bring Christian sisters and brothers into our household regularly as part of this expanded vision of family. If the waters of baptism are in fact thicker than the blood of biology, she wondered, then why wouldn't the church's practice of Eucharist prioritize God's household over the private household? We were rightly chastened by Maggie's response, and I've often been reminded of her words when our church celebrates Holy Communion.

Alongside baptism and the Lord's Supper, the New Testament tells us that the church of Jesus Christ is formed by other practices too. They devote themselves to "the apostles' teaching and to fellowship, to the breaking of bread and to prayer" (Acts 2:42). Through the ages, these elements have marked the local manifestations of God's kingdom. The meetings of Christ's disciples have always consisted of attending to the apostles' teaching, primarily through Scripture, to fellowship with one another, to bread breaking (perhaps an early reference to the Eucharist), and to prayer.

Acts records that the early church's devotion to these practices contributed to a common life of mutual self-giving, not just spiritually but also materially:

> And God's grace was so powerfully at work in them all that there were no needy persons among them. For from time to time those who owned land or houses sold them, brought the money from the sales and put it at the apostles' feet, and it was distributed to anyone who had need. (Acts 4:33-35)

Notice that the powerful grace of God is closely associated with the sharing and distribution of resources: "time, talent, and treasures, the trinity of possessions." God's household cares for its members as one would care for one's own kin, an intimacy of life and sharing of resources that is almost always reserved for blood ties alone.[9]

Going further, the church in Acts also refused to take up arms against their persecutors, never resorting to violence even in a desire to preserve their own lives. In fact, the stories of Jesus' first apostles are filled with suffering and indignities of all kinds: harassment, arrest, trials, imprisonment, torture, and execution. Paul summarized it memorably: "We are hard pressed on every side, but not crushed; perplexed, but not in despair; persecuted, but not abandoned; struck down, but not destroyed. We always carry around in our body the death of Jesus, so that the life of Jesus may also be revealed in our body" (2 Cor 4:8-10). Understanding their persecution to be a privileged means of participating in Christ's own suffering and death, the early church did not take up arms (Phil 1:29; Col 1:24). In response to curses, the church blesses; in response to arrest, the church sings; and in response to violence, the church prays (Lk 6:28; Acts 16:25; 12:5).

## Presenting Our Bodies Within Christ's Body

In all the instances described previously, we see that not only does the gospel of Jesus Christ save our souls, but it also redeems and transforms our bodies. Reception of and submission to the good news results in changes to our whole person—and our whole person in relation to other whole persons in the new household of God. Paul expresses the reality of our new life memorably in terms of "living sacrifice" to the church in Rome:

> Therefore, I urge you, brothers and sisters, in view of God's mercy, to offer your bodies as a living sacrifice, holy and pleasing to God—this is your true and proper worship. Do not conform to the pattern of this world but be transformed by the renewing of your mind. Then you will be able to test and approve what God's will is—his good, pleasing, and perfect will. (Rom 12:1-2)

What does it mean to offer your body as a living sacrifice? When I was a new teenage Christian, my youth group leaders applied this text to sexual morality. If you're offering your body to God, they said, then you aren't offering your body to illicit sexual behavior. It was also used to support the rejection of certain kinds of music, television, and films as hostile to the "renewing" of our minds. How will we ever learn to think on what's true and good and beautiful if we're dwelling on things false, evil, and ugly (Phil 4:8)?

At the time, I was (perhaps predictably) resistant to this line of reasoning, and to this day I remain unwilling to simply reject outright any art forms that aren't explicitly "Christian." Yet, to my teachers' larger concern, I now recognize their wisdom. They had a point! Interestingly, though, as an adult I've heard Paul's exhortation used to promote physical health and fitness—a kind of diet-and-CrossFit-for-Jesus approach. Perhaps this reading of Romans 12:1-2 is influenced by our social-media-saturated environment where we're trained to curate our appearance for public consumption. Wherever the view comes from, though, it is also missing the larger point.

I'm not against taking care of our bodies or being wise with our consumption, but both interpretations leave much to be desired. Paul was not talking about physical fitness. He is very much for bodily discipline, but that's never for the purpose of appearance (1 Cor 9:27). Body size and physical health are morally neutral things. Being able to bench press 250 pounds or run a marathon might be personal goals of yours, but there are no special rewards in heaven for such achievements. All bodies are good bodies because God made them, God loves them, and God redeems them. The purpose of bodies is relationship, not perfection.[10] In addition, Jesus' life and ministry seem to demonstrate a special preference for those deemed unhealthy and unfit by the majority population. Think of the master in the parable of the great banquet who, rebuffed by his initial list of guests, declares, "Go out quickly into the streets and alleys of the town and bring in the poor, the crippled, the blind and the lame" (Lk 14:21).

As important as both chastity and bodily discipline are, to interpret Paul's "living sacrifice" language in such narrow ways ignores a host of communal implications for the gospel.[11] They

keep our imagination in the realm of the individual, discon-
necting the individual body from the body of Christ. The formation of one redeemed people—Jew and Gentile—through
the power of the one Messiah is the overall theme of Romans.
So, it makes sense that when Paul exhorts the Roman church to
offer their bodies as a living sacrifice, he does so with communal,
social, and material implications in mind. In fact, this is precisely
what we see playing out in the story of Acts. Individuals are transformed, freed from the powers of sin and death, and freed for
the joining of disparate peoples into the church, which lives out
the kingdom of God on earth through tangible, bodily practices.

Described in this way, African American pastor and historian
Malcolm Foley is right to suggest that God's household, the church,
is created to offer a powerful threefold witness against the persistent evils of our world.[12] Against the narrative of "natural" superiority through things such as kinship, racialization, sex, gender,
class, and ability, the church offers a counternarrative of covenant
kinship under Christ's lordship—a family formed through baptism
and Christ's body and blood. Against practices of economic exploitation and wealth accumulation rooted in greed, the church
offers a counter economy of self-giving and wealth sharing, a family
in Christ that ensures all have what they need. And against practices of violence and domination, the church offers a community
of rightly ordered loves, which prioritizes the life of the other over
one's own life because of our future hope in Christ's resurrection.
When we "present our bodies as a living sacrifice," therefore, we
do so as bodies now united to other bodies in the whole body of
Christ, a sacrament of the kingdom in this present evil age.

## What's the Point Again?

So, the kingdom of God is manifested in the body of Christ made
up of Jews and Gentiles who are made kin through the waters of
baptism and the celebration of the Eucharist. But to what end?
What is the purpose or goal to which all of this is moving?

I agree with Anglo-American theologian David Fitch that the purpose of the church is to abide in God, to be a faithful presence of God in the world.[13] Yes, the church worships, prays, serves, gives, preaches, makes disciples, and so much more, but ultimately the church is *bearing witness* to the reign of God in their life together, loving God and loving neighbor, manifesting a glimpse of God's shalom within this present evil age. The point of our common life, then, is to be apprentices to Christ and his kingdom together through the power of the Spirit.

I realize this is exalted language. Some of us may have difficulty imagining a church where what I've described is lived out. It's one thing to say these things, it's another thing to do them. Maybe this is why Christians so often look to the martyrs like Perpetua and Felicitas for inspiration. In some ways, it's easier to imagine dying in a moment of courageous witness than living a whole lifetime with other fallible people seeking to be apprentices to Jesus together.

Unfortunately, no church is going to embody these realities perfectly. Even the early church described in Acts and addressed in the Epistles demonstrates all the flaws and problems you'd expect from an assembly of human beings: self-interest, anger, divisions, sexual immorality, greed, pride, drunkenness, and more. Until God's kingdom comes in its fullness, we will have to see the way of life I've described as aspirational—the end to which the Spirit is leading us—but one to which we will never fully arrive.

Thankfully, it is not an all-or-nothing scenario. The mystery of the incarnation shows that God is pleased to work in and through the world, which entails all the messes and mistakes that human beings assuredly make. It was Jesus, after all, who picked a bunch of Galilean fishermen, a tax collector, and some religious fanatics to lead his fledgling community. Amid all our failures to become the church described previously, we find hope in the fact that God's Spirit is always present, bringing order out of chaos and light out of darkness. The body of Christ made up of Jews and

Gentiles, slave and free, male and female, bearing witness to God's kingdom together is in fact God's mystery hidden in ages past and now revealed in Christ by the Spirit. This forms the framework for understanding the point of family today.

Over the past few years, our family has been part of beginning a new church in our community. It wasn't something we really set out to do. It kind of happened to us as we began meeting with a couple of other households for prayer and fellowship. Without any of the normal church planting methods, our little community has grown to around sixty people. The relationships we have formed through the slow process of becoming a church have transformed our family in multiple beautiful ways, but one of the most important is that each of us has found within our fledgling community the siblings we didn't know we needed. This is not to say it's always sunshine and rainbows; no community is perfect. Nonetheless, every day we're finding our love multiplied and expanded as we learn to join one another across differences of gender, race, class, ability, and more.

It's common today for such beyond-biology relationships to be characterized as "chosen family," and that's not necessarily wrong. But I think that label falls short of what Christians believe is happening. It's not that church replaces the nuclear family or that church is transformed into the nuclear family. Rather, such family-like bonds within the church are signs that all our households are manifesting (albeit imperfectly) our unity in Christ's body, our mutual inclusion in God's household. When this happens by the Spirit under Christ's lordship, each household finds its fuller, richer, more expansive significance as they are joined with other households in the church. Just as we as individuals become more fully ourselves as we join with others, so also do our families become more fully themselves as they join with others in mutual love, healing, and liberation. Together, we are all becoming more fully part of God's family, the church, which is at the center of God's kingdom in the world today.

# 4

# Family as Apprenticeship to Love

**One summer a couple of years ago** I was sitting in a packed auditorium listening to a fundraising pitch for a Christian organization. The speaker began with a slide that read, "Is it still possible to raise launchable eighteen-year-olds?" Next followed a brief description of the "boomerang generation"—children who go off to college and career but end up back in their parents' homes, either temporarily or permanently. The rest of the presentation flowed from there, explaining how their organization was doing their best to help produce "launchable" kids. The implication was clear: If parents will cooperate with the organization, contributing their funds and their children, then they will help produce adults who don't "boomerang" back to mom and dad.

Ever the theologian, and with not a little contrarianism, I sipped my coffee and wondered, *Is "launchable" eighteen-year-olds really the point? Is that what we're trying to do as Christian parents?*

I have nothing against the speaker or the organization in question. They have sound, research-based reasons for what they do, and I wish there were more organizations like theirs. But I haven't been able to shake the question that began the pitch because it contains multiple assumptions that merit interrogation.

What is the goal of parenting? What is adulthood, and by what standards do we determine that? What is the impact of ethnicity, racialization, culture, ability, and class on such standards? Do dominant cultural scripts about "launchability" coincide with Christian teaching? If not, how might that impact our approach to family, childrearing, and discipleship? Also, where is the church and what is its purpose in this launchability paradigm?

For instance, thinking of parenting in terms of raising launchable eighteen-year-olds assumes that the mark of adulthood is economic independence. And how is this achieved? By becoming a self-sufficient person who fits easily into the free-market labor system in our late-modern capitalist economy. Parents and caregivers achieve this goal by training children to become the kinds of people who succeed within such a framework. Parents then partner with schools, camps, and the like to discipline bodies and train minds, initiating them into habits that will cultivate the "virtues" required to become a "productive member of society."

On the one hand, this is fine. Developmental maturity typically leads to a child's psychological and bodily differentiation from their caregivers. Also, engagement in meaningful work is essential to a flourishing human life.[1] I want my children to be able to sustain themselves in our society, and that means educating them toward that end. There's nothing inherently wrong with that.

On the other hand, I'm mindful of the wisdom offered by American political theorist Kathy E. Ferguson, "When we are busy arguing about the questions that appear within a certain frame, the frame itself becomes invisible; we become enframed within it."[2] Many of us—and I'm talking first and foremost about myself—have left unquestioned the premise that paid labor is the only way, or at least the primary way, to demonstrate human worth. We've left unchallenged the supposition that the value of a person's work is determined by what the market is willing to pay for it. And many of us, whether we want to admit it, have learned to conceive of the relative success or failure of a person's work in terms of net income, material acquisition, and power. How does the family come to function with these assumptions in place? Stated bluntly, our families become autonomous sites of consumption trying to produce other autonomous sites of consumption.[3] But surely there's more to it than that!

All these thoughts lead to the one big question that undergirds all the others: *What is family for?* That families serve a variety of important purposes is not in question, but what families mean in the scope of God's providence—this is what nagged at me as we left the fundraising pitch and walked back into the parking lot.

## Humanity, Families, and Love

Human beings are made for communion—for union with God, self, and each other in the world God made. Communion is the way human beings and all creation participate in the eternal life shared by the Father, Son, and Holy Spirit. Such participation is possible only by God's grace through love—love for God, self, and neighbor. As Thomas Merton says, "Love is our true destiny. We do not find the meaning of life by ourselves alone—we find it with another."[4]

Communion is not a purely spiritual reality though. It is not a mystical realm that hovers above the particulars of our daily lives. Breakfast bodegas and morning jogs, oil changes and vacuuming, subway schedules and bath time—these are the sites where communion takes place, because love isn't ultimately a feeling. Love wills the good of the other. Love extends oneself for the purpose of nurturing the growth and well-being of the other. Thus, love is first and foremost a choice, an activity, a practice.[5]

The goal of human existence provides the framework for understanding the goal of human families. Families were made for humans, not humans for families. In other words, God's purpose for families serves the end of God's purpose for human beings.

In fact, all created things are meant to serve that end. Insofar as our interaction with the world is *not* ordered toward communion with God and others, we are missing the mark.

The point of families, therefore, is love. Families are born out of love–the triune love of God that is the foundation of the universe–and families are intended to be schools for love. Because it is love that makes for communion.

If part of you cringes at such a Hallmark-sounding claim, you're certainly not alone. But love is the deepest desire of the human person. Beneath our needs for food, water, sleep, shelter, and meaningful work is the need to know ourselves as beloved. Beneath our desires for achievement, pleasure, entertainment, sex, and more is the desire to be loved. So much of the world's pain and suffering is due to the lack of love.

## Family Wounds and Their Impact

Tragically, too many of us have experienced a lack of love in our families of origin. Ronnie and I were brought up by loving mothers who tried very hard to provide all that our young bodies and souls needed, yet we were regularly hurt and terrorized by the father figures in our homes. We learned a perverted and twisted form of love: love that meant constant self-effacing, suppressing feelings, hiding hurts, putting on a brave face, and soldiering on as if nothing were wrong. It was a love that meant nearly constant fear and an abiding sense of failure.

The 2006 film *Factory Girl* begins with drug-addicted socialite Edie Sedgwick, played by actor Sienna Miller, sharing about the abuse that took place within her apparently perfect family. She expressed her disillusionment like this:

> You know those photos of smiling families you always see on a mantelpiece? I can't even look at them because you never know what they're hiding. A *Life* magazine photographer came to our house to photograph the "ideal

American family." We looked happy and pretty, but underneath it just wasn't that way at all.[6]

I know the cynicism and disassociation that comes from living in an abusive environment. When you've known domination and exploitation from people who said with their mouths that they loved you, it makes sense that you'd snort derisively and move on. What's love got to do with anything?

Those of us who grew up without the safety, security, and constant love that our families should have provided find ourselves longing for those things in our adult years. Some of us struggle with the intimacy that relationships bring. We are drawn inextricably toward intimacy and repulsed by it at the same time. Some of us establish families hoping to correct the mistakes we experienced. We hope beyond hope that the intimacy we share with our chosen family will not result in more pain and sorrow. We cling to the promise of Psalm 27:10: "Though my father and mother forsake me, the LORD will receive me."

## Family Falsehoods and Their Impact

On top of the negative impact of our dysfunctional families, there have also been deficiencies in Christian teaching through the ages. One of the things that makes writing about families so difficult is that it is bound up with a host of assumptions about other things. Often those assumptions hide in the background, remaining unacknowledged. For instance, most of the church's early leaders assumed women were inherently inferior to men by every possible metric. It's not just that they believed in "male headship," to use contemporary language, but they believed women are mentally, emotionally, physically, and spiritually inferior to men, and that assumption was left unquestioned for many centuries.[7] Inevitably, such a view had an impact on how they interpreted and applied the Scriptures that pertain to families.

Other errors plagued teachers of the church too. Here are a few more:

- Children are not full persons.
- Physical punishment is a necessary part of childrearing without which children can't be taught.
- Hierarchy is essential to family relationships.
- Dual spheres—one for men and one for women—are a basic part of the world.
- The home is a haven from sin.
- Some families are simply better than others.
- Wealth is inherently neutral, so acquiring more and more of it is usually a good thing.
- Families are bedrock institutions that hold up society as it currently exists.

How can you discern what the faithful Christian family looks like if you are assuming falsehoods to be truths? You can't, at least not very capably. Yet, Western Christianity has been intertwined with ideas and practices counter to the way of Jesus for a long time, and it has influenced everything we've written, spoken, and built. Certainly, God has been present and at work amid our failures, but such instances are despite rank unfaithfulness. Thus, I think most Christians in my part of the world are still laboring to see Christian family practiced in a truly faithful, healing, and liberating way.

Thankfully, the point of Christian discipleship is not to replicate the lives and practices of Christians from previous generations. Just as I don't assume that modern folks know better because we are modern, I don't assume that ancient folks knew better because they're ancient. While we have much wisdom and insight to glean from Christians of times past, I do not think it is advisable or even possible to reproduce the ways of life present in prior eras. Our task is to accompany Jesus, led by the Holy

Spirit, in this time and this place, living out the kingdom of God as faithfully as possible right now.[8]

Peter tells us that in God's accounting a thousand years is like a day and a day is like a thousand years (2 Pet 3:8). Given that is the case, why would we look at two thousand years of church history and assume we've already fully understood the gospel and all its implications? What if we've only just begun day three in God's eternal timetable? What if, instead, we've only just begun to see things clearly and creatively respond to God's work in Christ? Dorothy Day said it this way: "We are only beginning, each of us, to practice the folly of the Cross, of trying to live as though we were brothers, and according to Christ's teachings."[9]

## Pro-Family Christianity? No and Yes

When we take a bird's-eye view of the New Testament and two millennia of Christian history, we can discern a general tension between two points of view:

1. Singleness is preferable for the sake of the already-inaugurated kingdom and its urgent mission, which was proclaimed and embodied first by the single Savior who established in himself, by the Spirit, a new household, the church, as a foretaste of God's kingdom. Those who can abstain from marriage and sex ought to do so for the sake of following Jesus more faithfully.

2. Marriage and childrearing are enduring institutions for the majority of the world's Christians, states of life that should be undertaken with discernment and prudence in imitation of Jesus as they await the coming fulfillment of God's kingdom. Those who cannot live faithfully as single people, which is most people, ought to marry and have children for the sake of following Jesus more faithfully.

During the first couple of centuries of church history there was major conflict between advocates of these points of view. Some, such as Tatian, were so antisex that marriage was seen as a "de-filement" alongside other worldly practices like pursuit of wealth and power. Some, such as Clement of Alexandria, taught that it was the duty of all Christians to marry and have children (with sex permissible only for the sake of procreation).[10] From the second and third centuries through the fourth and fifth centuries, these two perspectives were debated until a number of influential church leaders affirmed celibate singleness as the holiest state of life with marriage as a good backup.[11] This view remained more or less un-contested until the Protestant Reformation in the sixteenth century.

One reason for the early strain between the vocations of sin-gleness and marriage was the apostles' expectation that Christ's return was imminent. Paul's epistles make clear that he thought Jesus would return within his lifetime, and with Jesus' return would come a complete transformation of the created order (1 Thess 4:14-17). Such apocalyptic expectation influenced the ethical instruction the apostles offered to their converts as they proclaimed the good news. If the Lord is returning soon, then waiting in faithfulness becomes the primary ethical imperative. Whatever state of life you find yourself in, remain within it. Social and political institutions like marriage and family are passing away; God is going to make all things new. It's no wonder, then, that we are still debating what the good news means for mar-riage, sex, and family today!

While Christians today may not have the same sense of im-minent urgency that Paul did, we have certainly lived in the time between the times ever since Jesus' ascension, straddling God's already-inaugurated kingdom and God's not-yet-fulfilled kingdom. What are God's people to do in the interim?

Well, they seek to embody imperfectly in the present what we expect God to bring about perfectly in the future. Yet, even that aspiration cannot settle things because there remain countless debates over God's intended future. And to make things more complicated, when the church went from being a marginal, persecuted sect of Judaism to the favored, Gentile-dominant religion of the empire, the church assimilated in many ways to the social and political norms of Roman culture. When they did so, Christians began prioritizing the "natural" order, which included incorrect and highly problematic notions of sex, gender, children, and more. As Christianity spread throughout the world, therefore, it did so in conjunction with Roman imperialism, followed by alignment with other empires in subsequent centuries. So, the Christian tradition on "family" is not nearly as straightforward and clear as folks often imagine.

There is simply no uniform, unchanging paradigm for family that has existed from the beginning and continued unchanged into the twenty-first century. Rather, there have been varying forms of Christian family life that have developed over time as the church tried and often failed to maintain their unique Christian commitments and practices in various settings. What follows, then, is my perspective, assuredly incomplete and still in formation, on what family is and what it is for.

## What Is Family?

*Homo sapiens* have organized themselves into family units throughout their history. In this very broad sense, human families are "organized network[s] of socioeconomic and reproductive interdependence and support grounded in biological kinship and marriage."[12] *Biological kinship* means the human family is rooted in affiliation through reproductive lines with the parent-offspring relationship at the center.[13] *Marriage* means a consensual and contractual unity between kin groups for the purposes of reproduction and the continuation of cooperative relationships. All of this is very academic, but the basic point is this: throughout the human story, families have been organized around the rearing of children to maintain survival by managing resources.

This is a rather unromantic notion! Modern societies, especially in the West, tend to think of families as places of emotional intimacy and affection rooted in the romantic love of a married couple. (In Disney terms, think of the families in *The Parent Trap*, *The Incredibles*, or *Inside Out*.) But this has not been the universal norm. Far more ancient and influential is the large extended family united by a common blood ancestor for the sake of social and economic stability. (Think of the families in Disney's *Encanto*, *Coco*, or *Moana*.) In this model, romantic love may be present between spouses, but it is not essential and has little to do with the daily lives or long-term decision-making of the family. Even such families, though, involve contractual agreements between people. So, at the core of human families through the ages has been the rearing of children, meeting bodily needs, and consensual agreements.

This aspect of family is important and instructive, but Christians can't stop there. We confess that families originate and gain their meaning from beyond themselves—ultimately, from God. John tells us God *is* love (1 Jn 4:8). God's essential nature is love, eternally shared by the Father, Son, and Holy Spirit in an eternal relationship of mutual inter-existence.[14] We were created to share in the love of the triune God, eternal participants in God's abundant, joyful, and self-giving life. From early on, humanity broke faith and rejected God's love, alienating ourselves from divine life and harmony. While human life has since been marked by disorder and dissonance, sin and death, God's eternal purpose has remained, and God's will for humanity has been communicated through the created world, sacred Scripture, and finally in Jesus Christ. In Christ by the Spirit, the kingdom of God and the church as its outward expression manifests the eternal purposes of God—a people, Jew and Gentile, brought together to abide in God's eternal life of love.

Based on all the above, God's ultimate purpose for families is love. Love is, as American psychiatrist M. Scott Peck famously wrote, "an act of the will . . . an intention and an action."[15] Love is, in the language of Paul, conducting oneself with patience, kindness, and hope, forgiving faults, forgoing blame, protecting weakness, and rejoicing in the truth (1 Cor 13:4-7). Love requires what African American theologian Willie James Jennings calls "joining," the recognition that I can't become who I am without you, and you can't become who you are without me.[16] Thus, love is far more than affection, but, as bell hooks wisely observes, "a combination of trust, commitment, care, respect, knowledge, and responsibility."[17] Willing the good of the other in the "joining" of community is essential to being human, and family is assuredly one of the most important—if not *the* most important—places that such joining takes place. Whatever form the family takes, whatever society and culture they dwell within, families are born in the love of God, and the ultimate purpose of families is *love*.

What does this mean for real life? Families do important things for their members, especially vulnerable members such as children. In response to the long period of childhood vulnerability, families provide nurture and safety—the material stuff needed for survival and the protection of body and soul.[18] Providing such basic needs typically enables children to live long enough to individuate and socialize. They become their own persons, capable of independent thought and life (to varying degrees, depending on ability), as well as responsible participants of their communities (again, to varying degrees).[19]

Beyond the basic stuff of survival, contemporary scholarship on childhood has revealed that children fare best when they have several other social needs met. Children need at least one adult who is steadfastly involved in caring for them. They need someone who makes sure they get to bed on time and wear a jacket in cold weather and get their homework done. Also, children need developmentally appropriate expectations for their behavior and contributions in the family. This includes things such as maintaining the home, caring for their bodies and belongings, and caring for others in the household. Also, children need role models for how to be an adult and how to belong to a family. They need to learn how to say what they need, how to work through conflict, and how to apologize. Finally, children need to have their personal dignity and boundaries respected.[20] Those who have been shown unconditional love and respect by their caregivers are more likely to develop self-respect. So, children need people in their lives who let them be full and distinct persons with some say-so over their lives.

These social needs are recognized most clearly in the lives of children, but not all families or households include children. The truth is such needs are shared by all human beings regardless of age or stage of life. They are most acutely felt in children, but they persist throughout our lives. At the most basic level, our human families should be the places where such needs are met. They are contexts in which we learn that we come from love and are ordered to love as our goal, even if we wouldn't articulate it in precisely those terms.

## The Family and the Family of God

Christian families are temporal households within the eternal household of God, the church. They are finite communities of disciples within an everlasting communion created in Christ. Christian families live together in such a way that they bear witness to God's kingdom amid this present evil age. Like all families, love remains their origin and purpose, but now it is a love that, in Christ by the Spirit, has a cruciform shape. If the church's purpose is to be apprentices to love in God's kingdom, then the Christian family's purpose is essentially the same, but on a smaller scale. Some have even gone so far as to call families "domestic churches."

The Christian family's goal is to *be apprentices to love together*. Another way to put this is to learn to abide in the love of God. "Abide" is the language Jesus gives in John's Gospel for how disciples respond to the love he shares with the Father. "As the Father has loved me, so have I loved you. Now remain [abide] in my love" (Jn 15:9). Abiding in God's love means apprenticing to God's love, and vice versa. Both ways of framing the goal of family mean learning together how to inhabit our bodies, homes, neighborhoods, and communities *in Christ*. Whether they in-clude children or marriage, Christian families are communities of Jesus' disciples, kin to Jesus and each other through their commitment to "do the will of God" (Mt 12:50; Mk 3:35; Lk 8:21). N. T. Wright says it this way: "Love is not our duty, it is our destiny. Love is the language they speak in the new creation and we get to learn it here."[21] So, the practice of Christian family is learning in advance the loving way of God's new world.

## But What Kind of Love?

I have said that love is willed action that extends oneself for the purpose of nurturing the growth and well-being of the other. But more needs to be said about love within families because too often, due to sin and trauma, that family love has been misun-derstood and poorly practiced.

The first thing Christians often think with reference to love is self-sacrifice—and there's good reason for this. At the center of our faith is the self-giving love of God demonstrated in Jesus Christ. "For God so loved the world that he gave his one and only Son" (Jn 3:16). Without any reciprocity from humanity (not even the ability to reciprocate!), God acted decisively to deliver us from sin and death. Since we are called to love as God loves, we too will be called to imitate God's love in our relationships: "In your relationships with one another, have the same mindset as Christ Jesus: Who, being in very nature God, did not consider equality with God something to be used to his own advantage; rather he made himself nothing by taking the very nature of a servant, being made in human likeness" (Phil 2:5-7).

Because they are sites of daily neediness and vulnerability, families often require self-sacrificing love from its members. Hunger and thirst require sustenance. Nakedness requires clothing. Sickness requires tenderness and care. Weariness requires rest. Soiling requires cleaning.

The more limited in physical and mental ability a family member is, either temporarily or permanently, the more likely they will require self-sacrificing care from another. One spouse's auto-immune flare ups might lead to several days of solo housework for the other spouse. A time of disability for one family member might lead to another seeking additional work to make up the difference in lost wages. A dying parent or acutely sick friend might require round-the-clock care. While these situations might be made less difficult with additional support, there's no way to remove entirely the need for self-sacrifice, and the self-sacrifice undertaken can never really be repaid; it simply exceeds the bounds of tit-for-tat accounting.

Women have often been called on to serve in caring, clothing, tending, and other sacrificial roles. For much of history, in fact, there was an operative assumption that women are more naturally suited for such caretaking because they possess more limited minds, permeable bodies, and changeable affections. As a result, most bodily things—birthing, nursing, cleaning, cooking—were designated "women's work." Then, as the Greek and Roman Empires expanded, followed by other Western powers in the centuries to follow, the peoples they encountered were thought to be "barbarian" and "uncivilized." As a result, they were classed along with women as best suited to the work of hard labor, hospitality, and caretaking—credited, again, to their supposed inferiority.

Such assumptions about women and non-White peoples are sinfully sexist and racist and have no basis in reality. Thankfully, most Christians today understand this—at least in theory if not yet fully in practice. Still, the history of labor division continues to present a challenge to Christian families in two respects. First, we must be careful not to imagine that self-sacrificing love is the special domain of some people over others. Cruciform love is the responsibility of all Christians. Second, we must not assume that self-sacrificing love is the final goal of all loving relationships. Though essential and inevitable within families, self-sacrificing love is not an end in itself.

On the second point, I need to explain more. When Jesus was asked to name the greatest commandment, he responded by linking two commands: love God with all that you are and love your neighbor as yourself (Mt 22:37-40). The second command first appears in Leviticus 19:18, 34. In that context it is given to curtail revenge and applies only to those among the people of Israel, but when Jesus draws on it, along with his disciples after him, the command is joined with Deuteronomy 6:5 (to love God) and takes on universal significance (Mk 12:30-31; Lk 10:27). Furthermore, the love described in the second command is one that assumes love of self: "Love your neighbor as yourself" (Mt 22:39).

It is easy for Christians to miss self-love because we are so used to thinking of love purely in a self-sacrificing frame. But when Jesus enjoins us to love our neighbor, he grounds that love in *our prior love of self*. In other words, the neighbor love that Jesus teaches treats "the personhood, claims, and needs of the other as seriously as we treat our own."[22] American theologian Don Browning and others would call this kind of love *mutuality* or *equal regard*. The church is expected to love each other in precisely this reciprocal manner, grounded in God's prior love for us, "since God so loved us, we also ought to love one another" (1 Jn 4:11). The New Testament, therefore, is full of exhortations to love with *equal regard*:

- "May the Lord make your love increase and overflow for each other and for everyone else, just as ours does for you." (1 Thess 3:12)

- "Submit to one another out of reverence for Christ." (Eph 5:21)

- "Love one another with mutual affection; outdo one another in showing honor." (Rom 12:10 NRSV)
- "Through love become enslaved to one another." (Gal 5:13)

Even in the case of first-century marriages, where there was a preexisting social hierarchy of husbands/fathers over their wives and children, love is encouraged in a manner of reciprocity. The injunction in Ephesians 5:28-30 reframes marriage: "Husbands ought to love their wives as their own bodies. He who loves his wife loves himself. After all, no one ever hated their own body, but they feed and care for their body, just as Christ does the church—for we are members of his body." The husband's love of self becomes the basis of love for his wife, and the reciprocal love of husbands for wives is predicated on similar reciprocity manifested in the church: "Submit to one another out of reverence for Christ" (Eph 5:21).

What's vital about love as equal regard is that it does not rule out self-love. In fact, it assumes as customary, normal, and good that one has a desire for self-fulfillment. But love as mutuality requires that we give equal consideration to our neighbors' self-fulfillment as to our own. We love ourselves and we love our neighbor. Within family relationships, then, members must learn to regard or respect each other as full selves and persons—as ends in themselves, beloved children of God—and to will the good for them as earnestly as we do for ourselves.

So, as courageous and beautiful as self-sacrificing love is, it cannot be the end goal of Christian relations, let alone Christian family relations. Sacrificial love entails giving of oneself in such a way that it is not reciprocated. While this may sound romantic to some, a life of perpetual self-denial and self-abnegation is decidedly not. Sophia Tolstoy, wife of the famous Russian novelist Leo Tolstoy, married young and gave birth to his thirteen children. By her own testimony, she spent her life in total subservience to her "genius" husband and his needs. You can feel the tragedy of her self-obliteration in the diaries she left behind. One entry from March 13, 1902, is especially poignant:

> For a *genius* one has to create a peaceful, cheerful, comfortable home. A *genius* must be fed, washed and dressed, must have his works copied out innumerable times, must be loved and spared all cause for jealousy, so he can be calm. Then one must feed and educate the innumerable children fathered by this genius, whom he cannot be bothered to care for himself, as he has to commune with all the Epictetuses, Socrateses, and Buddhas, and aspire to be like them himself.
>
> I have served a genius for almost forty years. Hundreds of times I have felt my intellectual energy stir within me, and all sorts of desires—a longing for education, a love of music, and the arts. . . . And time and again I have crushed and smothered these longings, and now and to the end of my life I shall somehow continue to serve my genius.[23]

Thankfully, the love command of Jesus does not require constant, unceasing self-sacrifice. And if family is to be a school of love, then one or more members cannot always be in a self-sacrificing mode. Not only is such a life a subtle and slow-moving death, but it also prevents other family members from learning how to love in return. And that is, in the end, not loving—not willing the good of our family members.

While my children were infants and toddlers, it was right and good for me to provide them with all the food and drink they needed to survive, even when such care was to my personal and professional detriment. But now that they have become capable, semi-independent persons, to continue to serve them in the same way as when they were helpless would be harmful both to them and to me. I have a limited capacity, and they need to learn to make food for themselves and others too.

Likewise, during periods of intense challenge—such as a parent in crisis or a mental health emergency—sometimes friends and loved ones must give of themselves without equal regard for long periods of time. Such times are unavoidable, especially toward the end of life. But the work of love that only and always goes one direction is not the fullness of love God desires between persons. Love that is only ever self-sacrificing and one-directional and never mutually given and received is ultimately detrimental to all parties and works against the communion we were made for. This doesn't mean some of us aren't occasionally called to long-term self-denial for the sake of love. But such instances are tragic exceptions to the rule of reciprocal communion.

All members of a family are full human beings, beloved divine images, with agency and subjectivity of their own. Therefore, equal regard love or mutuality is the goal of family love. This is precisely the kind of love Jesus modeled and commanded for his disciples when he washed their feet: "A new command I give you: Love one another. As I have loved you, so you must love one another. By this everyone will know that you are my disciples, if you love one another" (Jn 13:34-35).

## The Challenges of Love

Although what I've laid out thus far may not sound particularly controversial, this way of thinking about family is challenging on a few fronts. First, it doesn't lend itself to a universal blueprint for families to follow. Apprenticeship to love, or abiding in love, doesn't tell you who should pursue paid employment, manage the bank account, or do the laundry. The goal of apprenticeship requires much more by way of daily improvisation than many Christians are comfortable with.

Also, what I've outlined, when taken to its logical conclusion, disrupts dominant ways of thinking about childhood and adulthood. If all family members, whatever their ages or abilities, are disciples of the same Lord and members of the same household, then all our domestic relationships are affected. Of course, childhood and adulthood have important social and scientific meaning, which should be considered as we establish things like household responsibilities. But the radical call of Jesus to "Follow me!" means notions of childhood and adulthood should also be reshaped in view of the gospel, the sacraments, and Jesus' own example. And that will inevitably affect our life together as family.

Likewise, if love is the Christian family's source and apprenticeship to love our primary aim, then we must actively resist a status quo where people are understood and categorized according to their economic worth. Among other things, this means that the formation of self-sufficient, "launchable" adults is not the central goal of Christian childrearing or Christian families in general. While the development of human capacities and meaningful work are part of the good life, family success cannot be determined by how well one's offspring attains Western middle-class standards.

Finally, framing families as communities of disciples removes from adult members the expectation that they can control the outcomes of their work. Yes, our families are embedded within God's household. God is our Father, Jesus is our brother, and the Holy Spirit is our comforter. Yet, sin still plagues families. The focus of the family is not achieving success. Rather, the focus is *faithfulness*—bearing witness as faithfully as possible to the kingdom of God inaugurated in Christ and embodied in his church. The outcome of each individual family, like the outcome of history, is ultimately in Christ's hands (Rev 5:7).

Those who promise certain results if only families will follow these steps or perform these gender roles or do schooling in this way are playing God. To promise happiness and success for conformity to a blueprint is a form of prosperity gospel and anti-Christ. Such promises offer divine rewards for good behavior and assume that the point of Christian family is personal comfort.

This is not the way of Jesus. The point of Christian families is not conformity to an ideal or the creation of a utopian home, but the cultivation of an outpost of God's kingdom—just one humble household in the eternal household of God.

## Launchability and Love

Is it necessarily wrong to want economic independence for your children? No, I don't think so. Given the structure and norms of Western society, it makes good sense to do what you can to raise children who will be "launchable." But launchability with all its socioeconomic implications cannot be the foremost goal for Christian families.

In Christ's body under God's kingdom, the ultimate goal of families is to become love's apprentices. That is our first and most urgent calling. So, which select soccer team your child is part of isn't nearly as important as how your family is learning to love by participating in that team. What town you live in and what home you buy isn't nearly as important as how your household is learning to love among your neighbors.

But remember: Such love is not a one-way street. Mutuality is always the goal. Therefore, we don't approach our teammates, neighbors, coworkers, and classmates as though we have all the giving, serving, and teaching to do. Rather, we recognize we're all on a journey into God's kingdom and apprenticeship to love is the way forward for all of us.

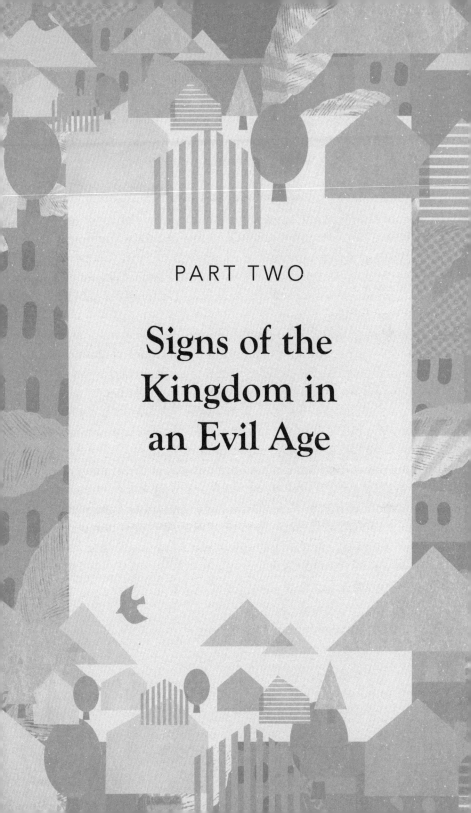

PART TWO

# Signs of the Kingdom in an Evil Age

# 5

# Families, Sin, and the Unjust Status Quo

**As I write, the streaming comedy-drama** *The Bear* is winning numerous awards. Set in present-day Chicago, *The Bear* follows its many characters as they run a restaurant and grapple with the challenges of family tradition and trauma. Season two's episode "Fishes" was especially poignant as it showed in excruciating detail the dysfunctional horror of an extended family that has molded itself around the whims of a mentally ill alcoholic, the main character's mother. The Berzatto family Christmas Eve spirals out of control as Donna (played masterfully by Jamie Lee Curtis), insists on carrying on the Seven Fishes tradition, cooking a complicated multicourse meal while drinking, smoking, and bemoaning her solitary labor despite being offered help repeatedly by everyone in the family. The episode concludes in an outrageous, but somehow still predictable, fashion when a distraught Donna drives her car into the house.

One of the things that makes *The Bear* so relatable for viewers is the extent to which it features the beauty and tragedy of families, as well as the hardships faced by emerging adults as they reckon with their origins and try to chart a healthier future. Every family is made up of members with personal histories, their own *tradition* and *trauma*. Tradition includes things such as language, rituals, and culture, encompassing everything from religious beliefs and holiday celebrations to how you spend your money and divvy up chores.[1] Trauma, meanwhile, is what happens when a person is "rendered helpless" facing an event that overwhelms "the ordinary systems of care that give people a sense of control, connection, and meaning."[2] Both individuals and communities experience trauma, and it is not unusual for family traditions to be connected to such experiences, like Christmas in the Berzatto home.

At the same time, all families are embedded in larger ecological, political, social, and economic realities. In fact, African American sociologist Andrew Billingsley identifies no fewer than twelve systems of society on which all families are dependent and to which all families contribute in one way or another.[3] It makes sense, then, why scholars say that the failure of families in large numbers is attributable, at least in part, to their environments. Trouble in families usually indicates a crisis in "the village," including things such as education, transportation, healthcare, employment, race and class and sex discrimination, and the exploitation of land. In the end, society is only as strong as its families, and families can only thrive in healthy societies.[4]

Our individual families can't restructure society, yet Christian discernment and improvisation require that we reckon with the broader society in which we're rooted. We cannot become apprentices to love anywhere but *here*—in our complex, sin-soaked, multilayered world. Some of our realities are simply the accidents of geography and history, while some (maybe most) are the result of decisions made generations ago. I wish it weren't so! I wish families were self-contained units that, through individual effort and grit alone, we could shape according to our convictions. But the truth is much more difficult. Most of what has created the broken world we live in isn't directly our fault. Yet it remains our responsibility to address the ongoing consequences as faithfully as possible under

Christ's lordship in God's kingdom. To do that, we must face the realities of evil and sin with which families struggle every day.

## Families, Evil, and Sin

In Jesus' preaching and teaching, he draws on the stories and categories given to him by the Hebrew Bible, which identify evil as that which violates shalom. Shalom is the "universal flourishing, wholeness, and delight" of God's reign over the whole world.[5] Shalom is shorthand for the way things ought to be under the rule of the triune God. Sin is the breaking of shalom, faithlessness toward God our Creator, defiance of God's law, which reflects God's will, and the violation of self and neighbor.

Those who commit sin are culpable, at least in part, for their participation in evil. As Ephesians says, "You were dead in your transgressions and sins, in which you used to live" (Eph 2:1-2). Though being "dead" seems to defy the exercise of agency, we also "used to live" in those "transgressions and sins," which suggests willfulness and therefore liability. At the same time, the New Testament also speaks of sin as having a mysterious agency of its own. In Romans 7, Paul speaks of sin as "seizing the opportunity," "working" in the body's members, enslaving people, and acting within them, apparently without their consent (Rom 7:11, 13-14, 20). In this sense, sin is a cosmic power that oppresses all under its dominion. The cosmic dimension of sin is linked to spiritual agents such as "the ruler of the kingdom of the air, the spirit who is now at work in those who are disobedient" (Eph 2:2). Ecuadorian theologian C. René Padilla says it this way: "[Human beings] are victims of an order that transcends them and imposes on them a detrimental way of life."[6]

Sin is multifaceted. Sin is something we do willfully, and sin is something acting in us against our will. We sin as individuals and as groups. We sin in our thoughts and our actions. We sin in things we do and things we fail to do. We sin against individuals in the present, and as the impact of sin ripples through our communities, we sin against unseen and unnamed others in the future. We are willful perpetrators of wrongdoing, responsible agents who must be held accountable. But we are also victims of the power of sin, sufferers who must be freed by Christ's work and the Holy Spirit's power.

Sin gets in the way of families being the loving incubators for individuation and socialization that they are meant to be in God's creation. Sin prevents Christian families from becoming the households of faith they are meant to be within the household of God, and sin, both inside and outside, obstructs the witness of Christian families, making them function more like signposts of the status quo rather than sacraments of God's kingdom. But sin is never generic, disembodied, or disconnected from the broader world. So, let's get more specific about the impact of sin on families.

## Sin Inside Families

First, there is the reality of sin inside families. Although it comes as a surprise to no one that families contain sin (and lots of it!), it doesn't seem to feature much within Christian books about families. Unfortunately, contemporary Christians tend to romanticize and idealize "the family," giving the impression that family is a sinless space in a sinful world.[7] Sermons and books often suggest that if family members will play their assigned "roles" correctly and seek to conform to the divinely given ideal, then sanctity and success is all but guaranteed.

Whatever we might want to be true, real families are sites of sin every day, both sins of commission and sins of omission. Some are relatively minor matters: an unkind word, a fight over the bathroom, a sarcastic dismissal, or a neglected bid for help. Such things are common and comparatively easy to remedy. But some sin within families constitutes major failures: persistent neglect of basic needs, regular physical violence, constant verbal battery, sleep deprivation, the parentification of children, or intentional social isolation. Such are the kinds of traumatic experiences that permanently injure individuals and their communities. Unfortunately, whether we're talking about minor matters or major failures, not a single family is exempt.[8]

Much of the human propensity to sin arises from anxiety about our existence—our finitude, relationships, wealth, social status, and more—the things with which we make sense of ourselves and seek to control our lives. Though anxiety about such things is not itself sin, we often try to insulate ourselves from it through aggression and control on the one hand or self-abnegation and enmeshment with others on the other. This means anxiety often saturates our most intimate relationships, and we try numerous strategies—some healthy and some not so healthy—to assuage it.[9] Given our human condition, it makes sense that our closest relationships would have the most propensity for sin. After all, these are the people who live with us when we are at our best and worst. Our spouses and children are there when we're ecstatically happy and defensively hangry. Our dearest friends are there when we're celebrating life's victories and struggling to get out of bed.

One place where sin can be most pronounced within families is in relationships where there is a significant difference of power. Power is the ability to direct or influence the course of events or the behavior of others, and our families are sites of diverse power dynamics. Consider the differences in power between parents and young children, older children and toddlers, wage earners and financial dependents, women and men, the elderly and the young, those with disabilities and chronic illness and those without. When you take the human propensity for anxiety and combine it with the complex interplays of power in the home, sin and its consequences can be easily overlooked, misunderstood, or exacerbated. When families are severely stressed, under-resourced, and isolated, then unacknowledged sin can lead to neglect, abuse, violence, and even death. In such cases, families become pernicious places, especially for the most vulnerable.[10]

Abuse in its various forms is a common feature of human families. Because of the long-standing expectation that women are children's primary caregivers, most child abuse is carried out by mothers. Also, psychological abuse, sexual abuse, rape, and incest are horrifically common. The abusers in such cases are not easily identifiable monsters. They are, in fact, regular people, "good people" even, showing little to no signs of the heinous behavior they engage in behind closed doors. Not only does abuse happen within families, but it also happens in the name of Jesus through the perverse use of the Bible and Christian practices.

I am a survivor of abuse. I have also witnessed instances of abuse in families. I have photographed the bruises following a friend's beating at the hands of her drunken husband. I have responded to another friend's panicked call when her soon-to-be-ex-husband was threatening violence while her terrified children watched. I have supported friends who had to cut off interactions with an abusive grandparent. I have listened to another friend as he shared the impact of his wife's verbal battery on his mental and physical health. I have heard stories of sexual abuse of younger siblings by older siblings, and the rape of wives by husbands.

It's hard to make sense of all this. On the one hand, family is created by God for the good of individuals, communities, and the world. They emerge from God's love and are for the purpose of learning, giving, and receiving love. Our best sociological and psychological research demonstrates the significance of stable, supportive, and well-resourced families for both human development and the cultivation of healthy communities. The truth of family's divine purpose and deep significance must be affirmed, and those things necessary for the health of families must be supported.

At the same time, families can be treacherous places. Sin is not just "out there" but also "in here." Families are not and cannot be sinless havens. In fact, the private nature of most families makes their exploitation for evil purposes easier and more likely to be covered up. Vulnerable people—especially children, women, people with disabilities, the elderly, and the chronically ill—are often exploited and oppressed within families. Such experiences don't just cause lifelong psychological, social, and physical problems, but also thwart the individual's and family's ability to enjoy the fullness of life in God's kingdom (Jn 10:10; Eph 4:13; Col 3:8-15)—a reality that sends tragic ripples from their homes into the world.

If the good news of Christ is good news for all, then it must bind up the brokenhearted and proclaim freedom to captives *within families*. Christ's healing and liberating power is for every member of the family, each of whom bears God's image and is indwelled by the Holy Spirit. Christians of all ages are saints-in-progress, and families are not sinless spaces, nor are they lacking in perilous power dynamics. So, as we learn to think about and practice Christian family, we must do so with the conviction that no family member should be obliterated so that others may self-actualize. Such is not the good news. Such is not the kingdom of God.

## Childhood Wounds and Trauma

The night my mom told me that she was divorcing my father, and we were moving out the next day, I was only ten years old. Still, I felt relief, not grief. The man I had learned to call "Dad" (he was not my biological father) had some positive points. He was charismatic and intelligent. He could be silly, fun-loving, and adventurous, and he had occasional moments of sensitivity and compassion. But overall, Dad's presence in our family had a terrorizing effect.

The combination of untreated mental illness and reckless alcoholism meant he was manipulative and controlling, and his moods were unpredictable. One minute we'd be cuddling on the porch talking about my school day; the next minute he'd be yelling at my brother to go pick a switch from the backyard. I remember, after one of his more violent blow-ups, telling my mother through tears that I was afraid one day he was going to kill us.

Though I only spent around nine years of my life living in the same home with my dad, his behavior left me with unseen scars written on my body and buried deep in my psyche. And I am by no means in the minority. Many adults trying to create families the best way they know how are seeking to do so while encumbered by family histories of dysfunction and abuse. Learning, therefore, how to become apprentices to love is complicated even beyond the "normal" challenges faced by fallible human beings. We have bodies, minds, and hearts shaped by abuse, but we must forge ahead anyway, trusting, as Spanish poet Antonio Machado says, *se hace camino al andar* ("the path is forged as one walks").

No one emerges from childhood without wounds of some kind: instances in our growing-up years where we experienced a failure to love. Such failures happen in the home and outside the home. They come from family members, friends, neighbors, and strangers, and such failures to love are hurtful and often stay with you throughout your life.

But I would distinguish childhood wounds from abuse. Abuse constitutes a pattern of harmful behavior (psychological, physical, sexual) that causes considerable long-term damage. Abuse often causes trauma: the result of an experience that is simply too much for a person to handle. Traumatic events "overwhelm the ordinary human adaptations to life."[11] Traumatized persons experience profound powerlessness, which undermines and jumbles their sense of self and the world. As a result, "trauma is not just an event that took place sometime in the past; it is also the imprint left by that experience on mind, brain, and body."[12]

Whether you've experienced occasional wounding, abuse, or trauma, you have likely grown up with patterns of thought and behavior that work against your flourishing and the flourishing of others. Many such patterns begin as vital coping strategies, but as adults we often find that such previously helpful behaviors no longer benefit us. Even less so when we are trying to form friendships, intimate relationships, and perhaps raise our own children.

Shortly after my youngest child turned ten, Ronnie was out of town, and I was putting her to bed. We followed our usual routine: Read a chapter from our latest book, pray together, sing or play a song (thanks, Spotify), and then make the sign of the cross on her head and bless her. Despite the familiarity of the ritual, as I spoke the words of blessing over her I found myself overwhelmed with a surprisingly powerful grief. Sitting there in the dark, I saw my mother in my mind's eye sitting on my bed informing me of the divorce and our impending move, and I could feel in my body the fear and sorrow of that disclosure. In my daughter's sweet face, I saw just how young and vulnerable I was at her age. By almost every metric, that was the last day of my childhood. Though I held myself together long enough to leave the room, I spent the next hour weeping. Thirty years later, my body was finally feeling the full weight of grief from all I had lost in my father's abuse and my parents' divorce.

Because none of us emerge from childhood unscathed, healing from childhood wounds, abuse, and trauma is a vital part of our life in God's family. What we've experienced leaves our bodies, minds, and souls in a state that is ailing and fragmented. As a result, we become more susceptible to the powers and principalities of the world. If we are going to be apprentices of love who resist the stories and practices that deform humanity and hold us hostage, then we must also submit to healing work within our minds, bodies, and souls.[13] More than likely, we will never be fully free of the impulses such experiences left behind, but if we are going to be apprentices to love within God's family, then we must come to terms with our wounds and invite the Holy Spirit to heal us—in cooperation with therapy, medication, and other helps. Such work is not tangential to our sanctification but very much part of it.

## Sin Outside Families

In addition to sin within the family, there is also sin perpetrated outside families. The paths our families follow are not just the product of what happens within individual households, as important as that is. Because all families are embedded in political, economic, and ecological realities, just as sin runs amok within homes, so also sin runs amok in neighborhoods and communities. And that sin impacts families too. In a sense, then, sin is never simply "outside" families.

We live in a western suburb of Chicago. Our city was founded as White households fled the increasingly more diverse city of Chicago during the Great Migration of African Americans from the South to the North.[14] As a result, it is a majority White community, something intentionally pursued by its founders and all but guaranteed by policies over the past century. Our busing and train schedules, not to mention their regular maintenance (or lack thereof), determine when adults can work, whether before- or after-school care is needed, and whether children and parents spend time together and get sufficient sleep. Moreover, the availability and affordability of housing in our city along with fresh food and healthcare immediately affects every household.

Our city exists within a state established by European settlers arriving from Kentucky after the US Revolutionary War. These settlers did not find unoccupied land on the central plains, but a vast number of extended families of the Peoria, Myaamia, and Potawatomi peoples who had been living there for hundreds of years. Yet, their personhood, sovereignty, and material needs were not respected by individual settlers or US law. In 1803, their territory was acquired by the United States through the Louisiana Purchase, and Illinois became the twenty-first state of the union in 1818.

Our family's country is a democratic republic with ideals of universal liberty and justice that remains a deeply inequitable work in progress. The United States was founded by landed White men for landed White men. It was built on a continent taken from Indigenous peoples through settler colonialism, and it was cultivated through the enslaved labor of African peoples and exploitative labor of peoples from Latin America, Asia, and the South Pacific. All this led to the mass accumulation of wealth surpassing anything the world has ever known. Inspired by Enlightenment ideals, confidence in divine favor, and a White supremacist ideology imported from Europe, US institutions and laws were established to protect the whiteness and male dominance of American society. Yet, the resistance and activism of racialized minorities and women through the centuries, painstakingly and with much suffering, has led to a more just but still grossly flawed union. This national history, too, has ongoing consequences, both for families who live in the United States, and for millions of households around the world. For good and for ill, all families are inheritors of the earth left for them by their foremothers and fathers.

Finally, there's a cosmic dimension to our places too. Alongside the oppressive power of sin, Scripture assumes the existence of other agents in the created order who oppose God's kingdom. Ephesians calls them "rulers," "authorities," "powers of this dark world," and "spiritual forces of evil in the heavenly realms" (Eph 6:12). The book of Revelation is perhaps the most forceful, revealing that behind the machinations of emperors and empires are cosmic forces aligned against God who have been given temporary freedom to deceive and destroy. Such powers and principalities exploit the structures and systems of human societies to oppress humanity and enslave people in idolatry.

Christians seeking to practice family within this present evil age must be able to see the many interlocking layers of sin so that they can learn how to survive, resist, and imagine something better. There is no ideal or generic Christian family; there are only *families*, and these families exist within socioeconomic, political, and spiritual environments that are profoundly complex, unjust, and even malevolent. The question is not whether evil powers and injustice persist, but rather how to address such realities and structure our family lives so that we can resist their influence.

## Families and the Unjust Status Quo

Unfortunately, the two-millennia story of Christianity demonstrates that Christians have often assumed an all-too-easy congruence between the family's purpose in Christ and the socio-political status quo: That the purpose of Christian family is to defend and uphold "the way things are" rather than offer an alternative. Maybe this is why Jesus spoke so often of the conflict between God's kingdom and the biological family. He knew just how tempting it would be to seek to conserve existing conditions, particularly when our families benefit from them.

The Roman Empire was the setting where the gospel first took root. The male head of household, the paterfamilias, was the leader of the traditional Roman family and his power was total and absolute. The emperor was viewed as the father of the empire's "extended family."[15] So the submission of household members to the paterfamilias was essential to ensure the submission of citizens and all conquered peoples to the emperor. As a result, the Roman family, like the empire, could be a brutal and oppressive environment.

In the first couple of centuries of the church, the Christian way of life was seen as a threat to the stability of the Roman family. Of particular concern were its prioritization of the church over kinship ties, the relativizing of gender-based roles, and the undermining of the master-slave relation. It also didn't help that Christians worshiped a poor Jewish criminal executed in the most humiliating manner Rome had on offer. If God's kingdom establishes a new household with Christ at the head, then the authority of the paterfamilias is weakened, and the family's order short-circuited. As the family is undermined, so is the empire. For this reason, early Christians were often treated as bad citizens and defiant subjects.

Eventually, though, Emperor Constantine converted to Christianity and determined his newfound faith would be useful for imperial unity. When church leaders agreed that it was God's providential will to become the empire's official religion, it was a natural next step for the Christian family to be viewed as the means to uphold, rather than subvert, imperial power. Once the emperor was seen as divinely appointed and the empire's structure God-approved, then the traditional form of family was rendered sacred too. The family became a tool of preserving empire rather than a revolutionary sign of God's kingdom.

Now, let's move forward in history a thousand years. Over the course of those centuries, Christians largely determined that slavery was not only permissible but good. Their desire for wage-free labor was wedded to a racial caste system that justified the exploitation of dark-skinned peoples due to their supposed natural inferiority and barbarism. So, European Christians began to systematically steal and purchase people from the African continent and traffic them across the Atlantic Ocean to work the land in their newly conquered territories. (What European conquerors and colonists did to the peoples already living in the New World is a further layer of heinous atrocity.)

We should not fail to think about the slave trade's horrors in terms of families. Countless African families, multiple generations' worth, were sundered in the kidnappings, ghastly voyages, and vicious treatment and illnesses found in the New World. Once forced into labor on plantations, *encomiendas*, and missions in the Americas, the families formed by enslaved persons were considered invalid. The only "family values" recognized by colonists and settlers were those of Europeans. In fact, for centuries the children of Native American families were sent to live in residential schools, orphanages, and White households to "civilize" and "Christianize" them.

All these horrors were carried out with the blessing of White Christian leaders. Theological heroes such as Jonathan Edwards were among the slaveholders who participated in the destruction of African families to support his own family. The truth is Edwards was only able to produce the sermons and books that are so lauded today because a young teen, Venus, a boy, Titus, and a woman, Leah, were forced to carry out the manual labor to sustain his household. And those are just the enslaved persons we know by name. Countless families—in Edwards's case, Black families—were wrecked and exploited so that White families could flourish, amassing multiple generations-worth of wealth, power, and influence.

In the nineteenth and early twentieth centuries, the United States undertook the expansion of its territories around the world in imitation of the British Empire. Part of that effort included the war against Spain, which resulted in the acquisition of Puerto Rico, Guam, and the Philippines in the aftermath. US politicians cast the procurement of these lands and peoples in explicitly religious and racist terms: a White Christian nation intervening to convert and civilize inferior Brown, heathen nations—never mind the fact that Puerto Rico, Guam, and the Philippines were already majority Christian.

But it wasn't just White supremacy at work in American imperialism—and this is what I don't want us to miss. Leaders strategized and communicated their plans by drawing on White patriarchal notions of the family. In the rhetoric of politicians and preachers, the United States would serve as beneficent father to the children of these inferior nations, training them to take their proper place in a rightly ordered world, and a key part of the civilizing process was enforcing the patriarchal family form on conquered territories.[16] Once again, millions of families were damaged through US military endeavors, and an explicit vision of family was used to prop up the unjust status quo.

Whether we're talking about fourth-century Rome, eighteenth-century Alabama, or twentieth- and twenty-first-century Puerto Rico, Christians have too often been happy to see "the family," both symbolically and functionally, bolster an unjust social and political order. Christian families today are inheritors of this tragic story and its present realities. At the same time, the gospel proclaims that the Word who became flesh as a poor, colonized Jew in Roman-occupied Judea is at work through his Holy Spirit to bring healing and freedom through God's kingdom today. Christian families can join God in that work only by telling the truth about the past and present, and intentionally seeking a new vision for the future.

### Back to the Berzattos

Returning now to the dysfunctional but beloved Berzatto family, I wonder how this chapter's description of sin in all its layered complexity might inform our interpretation of their plight. There is certainly plenty of sin within the family. Disordered desires have led to disordered relationships, which have yielded more disordered desires and disordered relationships. Family members have become so used to dealing with each other in dehumanizing ways that they can no longer see, let alone try to pursue, what they're missing. They either hide their wounds and illnesses from each other, or they ignore them even when staring them in the face, and their predicament is exacerbated by being embedded in Chicago under late-modern US capitalism where they are always on the razor's edge of financial ruin.

Yet there are signs of life, which is why viewers keep tuning in. Carmy is recognizing his mental illness in the wake of his family dysfunction, his abuse within the culinary industry, and his older brother's death by suicide. Through meaningful work, Richie is beginning to understand his worth and become a better person, even in the face of the still-devastating pain of his divorce. Natalie ("Sugar") and her husband, Pete, for all their flaws, are clearly seeking a healthier family life together, which will soon include a child. And Sydney—though not a Berzatto, she is part of The Bear "family"—is healing from the loss of her mother, a strained relationship with her father, and past business failure.

Of course, viewers don't know whether such changes toward the better will continue in the coming seasons. I'm not trying to suggest the Berzatto clan is Christian or in any way exemplary. But their story so far demonstrates the kinds of transformation—slow, halting, and piecemeal though it may be—that we should expect to see in families seeking abundant life in God's kingdom. As the Spirit of God renews the face of the earth, the Spirit also seeks the renewal of families, freeing them and healing them from all that chokes out life. Not every evil will be overcome, nor every sin stamped out. Nevertheless, families can offer faithful resistance in cooperation with God's household one day at a time.

# 6

# Apprenticeship to Love
# in a Fallen World

**On August 9, 1943,** a young husband and father was executed via guillotine in a Nazi prison. His crime was undermining military morale (*Wehrkraftzersetzung*) because he refused active service as a Nazi soldier. Franz Jägerstätter was a modest Austrian farmer living a quiet life with his wife, Franziska, and their three small children, but when Austria was occupied by Nazi Germany and annexed through the *Anschluss* in 1938, Franz was the only person in his village to speak against it. Dismayed by his community's support for the Nazis, he wrote, "I believe there could scarcely be a sadder hour for the true Christian faith in our country."[1]

Though he deferred military service multiple times and refused to take the oath of loyalty to Hitler, eventually Franz was called up to active duty and forced into direct confrontation with the Third Reich. He declared his conscientious objection to the war and was arrested immediately. Though neither his priest nor his bishop supported him, Franz refused to relent. Even the prospect of leaving behind a young wife and small children could not deter him. He was quickly tried, convicted, and executed without fanfare. Jägerstätter's last recorded words before his death were, "I am completely bound in inner union with the Lord."[2]

Fifty years later, Chantal Mujjawamaholo was a twenty-one-year-old student at secondary school in Nyange, Rwanda, many miles from her hometown. On March 18, 1997, just a few years after the Rwandan genocide, the Interahamwe, a Hutu-aligned militia, invaded the property. Students had just finished their dinner and were gathered in groups finishing the day's assignments. Brandishing guns, the rebels forcibly entered the classrooms and demanded that students divide into Hutu and Tutsi. Knowing the militiamen would execute Tutsis, the students refused to comply, saying, "We are all Rwandans." The rebels fired indiscriminately on the students and threw grenades into the classrooms. A total of thirteen young people were killed.

All the victims were taken home and buried in family plots, but Chantal's family lived too far away. She was buried on the school grounds instead. Unlike Franz, Chantal left behind no written testimony or last words. Her grave is marked with a simple stone inscription: "Chantal Mujjawamaholo. B. 24.04.1975. D. 18.03.1997."

Ugandan theologian Emmanuel Katongole reports that when he sought an explanation for the Nyange students' valor, he couldn't find a clear answer. The teachers told him the students had just prayed together following their evening meal and had been meeting regularly with a mentor to discuss Christian nonviolence. Yet somehow their life together at the Nyange school had shaped them into the kinds of people who could bear witness to Christian unity even unto death. Katongole writes: "In a world that is so enamored of grand strategies for how to end poverty and eradicate terrorism, the martyrs remind us that the journey of reconciliation is a journey of tactics and gestures—a story here, a lesson there, and some insights along the way."[3]

What would make Chantal give up her life—one just barely begun—to protect her friends? What would compel Franz to resist to the point of leaving his wife widowed and their children fatherless? Apprenticeship to love showed them a different way. Chantal was on the "journey of tactics and gestures" with her classmates in the rhythms of life and learning. Their meals, prayers, and discussions pointed her toward a different world beyond the ethnic violence of her home country. Franz served as sacristan in his local church, assisting regularly with the sacraments, and had joined the Third Order of St. Francis, a fraternity of Catholic devotion. Doubtless his life of farming and childrearing had also inculcated habits that deepened his loyalty to Christ's body.

Franz and Chantal were both involved in the reconciliation of God's family through the activities of their daily lives. Though in a different time and place, a similar route is required of us as kingdom citizens today. Christian families must learn the tactics and gestures Katongole speaks of—"a story here, a lesson there, and some insights along the way"—that help us to practice the kingdom. We may never face military conscription or a rebel militia, but we certainly face other corrosive evils every day, and the same habits that empowered the church's martyrs for a faithful death also empower us for a faithful life. Rather than a culture war, therefore, what's needed are mundane yet sacramental acts of Christian faithfulness. Though relatively small and unremarkable, such actions can subvert the powers that reign in this age and embody the kingdom of God here and now.

Outward conformity is not enough, though. We need a change, a conversion by the Spirit's power that transforms our desires. This is no small task! We are desiring creatures made for communion with God, self, and others, but our loves, our desires, are disordered by sin—personal sin within us and social sin all around us. This means our desires are cultivated and shaped every day by innumerable things, many of which are beyond our control. Still, by the Father's power, in Christ, and through the Spirit, families can become settings in which we learn another way. There is no formula for such kingdom apprenticeship, nor is there a set curriculum, but Christian families can at least begin with the helps provided by Scripture and the practices of the Christian tradition.

## Families and Formation

As I've said from the start, families have a created, natural purpose within God's world. Central to that purpose is to help meet the needs of its members, especially children, and provide them with tangible and intangible goods. We need food, clothing, shelter, rest, and we also need friendship, socialization, and opportunity for self-actualization. When such things cannot be provided, individuals and their communities suffer.

But meeting needs, as important as that is, remains insufficient for a Christian practice of family. Yes, such needs must be met—and met by church and society when families are unable to do so—but it remains true that the proper drive to meet needs is easily co-opted by powers and principalities. The necessity of shelter and sufficient living space easily turns into the drive to find an unnecessarily bigger home filled with nicer furniture and better electronics. The necessity of opportunities for a child's self-actualization easily turns into the desire to play every sport, join every league, and spend every waking hour in organized activity. The necessity of rest easily turns into exorbitant spending on elaborate vacations, which are often built on unseen exploitative labor and racialized colonization. In each of these ways, we see that sin, both individual and corporate, thwarts families as they seek to be apprentices to love. In the face of such challenges, we need not only to meet one another's needs, but also to train our desires so that we learn to love as God loves.

Yet, our desires are not naturally ordered toward God and his kingdom. Instead, our desires are twisted by sin, restless and wandering and looking for satisfaction. Within a consumer capitalist society in the twenty-first century, our desires are never lacking in opportunity to chase both lesser goods and outright evils. Such perverted restlessness leads us to harm ourselves and our neighbors because we are incapable of loving ourselves and others well. As Augustine famously confessed, "You have made us for yourself, O Lord, and our heart is restless until it rests in you."[4] To have our heart rest in the Lord is not a one-time thing. Rather, it must be pursued as a lifelong journey out of the reign of sin and death and into the reign of God. Though it is a long and by no means straightforward process, the pursuit of rest in God—having our desires reoriented by the Spirit under Christ's lordship—is ultimately for the good of ourselves, our families, and our communities.

How does this journey of transformation take place? It begins with the initiative of God to love us, claim us, call us, indwell us, and transform us. So, even as we take responsibility for our habits and seek virtue's growth in our lives, we always do so by the enlivening and empowering work of the triune God. In other words, we are sanctified in the same manner we are justified, by grace through faith, even as we acknowledge the need for human effort. As Anglo-American philosopher Dallas Willard has said, "Grace is not opposed to effort. It is opposed to earning."[5]

Understanding that all transformation begins with, is fueled by, and ends with the Holy Spirit's power, we can then acknowledge that the disciplining of desire happens primarily through the cultivation of our habits. We understand the importance of habits instinctively when it comes to sports, music, and art. If you want to learn how to pitch fast balls, you must practice, build your muscles, train your mind and body, preferably with the oversight of a skilled coach, so that over time you can throw a fast ball on demand. If you want to learn to play Bach's Cello Suite #4, you must practice, train your mind and body, preferably with the help of a skilled teacher, so that over time you can play it. Once learned and played repeatedly, you might not even need to read the music carefully anymore. Muscle memory, a trained ear, and thorough familiarity will lead you through the piece to its conclusion.

Christian virtue is developed in an analogous way. The Holy Spirit is given to us as a gift to mark us as Christ's own forever, and the Spirit infuses us with God's grace. The grace of God then works in, with, and through our bodies, minds, and souls to produce virtue. God's grace flows into us like a stream from the Holy Spirit. Our job individually and collectively is to learn to become an open conduit for God's grace.

Sadly, there are a million ways we close ourselves off from God's grace. We forget what we know to be true and wallow in disbelief and doubt. We keep a tight fist on our money and refuse to give to those who ask for help. When provoked, we choose to say spiteful, hurtful things rather than control our tongues. We refuse to empathize and show compassion for the suffering of one whose life experience is unlike our own. But our habits, even when undertaken in an unenthusiastic and rote way, keep us returning to a posture of openness and readiness to God. The Spirit operates on our hearts through our habits, and over time we might even begin to produce the fruit of the Spirit: love, joy, peace, patience, kindness, goodness, faithfulness, gentleness, and self-control (Gal 5:22).

Still, I want to be careful. What I have sketched previously sounds like a straightforward process, but the reality is almost never straightforward. Virtue's development is not like the climbing value of tech company shares on the New York Stock Exchange. Growth of virtue cannot be reduced to a chemical formula or mathematical equation, nor does it present itself in obvious ways. The fact is some habits work for some people and not for others. Sometimes change comes rapidly and sometimes slowly. Sometimes change is visible and sometimes invisible. Sometimes you live your whole life falling and rising again, never fully escaping a besetting vice, as much as you beg and plead for God's help. Sometimes the only hope for freedom and healing we can see is God's final intervention in the age to come.

Such realities underline the fact that God's transforming work in our lives is not ultimately under our control, nor can we manipulate God (or ourselves) toward our desired outcome. Nevertheless, the numerous commands of Scripture to repent and believe in Jesus, to obey all he has commanded, to offer our bodies as a living sacrifice, and to walk worthy of our calling all suggest that we have a responsibility to pursue transformation even as we acknowledge our ever-present and inescapable limitations (Mk 1:15; Mt 28:20; Rom 12:1; Eph 4:1).

Even though Christians have been rescued by God's great mercy and ushered into the kingdom of his beloved Son, our minds, bodies, and souls are still marked by our traumas and suffering, as well as the patterns of our fallen world. Sometimes an area where we have been sinned against by another becomes a wound that festers and grows. From that infected place, we then injure and hurt others, creating a habit of sin linked to the untreated wound from the past. As Paul says, sin dwells in our members and works against our efforts at transformation (Rom 7:23).

Also, even as God's kingdom is inaugurated in Christ, the anti-kingdom continues to grow (Mt 13:24-30). Through spiritual and material means, this world's powers and principalities are seeking to undermine the church and stymie God's kingdom (Eph 6:12). We see it everywhere: advertising, cable news networks, commercial development, political campaigns, school boards, and more. Christian families seeking to be apprentices to love must work against challenges that are both internal and external, individual and social, spiritual and material.

In the Chicago suburbs where we live, my family struggles daily to keep the priorities of God's kingdom at the forefront of our lives. The busyness of extracurricular activities can hinder us from showing neighbor love through hospitality and other forms of care. The suburban tendency to isolate from our actual neighbors affects us no less than others, and we have certainly internalized expectations from US middle-class norms about how our home and lawn should look. We are constantly comparing ourselves, both online and in real life, to what others have and do and produce. But I'm not just talking about Instagram or TikTok envy. I'm talking about our deepest desires, which we want to be oriented toward God and God's kingdom, being constantly pulled toward things we *know* will not last.

First-century Christians faced the same challenge, though without the lure of social media:

> Do not love the world or anything in the world. If anyone loves the world, love for the Father is not in them. For everything in the world—the lust of the flesh, the lust of the eyes, and the pride of life—comes not from the Father but from the world. The world and its desires pass away, but whoever does the will of God lives forever. (1 Jn 2:15-17)

John's warning is so stark because our deepest desires will assuredly determine the direction of our lives, motivating our decisions and leading to the formation of our character. The good news is that the triumph of God's kingdom is certain. Though we may lose the battle, God will not lose the war. Still, there remains a life of flourishing to pursue here and now within the families we currently have as we await the fullness of God's new creation. To undertake that journey of transformation, we must see and name some of the most entrenched challenges facing Christian families today.

## Apprentices to Love in a Fallen World

Resources for Christian family life tend to focus on trials that are either internal to the family or, if they do turn outward, focus on a narrow set of external things. Often, they will mention technology and social media, the ubiquity of pornography, the availability of drugs, and the secularism of public education. Sometimes they might include communication, the wise use of wealth, and mindfulness amid busyness. All these concerns are valid and worthy of discussion. But I want to broaden our vision to include even larger, all-encompassing realities in which these things are embedded. Despite having an immense impact on our daily lives, they often remain invisible and unaddressed. One of the reasons for this is that in the wake of the Enlightenment, Christianity in the West tends to be individualistic and therapeutic. Because of the focus on the individual's needs and well-being, broader social, political, and economic matters are often ignored. But such things are vital influences on our households, whatever form they take.

The first thing we must see is the ongoing impact of European and US imperialism. Imperialism is, in short, the practice of one nation establishing control over other areas and peoples through territorial acquisition or political and economic control. It almost always includes the expansion and growth of wealth, the sense of racial and cultural superiority, and even some divine right, responsibility, or calling. For example, the establishment of the Spanish, French, and British colonies in the New World was a result of imperial expansion, as was the United States' genocidal subjugation of Native Americans. US imperialism has also been demonstrated in its wars—those declared and undeclared—as well as its political and economic dealings with countries in Latin America, Africa, Asia, and the Middle East. In every case, US imperialist efforts have been buttressed with Christian rhetoric from politicians and church and community and church leaders.

Empire-building is nothing new in world history, of course, but that doesn't change the fact that the ideologies and methods of imperialism are counter to the kingdom of God. To put it another way, the gospel of Jesus the Messiah confronts and repudiates imperialist systems and practice. Still, due to the particulars of our history, US Christians are especially prone to conflating their allegiance to God's kingdom with allegiance to the empire. Catholic theologian David Matzko McCarthy notes that we are especially tempted to (1) assume that God's work is allied with the successes and progress of the US economy, (2) assume that US military supremacy is part of God's plan, and (3) see God's will for the world working through US democracy.[6] Resisting and countering these tendencies will take more than individual families and households, but it must at least begin there with truth-telling about the empires we find ourselves in. Apprenticeship to Jesus requires it.

The second aspect of modern society with which families today must grapple is the interrelated sexism and racism that's been entrenched for centuries. Sexism and racism are not the same thing, of course, but they often appear in intersecting and interlocking ways. Stories about the inherent inferiority of women to men or one people to another serve a terrible but necessary function within imperialism, especially for Christians. How can followers of Jesus of Nazareth justify the subjugation and enslavement of other people? Only through a compelling myth about human beings that vindicates their exploitative practices. Then Scripture and other resources are leveraged in support of gender- and race-based subjugation. Along the way, the revolutionary, hierarchy-subverting gospel of Jesus Christ gets traded for an anemic "gospel" for saving souls alone. How convenient for slaveholders, conquistadors, and Puritan settlers that the good news of God's kingdom meant only life after death for specially chosen souls rather than fullness of life—souls and bodies—for *all* beginning here and now.

As with imperialism, racial castes or hierarchies have been around for a very long time. But the modern one in which Westerners live is mapped on a Black-to-White spectrum with other non-White peoples arranged in between. They are "ranked" according to lightness of skin and perceived assimilation into White culture. The racist hierarchy is intertwined with long-standing gender hierarchy such that White, able-bodied, straight men are the perceived human norm against which everyone else is measured. Thus, masculinity is generally associated with the soul, strength, reason, power, and control, while femininity is generally associated with the body, weakness, emotion, submission, and subservience.

At the intersection of gender and race, though, we find exceptions to the binary. Black and Brown women have been historically de-feminized in the White imagination to justify their brutal treatment. Black and Brown men have been historically punished for their masculinity, forced to take a feminized, subservient status in order not to threaten White masculinity. In fact, in the complicated story of gender and race in the West, we find racial castes being gendered in particular ways in one setting only to be rendered differently in another. The larger point, though, is this: sexism and racism are interlocking realities with which Christian families are contending on a regular basis, and they undermine our collective apprenticeship to love.

The last aspect of modern society with which Christian families must grapple is advanced consumer capitalism. Over the past couple centuries, the great industries of the world have ushered us into a global consumer society. Private property is in the service of personal enrichment and our daily lives are structured primarily around what's good for business proprietors. Mass media, meanwhile, especially the internet and social media, shapes people into consumers who, as C. René Padilla says, "work to make money, make money to buy things, and buy things to find value for themselves."[7] Advertisers offer us stories that appeal to our sense of beauty and goodness, which then reinforce the cultural and social status quo. We learn early on that "to live is to possess," and constant work is the price we pay for pursuing satiation. Meanwhile, there's no margin in the never-ending grind of "the economy" to ask questions about the goals of human life and society.[8]

I am not saying all Christians must throw off free markets. Still, Christians must be clear-eyed about the malformations caused by generations of living in such an environment. As Rodney Clapp has said, "The deepest, most compelling aim for the church is not to support one economic system or another, but to measure the system one lives with against the claims of the kingdom and attempt to live faithfully in light of the consequent tension."[9] When we do that measuring, we find that capitalism's material success for some has resulted in the impoverishment and disenfranchisement of countless others.

Furthermore, families have irreparably changed living under the tyranny of the market. The arrangement of our days, weeks, and months is dictated primarily by the market's "needs"—what is and isn't profitable for shareholders and CEOs—and not by the needs of human beings. People are viewed primarily as consumers to be capitalized on and, if they're in the workforce, commodities to be used. Since there is no shared notion of the good life, what is profitable and expedient tends to be valued above all else. The prospect of taking profit losses to attain higher goods for persons, families, or communities is so unusual as to be newsworthy for weeks.

The technological advancements of the past century, from laptops to smartwatches, have only increased consumer capitalism's chokehold on the Western psyche. There's no doubt that the great capitalistic industries have produced affluence unlike anything the world has ever known, but at the same time they have produced a society that largely believes "to live is to possess."[10] Everything has been recast in market terms: marriage, family, friendship, education, health, vocation, church, and more. For most Christian households and churches today, you'd just never know that Jesus said you cannot serve both God and Mammon.

If to live is to possess, then it can make sense to use coercion and violence to protect what one has, whether individually or as a nation. And if we're going to use coercion and violence, then we're going to need a justifying narrative about protecting ourselves and our superior way of life. Which brings us back to imperialism. Under the reign of sin and the world's powers and principalities, economic exploitation is enforced by violence, which is then justified by sexism and racism and other myths that justify dominance. Dr. Martin Luther King Jr. named these as mutually reinforcing social evils, a "demonic cycle of self-interest" that assuredly continues today.[11]

Willie James Jennings has written insightfully about how the evils of racism, economic exploitation, and violence were spread in the New World largely through the work of merchants, soldiers, and missionaries.[12] Most of us wouldn't link these three vocations, but in European and American imperialism they were closely connected by design. Merchants sought out new resources to turn into riches, separating people from the land they lived on in order to possess both. People became slaves or cheap labor, and the land with its creatures and other resources became additional sources of wealth.

Alongside the merchants came soldiers because all who encountered the New World found places and peoples that were strange and unfamiliar. The people were usually unwilling to be exploited for material gain and would not cooperate with their own subjugation. Thus, steel and guns were required to enforce the European will-to-power, so soldiers protected European persons and goods while also suppressing and controlling Indigenous peoples.

Finally, with the merchant and soldier came the missionary. This is uncomfortable to acknowledge. I am an evangelical, which literally means "good news people," and I believe in the proclamation of the good news of Jesus Christ throughout the world.[13] But that doesn't change the historical reality that wherever European imperialism spread, so did Christian missionary efforts. Because the peoples encountered were interpreted as non-White and "uncivilized" (not conforming to European cultural and political norms), Christian missionaries united their "evangelizing" efforts with "civilizing" efforts—seeking to assimilate Indigenous peoples into European (more specifically, English, French, Dutch, etc.) ways of doing things.

It wasn't just a European thing though. The United States was also happy to use missionaries and other church leaders to evangelize and "civilize" Native Americans. At first, US policy was one of Native extermination, but the strategy shifted in the 1860s to one of "pacification" and assimilation. The so-called peace policy mandated the confinement of Native tribes to reservations and forced their assimilation into the "more advanced" US society. Leaders of these efforts saw civilization and Christianity working together. American military general Richard Henry Pratt infamously articulated their mission this way: "kill the Indian in him, and save the man." Repeatedly, therefore, the US government allocated funds to Christian organizations to facilitate the simultaneous evangelization and civilization of Native peoples.[14]

The cooperative work of merchants, soldiers, and missionaries moved toward a particular goal: possession, mastery, and

APPRENTICESHIP TO LOVE IN A FALLEN WORLD

control. In other words, the ownership of, supremacy over, and domination of the land, its resources, and its peoples.[15]

Perhaps it's stating the obvious, but I'll do so anyway: Love cannot operate with such goals. If love is willing the good of the other, treating "the personhood, claims, and needs of the other as seriously as we treat our own," then love is wholly incompatible with possession, mastery, and control. Yet so many Christians in the European and American contexts have been shaped by the cooperative work of the merchant, soldier, and missionary such that we cannot see how it hampers our attempts at love, even at the level of our families and households.

## So, Now What?

At first blush, Christians should have no trouble identifying the evils I've described previously as contrary to the gospel. They violate the witness of Christ's church and defy the shalom of God's kingdom. The policies and practices that contribute to the these evils should be abhorrent to Christians. But we know historically this has often *not* been the case. Instead, Christians have been the ones offering justification and support for such things.

Protecting "American families" has been used to justify numerous horrors, including lynching, the reservation system, racial segregation, eugenics, internment camps, the nuclear bomb, the war on drugs, the war on terror, and, perhaps most ironically, family separation at the US-Mexico border.[16] "Family values" has been used repeatedly to rally citizens in support of not only a particular moral vision but also policies, tax structures, criminal laws, and wars that perpetuate the demonic cycle of self-interest. And that's just at the national level. There are myriad local situations in which Christian families participate in the cycle of self-interest, too, and they are often convinced it is the right and just thing to do because it is in defense of "the family."[17]

What all this means for us today is that things are far more complicated than we realize. On the one hand, the world is more corrupt than we may have previously grasped, and our families are impacted by this corruption in ways we can't yet identify. When you see the extent of the darkness within us and all around us, it's easy to despair. On the other hand, many of the challenges with which we wrestle daily—how to spend money justly, how to practice sabbath, how to raise our children, and more—are linked to these broader social realities. The truth is nothing has escaped the influence of imperialism, sexism, racism, and consumer capitalism. It's not just us. It's not just me or my spouse or my roommates or my mother- and father-in-law. If we're struggling, we're not simply failures, merely lacking the necessary determination and grit. Rather, we find living under God's reign today extraordinarily difficult *because it is*. By diabolical design.

If cosmic forces have indeed worked through human self-interest, pride, and greed to entrap people in systems that undermine their dignity and thwart their flourishing, and if we have failed to see the ways that powerful institutions allied against God's kingdom are shaping us in practices of consumption, exploitation, and violence, and if Christian families are both victims of and complicit parties to these evils, then we should expect life to be hard and to see signs of the dire situation before us.

Perhaps we'd see zero-sum thinking about resources and opportunities combined with plummeting rates of happiness and life satisfaction. Perhaps middle- and upper-class families would compete against each other, always one-upping with activities, tutoring, and coaching in constant pursuit of the best situation for their children. Perhaps impoverished, immigrant, and refugee families would be demonized and blamed for the struggles of other families, and their bodies and lives made a spectacle of in gross political stunts. Perhaps emerging adults would lead lives of excessive busyness, overwork, and underrest seeking to escape crippling debt and find financial security. Perhaps there would be increasing rates of family alienation, as well as isolation, loneliness, and fear about the future. Perhaps we'd see rising rates of mental illness, drug addiction, mass shootings, and deaths by suicide.

Are these not the besetting problems we face today? Do they not suggest that something is deeply wrong?

Christians have a responsibility to face, name, and seek to remedy the social diseases that produce such devastating symptoms. But it's important to be clear about what can and can't be done at the family level. Liberation and healing from society's sins won't happen as a solo effort, not least because imperialism, sexism, racism, and consumer capitalism are part of the world's powers and principalities. They require the Holy Spirit's presence and the community's creativity *just to survive*, let alone to resist. Sometimes what our families can do given the limitations and complications of our lives seems so small as to appear ludicrous; but they are our mustard seeds of faith, our seeds growing secretly (Mt 13:31-32; Mk 4:26-29).

For example, in my household, we insist on having a family sabbath in which we set aside our devices and do things that are intentionally "unplugged." We have dinner with non-family members at least twice per week. We prioritize sleep and taking time to rest, even when deadlines are looming and to-do lists are long. We regularly offer our spare room to people in need of temporary lodging. We purchase most of our clothing used, and we worship every week with our little church. Are any of these things going to reform our tax structure or remake our criminal justice system? No. But they are the "tactics and gestures" that lead to changed lives and faithful witnesses. They are the way Christians are apprentices to love in this present evil age.

Thankfully, the way things have been is not the way things have to be. We serve a crucified and resurrected Lord who has given us his Holy Spirit as a foretaste and preparation for his coming kingdom. All baptized believers have sworn allegiance to this Lord, trusting that he reigns over all right now and by his Spirit he is making all things new. Among other things, this means the horizon of what's possible is not limited to what we've always done. It never has been and never will be.

# 7

# Singleness and Marriage

**The Covid-19 pandemic** was extraordinarily stressful for every household, but each in its own way.[1] Much that had been kept in the dark was brought into the light, either because we were forced to be together or because we were forced to be alone. And some of us didn't like what we saw.

Conversations with my single friend Christina were especially enlightening. I am an introvert who needs a lot of alone time, but suddenly I found myself unable to be alone. Meanwhile, Christina, an extrovert, was unable to escape her solitude. As the weeks stretched on, she became desperate for human voices, real eye contact, and basic physical touch. My household had to implement a schedule to limit the chaos of five people trying to work at the same time. Christina had to create a schedule too, but for the purpose of resisting loneliness and dissociation. I worried about who would care for my kids if Ronnie and I got very ill or had to be hospitalized. Christina worried whether she'd be able to care for herself. Would anyone be willing to risk illness to help her? Who would care for her dog if she were hospitalized? Most fearfully, would she end up dying alone?

Of course, the differences between single and married households were present before the lockdown, but the compounding pressures of the pandemic exacerbated all preexisting realities and brought them to the foreground in a new way. Not all families have marriage at their center, nor do all members of God's household have spouses and children. Yet, many do. While our daily lives may look different, all Christians, single and married, are apprentices to love within the household of God. Still, it's not uncommon for single and married Christians to struggle to connect and fellowship across vocational lines. There are many reasons for this failure to join one another, but one important factor is the contradictory nature of the messages we receive about marriage and singleness today.

For centuries, romantic love has been elevated to the highest place in our social and cultural imagination. It is especially apparent in the stories we tell in our television shows, films, and novels. "Westley and I are joined by the bonds of love," Buttercup declares, "and you cannot break it, not with a thousand swords."[2] Nothing can stop true love, we're told, not even death, black holes, or the passage of time. Yes, the love of family and friends is powerful, but the greatest prize, the peak of human existence, is romantic love. Or so the past few centuries would lead us to believe.

At the same time, the late twentieth and early twenty-first centuries have seen a shake up in the valorization of romance. Western culture still hasn't quite given up on "The One," but more and more people are finding the notion impracticable in an overworked and debt-shackled economy. Online dating, as convenient as it is, leads to as much despair as the hope of finding a suitable match. At the same time, fewer people are taking their romantic connections to the "next level" of marriage. Raising children together remains a primary motivation for couples who do get married, but even that varies based on socioeconomic status. Many singles in their twenties, thirties, and forties are rather cynical about the notion of enduring romantic love—and marriage is becoming less common as a result.

Meanwhile, contemporary messages about singleness are also contradictory. On the one hand, the single life is held up as liberating, fun, and something to be celebrated. Such portrayals often assume an elevated class status that permits a high level of independence, mobility, and consumption. On the other hand, in parts of society that still valorize lifelong marriage and children, women especially feel they must constantly defend their singleness and resist the stereotype of the lonely spinster. And, despite the examples of Jesus and Paul and many of the saints, some of the most vocal condemnations of singleness come from within Christian circles. Meanwhile, both women and men are regularly treated as not full-fledged adults because they are unmarried and childless. Such infantilization of singles goes beyond Christian circles, too, as many cultures prioritize marriage and children so much that to remain unmarried is to bring shame to the family and fail one's elders and community.[3]

Amid the contradictory messages, the Christian faith offers a unique witness—or at least it's supposed to. Based on the proclamation of the gospel, Christian faith reorients all states of life, including marriage and singleness, around apprenticeship to Jesus and reframes everything under God's reign. Certainly, singleness and marriage can offer many positive things that are valuable and beneficial in themselves, but singleness and marriage find their full meaning as they are submitted to the lordship of Christ in God's kingdom. What singleness and marriage share, therefore, is the capacity to bear witness to God's faithful, covenantal love revealed in Christ.

The gospel, then, doesn't pooh-pooh romantic love or deny the pragmatic benefits of singleness or marriage today; in fact, it takes them quite seriously. But the gospel does sublimate everything to loyalty to Christ and his kingdom. The reprioritization of all lives, whatever their particulars, means that Christians ought to think of both singleness and marriage in ways distinct from the world. In view of Jesus' life and teaching, we can affirm both singleness and marriage are equally valid, fruitful, and meaningful states of life. Both are complementary gifts to Christ's church, both image God's covenantal love, and both ways of life have mutuality or equal regard as their goal.

## Singleness: Bearing Witness to God's Fidelity

I remember the first time we had our friend Brandon over for dinner. We had just met at church a couple weeks before and discovered we were all new to the congregation. We made a pasta dish and Ronnie baked bread. Brandon brought a lovely bouquet of blue hydrangeas.

Over the course of the evening, Brandon shared about the challenges he faced as a single person in the church. He was especially frustrated with the treatment he received in "family-oriented" churches, the kind where everything seems to be family worship, family communion, family discipleship, and family retreats. He was often excluded from such activities and events because the organizers assumed he had no interest and only planned for those with spouses and children to attend. "I don't have a wife and kids," Brandon said, "but I'm also a family. I am a family!" Even though I sympathized with his frustration and sense of alienation, at the time I found his insistence puzzling. How can one person be "a family"?

Now, however, with almost seven years of friendship between us, I understand better what he meant. Brandon was insisting that even though he didn't have a spouse or children, he is a legitimate household within the church, the household of God. He is a "family" in the sense that he, too, as a single head of a household, must navigate many of the challenges that other families with marriage and children at their center must navigate. How to manage limited resources and time, how to maintain faith in a world that undermines it, how to be in community with others, how to practice hospitality and compassion, and more.

He does all of this without the benefit of a "built-in" partner with whom to strategize and share burdens. When Brandon insisted, "I am a family," he was asking to be treated as a legitimate, whole, and valuable part of the body of Christ—as he very well should be.

When folks read carefully what the New Testament says about marriage and singleness, they are often surprised that Jesus speaks in ways that show a clear preference for singleness. But it can be easy to miss because it emerges within a debate about divorce and marriage. When asked about the permissibility of divorce, Jesus responds by emphasizing marriage's permanence. He disallowed the possibility of men discarding their wives for any reason they please (Mt 19:4-9). In a society where women were as a group much more vulnerable than men economically and socially, Jesus stands up for women and tells men that they cannot simply dispense with their wives for no reason without violating the covenant law against adultery.

Jesus' disciples were troubled by his response, though, and their reaction inadvertently revealed the hardness of their hearts: "If this is the situation between a husband and wife," they said, "it is better not to marry" (Mt 19:10). In other words, if marriage obligates me to be faithful to and responsible for my wife for life, then it's better not even to try.

The funny thing is Jesus does not directly contradict them. If they expected him to soften his stance, they were sorely disappointed.

> Jesus replied, "Not everyone can accept this word, but only those to whom it has been given. For there are eunuchs who were born that way, and there are eunuchs who have been made eunuchs by others—and there are those who choose to live like eunuchs for the sake of the kingdom of heaven. The one who can accept this should accept it." (Mt 19:11-12)

In the ancient world, eunuchs were incapable of bearing children either because of an in-born irregularity in their bodies or castration by others. Although eunuchs could be found everywhere in ancient societies, they were often seen as valuable members of royal households because of their inability to reproduce. With no progeny of their own, it was thought kings could expect wholehearted devotion from eunuchs and need not fear a challenge for dynastic succession. In other words, with the option of personal honor via procreation already foreclosed, eunuchs could serve the king and his kingdom single-mindedly.[4]

When Jesus calls up the image of a eunuch, therefore, he's drawing on a royal office with which his disciples were already familiar. But Jesus also goes further to say that some people *make themselves* eunuchs for the sake of God's kingdom. That is, they are single and celibate by choice for the sake of undivided devotion (Mt 19:11). Here Jesus seems to be alluding to the prophet Isaiah's promises that eunuchs, previously barred from the temple and presumed cursed, have an eternal place in God's promised future: "To the eunuchs who keep my Sabbaths, who choose what pleases me and hold fast to my covenant—to them I will give within my temple and its walls a memorial and a name better than sons and daughters; I will give them an everlasting name that will endure forever" (Is 56:4-5). As a result of God's promises, therefore, Jesus admonishes his disciples: "The one who can accept this should accept it" (Mt 19:12).

What precisely does Jesus mean? Is "this" referring to Jesus' overall teaching? Or is it specifically referring to Jesus' latter point about some choosing to be eunuchs for the kingdom? The text is unclear—and most of our English translations reflect the ambiguity. Considering Jesus' relativizing statements about kinship elsewhere in the Gospels, it seems more likely that Jesus is urging those who can remain single to do so. In view of the inbreaking kingdom of God, which demands total loyalty to Jesus, and the promises of God to eunuchs, singleness is the preferred state of life for those who can "accept" or "receive" it (Mt 19:12).

It's not only Jesus who prefers singleness. In 1 Corinthians 7 the apostle Paul also elevates the single state for explicitly pragmatic reasons. "I say: It is good for them to stay unmarried, as I do," Paul says of those who are widowed and unmarried (1 Cor 7:8). But if the self-control required for celibacy is too much for them, he says, "they should marry, for it is better to marry than to burn with passion" (1 Cor 7:9). Paul explains his reasoning on this point by making the general statement, "Each person should remain in the situation they were in when God called them" (1 Cor 7:20), and he illustrates further with a comparison to those who are uncircumcised or enslaved. Neither state, he says, is a hindrance to following Christ. "Each person, as responsible to God, should remain in the situation they were in when God called them" (1 Cor 7:24).

Remember: Paul is expecting the imminent return of Christ. So, he thinks it's better to remain in whatever social station the Corinthians already find themselves in. For, he says, "the time is short" and "this world in its present form is passing away" (1 Cor 7:29, 31). Paul wants his sisters and brothers in Corinth "to be free from concern," which is inevitable for those who marry and have children (1 Cor 7:32). He says they are free to marry or remain single, but the end is coming soon and the priority for everyone is obeying God's commands (1 Cor 7:19). Therefore, it will be easier for those who remain single as they will experience less anxiety and stress due to family obligations (1 Cor 7:32-34).

Paul concludes this section with an important insight into his motives: "I am saying this for your own good, not to restrict you, but that you may live in a right way in undivided devotion to the Lord" (1 Cor 7:35). To *live in a right way in undivided devotion to the Lord*. Whatever serves that purpose, he says, ought to be affirmed. Hence, his pragmatic preference for singleness. Still, Paul makes it clear that he considers both singleness and marriage to be legitimate states of life for Christians; both are "gifts," which come from God (1 Cor 7:7).

In the first few centuries of the church, pastors and theologians elevated singleness as the way of life most appropriate for imitating Christ. Elsewhere in the Gospels, Jesus tells the

Sadducees that the future state of human beings will be one in which "people will neither marry nor be given in marriage; they will be like the angels in heaven" (Mt 22:30). Later theologians reasoned, therefore, that imitation of Jesus in his chaste singleness is a living picture of God's new creation, which isn't dependent on marriage or biological procreation. As Pope John Paul II said, "The celibate person thus anticipates in his or her flesh the new world of the future resurrection."[5] And why wouldn't Christians want to begin emulating our future state right now?

Within the Greco-Roman world, the early church's preference for celibacy was countercultural—so much so that it created a scandal. Because marriage was seen as a hindrance to faithful discipleship, there are many stories of saints taking vows of celibacy and fleeing arranged marriages. As Asian American Al Hsu observes, "As surprising as it may seem to us, it was the church that provided an escape from the [cultural] pressure to marry and reproduce."[6] Even so, when Christians attempted to exercise agency in that way, they were often opposed by their families. In the cases of young women, especially, their fathers or fiancés sometimes resorted to violence, either to force their conformity or punish their resistance.

In contrast to the Christian tradition's valorization of singleness, many contemporary Christians imagine singleness to be a deficient and even morally aberrant way of life. For them, as Australian author Danielle Treweek notes, Christian singleness is characterized primarily by lack: a lack of romance, a lack of relationships, a lack of sex, and a lack of fulfillment because, as the contemporary imagination assumes, fulfillment isn't possible without sex and romance, and without sex and romance, there are no intimate relationships. These assumptions are, of course, patently false. But for those who hold this view, the only legitimate forms of singleness are those which are considered a specially empowered calling, a limited transitional phase (preceding marriage), something tragic (like widowhood), or a heroic choice based on a unique mission. Singleness is generally not looked on as a worthwhile state in which Christians may freely choose to live—a form of life with inherent dignity.[7]

So, let me be clear: Singleness is a honorable and worthy station in God's kingdom. The new covenant in Christ makes us children of God "not of natural descent, nor of human decision or a husband's will, but born of God" (Jn 1:13). We are remembered in eternity, our names written in the book of life (Rev 20:12), not because of offspring (or career or wealth or property ownership), but because of God's gracious action on our behalf. There are no bonus points in heaven for marriage and children, and all are adopted into God's family, the church, regardless of one's marital status. As Paul says, "If you do marry, you have not sinned," but also, "those who marry will face many troubles in this life, and I want to spare you this" (1 Cor 7:28).

In view of the coming bodily resurrection and new creation, singleness is a sacramental sign of God's kingdom. Whereas the first human, Adam, was given a partner, Eve, from his own side, in an earthly union that produced children, the consummate human, Jesus Christ, had no such earthly partner. His "wedding" took place through his death and resurrection—and from his body God brought forth the church, his bride, with whom he is united forever (Jn 19:34; Rev 21:2). Single Christians, therefore, testify in their bodies to God's covenant fidelity to God's people and demonstrate their faith in the eternal marriage that awaits all in Christ's bride. In addition to the many possible benefits of remaining single, the love shared, given, and modeled by a single person's life speaks truth to the world about God and God's fidelity to us.

As meaningful as such a theological understanding of singleness may be, the modern industrialized world presents serious challenges to Christian singles. Under the conditions of consumer capitalism, Western people are often forced to move all over to find suitable work. Such moves take people away from family, friends, and church, leaving them more vulnerable in almost every way. The economic situation since at least the early 2000s has been such that emerging adults headed into the workforce often find it difficult to sustain life on one full-time job. Rent and home prices are high, student loan debt is a national crisis, medical care is astronomically expensive, and the cost of living keeps rising. We live in an age where people are forced to turn to GoFundMe for lifesaving cancer treatments and organ transplants. One understands, therefore, why, contrary to the perspective of Paul and the early church, singleness looks to many like the opposite of a "gift" (1 Cor 7:7).

The answer to a society inimical to singleness, though, is not to abandon such a fruitful and sacramental state of life and encourage everyone to marry. Rather, the answer is for Christians and churches to use their sanctified imaginations and resources, however limited they may be, to pursue more communal and interdependent ways of life. If we want to take the New Testament's language about God's family seriously, then we ought to intentionally seek ways to put it into practice. Such a church will encourage friendships across vocations and the mutual sharing of time, space, and resources to facilitate the true joining of siblings in God's household.

I have seen this done before. The church my family attended before establishing our current congregation had an unusually high number of lifelong single people, and not just single people "in the pews." One of the deacons was a single woman, and the church was served by several single spiritual directors and leader volunteers. The vestry (our version of a governing board) had multiple single members. The most striking thing to me, though, was the way the single households and married households were interwoven. Yes, the single people shared unique experiences, needs, and concerns, but they were also close friends of married folks in the congregation, regularly attending shared gatherings and caring for one another in times of need.

I don't think there was a strategy that led to this beautifully interdependent community, but it was clear these disparate families had been living together for a long time. After a decade or more of stability, going through life's highs and lows while staying in the same place, they had been joined to one another in a way that defies the typical marriage-based segregation that happens in many churches. May their kind increase.

## Marriage: Also Bearing Witness to God's Fidelity

Despite the preference for singleness in the teachings of Jesus, Paul, and the early church, marriage was by no means rejected. Jesus affirms that marriage is part of God's good plan for humanity, even if it will not be part of the eternal kingdom (Mt 19:4-9; 22:30). Paul acknowledges the practical limits of marriage but says that those who marry are not sinning (1 Cor 7:36). Those who are married ought to live faithfully in the married state (1 Cor 7:17), and Ephesians 5:32 reframes marriage as a "mystery" that reveals something about Christ and the church. The rest of the New Testament also provides ample evidence that a significant number of early Christians were married, and it seems clear that the apostles and their disciples expected that marriage and childrearing would continue into the foreseeable future. So, rather than forbid marriage, they taught how to think about and practice marriage in light of the gospel.

Even so, the Christian tradition has been debating the purpose of marriage for a long time. But what we're debating and why has changed considerably over the years. Early church leaders fought about whether marriage was inherently sinful because of sex. Contemporary churches, by contrast, largely assume sex is good (not sinful) and fight instead about gender roles. Early church leaders fought about whether divorced and widowed spouses could remarry. Contemporary churches largely ignore that question and fight instead about who can get married to begin with. Doctrine and practice develop over time, influenced by many complex factors, so these changes in discourse are understandable, but it's important to remember at least some of the early church's deliberations about marriage and sex to understand better some of the challenges in our day.

The early church was deeply uncomfortable with sexual desire and sexual relations. This doesn't make intuitive sense to us because over the past century and a half, most Christians have come to think of married sex as an inherent good. But most of the early church fathers prized celibacy and looked down on marriage as a lesser calling because it involves sexual intercourse.[8] Why was this a problem? Sex was always thought to entail inordinate bodily desire. The fancy word for it was *concupiscence*. In sexual relations, they reasoned, bodily desires almost always overcome the rational mind and lead to actions not wholly governed by the will. Thus, they concluded, such inordinate desires must be sinful, and marriage must always include some measure of sin because it includes sex. In fact, as bizarre as it sounds to us, it was considered the ideal scenario for married people to voluntarily cease sexual relations for the sake of holiness.

At this point it is fair to ask: Why would a Christian get married and have sex if it always included sin? Here, Augustine enters the fray in the fifth century to defend the good of marriage despite its association with sex. During a time when the church valorized celibacy above all else, Augustine tried to reason through and synthesize biblical teaching on marriage and sex to show that it is, in fact, given by God for good reasons.

In summary, Augustine taught that marriage is for three purposes:

1. Procreation through the male-female union, fulfilling the Creator's mandate to "Be fruitful and increase in number" (Gen 1:28) and to raise children to know and love God

2. Faithfulness or fidelity in which husband and wife pursue oneness with each other and only satisfy their sexual desires within their union

3. A sacramental sign, where the spouses are an embodied icon of the indissoluble relationship between Christ and the church (Eph 5:32; Rev 19:7, 9; 21:2)

For Augustine, the three goods of marriage outweigh or nullify the sin that is surely present in the married couple's sexual acts. In other words, for Augustine, the inordinate desires present in sexual intercourse are excused within marriage because they are directed toward procreation, they take place in a monogamous union, and they help create the sacramental sign.

This way of thinking about marriage and sex is foreign to many Christians today. Yet given his context and his own preference for celibacy, Augustine's defense of marriage is remarkable. It laid important groundwork for later theologians to conclude that marriage is, in fact, a good and worthwhile state of life for Christians. Not all holy lives are single and celibate lives. Thanks be to God! Virtually every Western theologian since Augustine has built upon or had to contend with his vision.

Still, I think Augustine's theology has passed on some serious deficits—deficits that remain at work in Christian teaching today. First, Augustine was working with a prescientific view of women's and men's bodies. Much of what he and his contemporaries thought about bodies came from Aristotle, and that inevitably colored his view of gender, sex, and marriage. Augustine thought that the man's semen was the source of life. The woman, by contrast, was understood to be an empty vessel to receive man's seed; one worthy of honor and respect, but an empty vessel, nonetheless. Thus, the *telos* of the sexual act—its ultimate goal—was the man's ejaculation inside the woman's vagina. Absent from Augustine's vision is any sense that women's bodies contribute more than materially to the procreative process, that sexual relations could be more than intercourse, or that sex could have a goal distinct from the release and reception of seminal fluid. This isn't limited to Augustine. Most who wrote on marriage prior to the modern period operate with similar limitations. Such a flawed understanding of women's bodies and women's experience of sex has remained widespread in Christian writing and teaching ever since.[9]

Going further, Augustine assumed that all sexual intercourse is sinful, but especially sexual intercourse not intended for procreation. In other words, if some kind of contraception is used or if nonpenetrative sex results in "seed" not being deposited correctly, then the sexual act is perverse and sinful. Again, I realize many Christians today don't hold this view, especially among Protestants. The moral teaching of the Roman Catholic Church, however, continues to be that contraception is sinful, and many others continue to function with Augustine's view of bodies and sex in subtler ways.

For instance, despite a sizable amount of research on the topic, and despite the existence of the clitoris (the only known human organ whose function is solely for pleasure), some continue to teach that women in general can't desire sex or can't enjoy sex. This perspective is wrong, and the error has serious consequences. Furthermore, Augustine and others concluded that sex is primarily for procreation because their predominant lens for interpreting sexual relations was the male bodily experience. When the climax of the male experience is the pleasure of ejaculation, then it makes sense that moment would be viewed as the most important among men writing theological accounts of sex and marriage. Now that we know better, however, it is possible to theologize better and do better.

We now know that women's bodies are fertile for a very small window of time every month and that monthly window can be unpredictable. When a sperm does meet an egg within that window of time, a significant percentage of those conceptions result in natural miscarriages. In addition, we now know women can experience sexual pleasure and orgasm in ways that don't include penetration or ejaculation at all. When all these details are considered, we see that Augustine has made one of the possible results of sexual intercourse—and one that occurs only in a small percentage of cases—into the primary purpose of sex. Not only has Augustine made it the primary purpose of sex, but he's also made it the primary purpose of marriage. But as most people know well, marriage is *so* much more than sexual intercourse and procreation.

Besides the problems with Augustine's view of bodies and sex, I don't think his account of marriage is fully coherent under the new covenant. In Christ by the Spirit, Christians anticipate a future kingdom based *not* on biological procreation but on adoption into God's family. Of course, it is still a good thing to have children via procreation. Such fruitfulness remains an inherent good, just as children are inherent and unequivocal blessings from God despite the sometimes-difficult circum-stances they are born into. Procreation certainly remains part of the good purposes of sex within marriage, but in my view, it is not the central purpose of sex within marriage. In view of new creation, procreation no longer holds the central place it once did in the old order.

Finally, it's important to recognize that Augustine understood women and men in largely essentialist and hierarchical terms. Alongside others, Augustine assumed that men are naturally superior to women. As a result of their superiority, men ought to rule over women. The male is the active partner—the dom-inant, ruling leader—and the female is the passive partner—the submissive, weak dependent. Such essential differences based on one interpretation of sexual intercourse led to a vision of gender where womb and penis become integral to who women and men are and what roles they are designed to perform in the world.

Despite its ancient origin and mistaken biology, Augustine's (and Aristotle's) vision of women and men remains founda-tional to some visions of gender today. Yet, a gender-based assignment of "roles" in marriage is foreign to the teaching of the Bible. Certainly, one can find plenty of biblical texts to use in support of patriarchy (or male headship) because it was the context of the authors. So, too, was a patrilocal lifestyle where all live in proximity to the oldest male relative, and a patrilineal heritage where one's rights and property are traced through the male line. But Jesus' life and teaching do not support patriarchy as a God-ordained structure. In fact, he tells his followers not to attempt to rule over each other, but rather to serve each other as Jesus himself serves (Mt 20:25-28). He also tells them not to take the titles "Rabbi" or "Father" because they are all disciples of one Teacher (Christ), and all "brothers" with one Father in heaven (Mt 23:8-12).

Still, some interpret Genesis 1–3 and Jesus' teaching through the lens of a few passages in the New Testament, especially 1 Corinthians 11:2-16; Ephesians 5:21-33; Colossians 3:18-19; 1 Timothy 2:11-15; and Titus 2:3-5. Though each of these epistles was written to different churches in a variety of contexts, some interpreters find within them a universal affirmation of male headship and a divinely ordained gender-based hierarchy in marriage and church.

It is not necessarily wrong to use certain Scriptures as frames through which to understand Genesis 1–2 or the rest of the Bible for that matter. As Anglo-American scholar Scot McKnight says, "Everyone picks and chooses."[10] Everyone arranges the narrative of Scripture in the way they think is most faithful to God's revelation across the canon. That necessarily means prioritizing some texts and de-prioritizing others, and there is firm precedent for Christians to read the Old Testament in light of the New. The problem arises when Paul's epistles are understood to be blanket endorsements of patriarchal marriage and family. Instead of recognizing that Paul is teaching Christians how to live within already-established marriage and family structures (those of Greco-Roman society), many assume Paul is endorsing the structures themselves as God-willed, and then they read those structures back into the first few chapters of Genesis and the teaching of Jesus.

But such interpretations miss the mark and distort how the rest of the Bible's story is told. As a good church planter and missionary, Paul applied the good news of Jesus Christ to the lived experiences of his people in their specific places and circumstances. He described how Christians ought to conduct themselves in their various situations, as wives, husbands, children, enslaved people, and slave owners in view of Christ's lordship and the coming kingdom of God, and this pattern is very much in keeping with the way Jesus himself preached and taught.[11]

In the end, I reject gender-based hierarchy in marriage not despite the biblical witness but because of it. What is popularly called complementarianism is based on a dubious telling of the Bible's overarching story and inconsistent theology. To read Genesis 1–2 as divine design for patriarchy is to read the Roman *paterfamilias* that Paul assumed in his epistles back into the Genesis creation narratives. On its own terms, Genesis 1–2 does not assume patriarchy, nor does it ask its readers to see the first woman and man as universal ideals. Moreover, to read Genesis 1–2 as an account of gender roles assumes the context of marriage is required for performing one's gender, but plenty of human beings, including Jesus the Messiah, live their lives as single persons. Regardless of the circumstances of their singleness, those who remain unmarried are fully women and men even without a romantic partner. They do not need another human to complement them, complete them, or make them whole.

We ought to be suspicious of theological models that struggle to make sense of Jesus as a person, not to mention his teaching on the kingdom, church, family, and children. Jesus was a single man who never had children, never promoted gender roles, and never called women or men into patriarchal families. Rather,

Jesus taught the priority of discipleship and allegiance to him over and above the bonds of biological kinship. Instead of patriarchy and gender-based roles, Jesus and his disciples follow a trajectory of freedom in view of God's kingdom. The basis for such liberty is that we all have received "one Lord, one faith, one baptism," and been joined in "one body and one Spirit," destined for one future: God's new creation (Eph 4:4-5).

In Christ we are no longer limited by this world's divisions, and we are not required to perform such divisions within marriage and family. Rather, "In Christ Jesus you are all children of God through faith, for all of you who were baptized into Christ have clothed yourselves with Christ. There is neither Jew nor Gentile, neither slave nor free, nor is there male and female, for you are all one in Christ Jesus" (Gal 3:26-28). The call for married Christians, then, is to learn to live as mutual apprentices in God's kingdom, sharing a life and household that images the household of God: submitting to one another out of reverence for Christ (Eph 5:21).

So, if marriage is not, as Augustine said, primarily for procreation, and if marriage is not, as some say, for acting out prescribed gender roles, then what precisely is marriage for?

When Jesus refers to God's original intent for marriage, he points to the relational unity of the partners based on the shared essence of women and men: "That is why a man leaves his father and mother and is united to his wife, and they become one flesh" (Gen 2:24). Marriage provides a unique setting in which humanity's relational essence is manifested. Going further, though, Paul says marriage symbolizes in a mysterious way Christ's love for and unity with the church (Eph 5:32). Through their faithful, lifelong union, which includes sex and sometimes children, married partners point to God's fidelity to God's people. In addition to the many possible benefits of such a union, the love shared, given, and modeled by married spouses speaks truth to the world about God and God's fidelity to us.

Of course, this is not to say that marriage can't also be socially and economically advantageous. For most of human history, in fact, marriage has been pursued for precisely such benefits.[12] And it's not to say that marriage can't be personally fulfilling and emotionally satisfying. Certainly, those things are not only possible, but also well worth pursuing.[13] But because of its sacramental aspect, what we are saying yes to in Christian marriage is an indissoluble partnership with one person for life. The yes of our vows signifies the will of Christ through which his union with the church took place. So there's a way in which the direct object of consent in marriage vows is not one's particular spouse but one's *enduring union with* the spouse. In other words, a marriage is not created by consent to a particular person, but to an indissoluble union with a particular person.[14]

The major challenge, though, is that no one who marries can possibly know all the implications of their "I do." They have no control over what successes and adversities they will encounter, what disasters they will have to weather, what gains and losses will come to pass, and who their spouse will become on their journey. As Anglo-American ethicist Stanley Hauerwas says, "You always marry the wrong person."[15] Yes, marriage takes commitment and work for it to remain good and healthy: attention, communication, mutual love, and more. At the same time, marriage is a little bit of a crapshoot. Life is unpredictable. Horrors are real. The weaknesses of humanity and our existence in a fallen world are such that some relationships can't endure all that is thrown at them, and some people find themselves married to people who subject them to such degradation that they cannot continue in the union. God has made merciful provision for such circumstances through divorce, even if the sundering of the relationship is tragic.

Marriage entails a great deal of risk, as much perhaps as remaining single. Both states of life entail significant dependence on other people—spouse, friends, neighbors, family, therapists, and more—who are not under our direct control. Both states of life require deep trust in the goodness, guidance, and provision of God, a virtue that will require significant growth and maturation over the years. And both singleness and marriage call on God's household, the church, to provide support and provision to help people in either state to continue walking faithfully with Christ.

## Singleness, Marriage, and the Family of God

Every family must determine how to be apprentices of love together. Undoubtedly, daily life will take different shapes depending on whether household members are married—or some combination of marrieds and singles. I have lived as a single woman with roommates, a married woman with single friends in a shared home, and a married woman with children. Sadly, it wasn't until we had children that I began to approach the daily aspects of our life together with real intentionality in view of the gospel. With little ones to disciple in the faith, suddenly the importance of routines and rhythms became obvious in ways that I couldn't ignore.

I wish I had brought the same thoughtfulness to my life as a single person with roommates and a married person with housemates. All these states entail being apprentices to Jesus together and, therefore, all require sharing, planning, and organizing to cultivate the practices necessary to build that kind of life. If mutuality—reciprocal love, generosity, and joining—is a central aspect of our apprenticeship, then households must commit themselves to the interpersonal and communication dynamics necessary for creating real mutuality.[16] It's not enough to say you believe in mutuality regarding meals, chores, errands, caregiving, and emotional support. You must do things that help to create a culture of mutuality in the home.

In our current season, family meetings provide regular opportunities for members to voice hurts and concerns and for us to seek remedies together. I know a single friend who lives alone.

Even though she doesn't share household duties with anyone, she has a weekly and monthly schedule of communal activities, including tea with friends, meals after church, and walks in the park with neighbors. I know a couple of single friends who bought a home together and they have developed a schedule of shared chores so that they truly share their housework. The schedule can, of course, be modified as things come up and seasons come and go. The point is that the household is committed to mutual love, which isn't just a feeling but demonstrated in a way of life.

As I've said from the beginning, there is no blueprint for how to live as married and single people—as much as we might wish we had one. Instead, we have a diagnosis of what ails us as individuals and society, and a cure in the person and work of Jesus Christ who has brought about God's kingdom by the power of the Holy Spirit. Thankfully, Christ has given us his way of life through Scripture, a way marked by work and rest, eating and sleeping, listening and sharing, serving and receiving service—all under the reign of God. Christ has bestowed on his people some vital practices that can serve as touchpoints for family life in whatever form they take. Rooted in such practices, which we receive through Christ's church, families can improvise with the Spirit's guidance a way of life that better emulates God's reign, and gestures to the world the love we are meant for in union with God. I say more about such practices in part three.

# 8

# Children and Childrearing

**Among the photos, icons, and artwork** in my office hangs a note from my oldest child. It was written in pencil when he was in first grade and still learning to form his letters. There's a vowel missing and multiple misspelled words, but the message is discernible: "Nevr lose hopy. Donot geve up. God is with you."

When my six-year-old son handed me this piece of folded scrap paper, he couldn't have known how much I needed his words. I had held my PhD for two years and had been searching for an academic post for three years. Application after grueling application resulted in nothing. I was working a full-time job that paid well, but for which I was ill-suited. I was grateful for employment but deeply unhappy, and my disillusionment was slowly eating me up inside. Like my not-yet-begun academic career, my faith was languishing, and into this dark and lonely period of testing, God's Spirit spoke through my son. In his awkward scrawl, I heard God's voice: "Fear not. I am with you."

Not all Christian families include children, but many do, and those who do have received a tremendous gift. The contexts into which children are born can be complex and fraught, and caring for children can be difficult, but children are a blessing from God.

Scripture is unambiguous on this point. Still, it takes faith to receive children as a divine gift. It takes faith to welcome a child into your household. It takes faith to move at a child's pace and to allow a child to make demands on your body, time, and resources. Specifically, it takes faith in the God who raised Jesus from the dead and is always present and at work.

Because children come into the world vulnerable and ignorant, they will not survive without adult nurture and protection. When they welcome a child into their household, caregivers assume a new role in what British American poet W. H. Auden calls "the New Order": "To supply and deliver his raw materials free."[1] Sometimes war, natural disasters, and other catastrophes interfere with adults' ability to provide the "raw materials." Sometimes adults can't earn enough to provide for basic needs. Children are a blessing, yet what children require is neither free nor cheap. Significant time and resources are needed to offer healthcare, education, space to explore and play, and, for Christian families, formation in the faith.

The care of children is too costly and important to be left to individual households to undertake alone—and God does not mean for us to. Studies show the ability of families to cope with stress and setbacks depends in large part on their networks, and God's household, the church, is responsible for the growth and well-being of all children in their midst. Whether in the legal custody of parents, grandparents, foster parents, aunts and uncles, or some other relation, children are a sacred trust to the body of Christ. Going further, Christians who affirm the gift-nature of children also have a moral obligation to ensure the societies in which they reside are doing all they can to care for children, the most vulnerable of "the least of these" (Mt 25:40).

## The Weight of Childrearing

One reason Christians find childrearing so heart-wrenching and anxiety-inducing is due to the sincere desire to pass on the faith. As full persons with wills and consciences of their own, children will have to decide eventually whether to trust in Christ for themselves. Sometimes the immense weight of that responsibility leads us to think we own our children, that they are our projects, and that their lives are affirmations or denials of us as persons. Not only is this not true, but also it is an approach to childrearing that will be detrimental to all. We do not own our children. They are not commodities or accessories, they are not our clones, and we must resist words and practices that suggest otherwise.

Children belong to themselves and to God. They are full persons with their own minds, hearts, and wills. Still in development, yes. Immature, yes. But full persons, nonetheless. Yes, we are morally and legally responsible for their care—work we must not take lightly. We hope as their caregivers that they will, led by the Spirit, offer their whole selves to Christ in allegiance to God's kingdom, but that is not ultimately within our control. Their stories are not ours to craft, their lives are not ours to live, and their choices are not for the sake of our validation. All parents experience this, but the parents I know who care for children with traumatic histories or significant neurological differences know this in a unique way.

Remember the goal of Christian households as part of the larger household of God: To be apprentices to love. Earthly families, as beloved and important as they are, are temporary institutions that will pass away when the resurrection comes and new creation begins. The body of Christ, however, will endure forever.

One way to practice the truth that our children aren't ours is to share childrearing with trustworthy family and friends, as well as a safe local community of believers. Whenever and however a child's trust in Christ emerges, children are part of the community of disciples, joining older, more mature believers in their practice of faith. Not only do they benefit from the example of older believers, but they minister to older believers through their nascent faith, as my son's note so vividly illustrates. Apprenticeship to love requires more than just the nuclear family, and children need more mentors than just the people they live with. At its best, the discipleship journey takes place in the accompaniment of other apprentices in the church.

What we are preparing children for is not simply life in our home or at school, a university, or a national economy, as important as such things may be. Rather, we are preparing children for life in God's kingdom, both now in the local manifestation of the kingdom (the church) and in the age to come. The kingdom of God is not disconnected from the spheres of home, school, business, and nation, so such things are not left to the side. In fact, we trust God's kingdom is being manifested through the specifics of such spheres as Christians seek the Spirit's creative guidance in each, but each realm must be approached considering the purpose and aims of the eternal body of Christ and God's already-not-yet kingdom.

In children's earliest years, their caregivers are the primary means by which God speaks love to them. Through cotton blankets and cheese quesadillas, back scratches and raspberry kisses, God initiates a relationship with children, and they begin to learn of God's provision and care. As children mature, the rhythms of church life and family life teach them to speak the language of Christian faith and experience the affections that come with it. The hope is, as my friend Aubrey Spears says, that a child would never know a day apart from Christ. That they would look back and recognize that they have always been accompanied by God's loving presence.

What I've described is the best-case scenario, but the best case isn't always how things work out. Families are complicated, and our work within families are impacted by many layers of complexity. Our best childrearing efforts can fall short of what's needed due to personal weakness, scarce resources, poor schools, negligent social services, faulty medical care, and so much more. In fact, it's more than a little frightening just how many factors that affect the lives and trajectories of our children ultimately lie beyond our control. And even the thing over which we *think* we have control—ourselves—sometimes betrays us.

Because of the weightiness of the childrearing task, many parents and caregivers go looking for fail-safe plans to guarantee good outcomes. But just as there is no precise formula for success in marriage and friendship, there is no precise formula for raising children. Despite adults' best efforts, children will make countless decisions throughout their lives that form their character and set their future course. We know the Christian life is not one ultimately creditable to human design or power, anyway. "For it is by grace you have been saved, through faith," Ephesians says, "and this is not from yourselves, it is the gift of God" (Eph 2:8). There is no guarantee of faith in children, nor of the development of hope or love or the rest of the Spirit's fruit.

My friend Renée once told me that her greatest temptation as a parent is to treat each of her children as though they have a sticky note on their foreheads. What she meant by this is that she tends to see her children as a to-do list of necessary changes—be more punctual, stop slouching, take more initiative, grow in confidence—rather than full persons with much to offer her household right now. Holly Taylor Coolman warns, "Too often parenting . . . slides toward imagining something that parents are doing *to* their children. Parents can get pulled into something perhaps better described as management of children." But children are persons, not products.[2] So instead of walking to-do lists, how are we to think rightly of the children among us? We do well once again to begin with Jesus.

## Jesus and Children

Jesus was not a parent and he repeatedly relativized biological kinship in view of his new family of disciples. Yet, his affection for and rapport with children must have made a lasting impression. The Gospels tell multiple stories about Jesus and children, and his teaching about children and discipleship are recorded in three out of four Gospels. Perhaps we have become so accustomed to images of Jesus blessing children that we've forgotten how unusual both his posture and teaching were in the first century.

After Jesus' transfiguration, his closest disciples begin to argue among themselves who is the greatest or will be the greatest in the kingdom of heaven. Matthew, Mark, and Luke each relate the ensuing exchange in different ways, but all agree that as part of his response to the disciples' squabbling, Jesus places a child in their midst (Mt 18:2; Mk 9:36; Lk 9:47).

Imagine the scene with me: Jesus gestures for the Twelve to circle up around him. Some of them are scowling, still indignant and tense from their argument. Some of them look sheepish, suspecting they're about to be rebuked. But the men gather in a reluctant cluster. As Jesus looks about the circle, they wait in mounting tension for him to speak. But then something catches his eye. Looking between their heads and beyond the group, Jesus' expression brightens, and he smiles. They turn to see what he's looking at, but Jesus walks through them. "What's he doing?" they whisper to each other, as Jesus approaches a child a few yards away. They hadn't even noticed someone was there.

Who is the child? Maybe she's a fisherman's daughter taking a break from her chores. Maybe he's a boy with Down syndrome mending nets in the sunshine. Maybe he's Jesus' own preschool-age cousin. Whoever the child was, whatever reason he or she was there, the child certainly wouldn't stand a chance at being "the greatest" in God's kingdom. But there's Jesus, his back to the disciples, bending to bring himself to eye level with the child. They speak quietly for a moment and then share a laugh. Standing back up, Jesus takes the child's hand, and they stroll back to the group. As Jesus continues to teach them of God's kingdom, the child stays close, Jesus' calloused hands resting gently on the child's shoulders.

Asked to resolve a one-upmanship dispute, Jesus centers the child. Asked about the nature of God's kingdom, Jesus centers the child. This is more remarkable than we realize.[3] The ancient world wasn't particularly fond of children. Though modern people might associate children with innocence and wonder—happily oohing and aahing over their antics on Instagram or TikTok—the

Greco-Roman world didn't see children this way. Certainly, most parents loved their children and valued them as vital to their household, but the ideal human being was the free, adult, male citizen. So, children occupied one of the lowest rungs on the social ladder. They were considered needy, vulnerable, immature, foolish, impulsive, and irrational. Their value lay mainly in what they might one day become—the value and honor they might bring to their families in the future. Thus, children weren't considered full persons and had no rights under Roman law.

The Jewish tradition was a bit more child friendly. They valued children as signs of God's blessing and inheritors of the divine covenant. Children had covenant responsibilities and were expected to learn the stories of their people and uphold their laws and traditions, and Jewish teachers shunned the brutality of Roman practices toward children like abortion and exposure. Even so, children were not idealized as they are in modern societies. Throughout the Hebrew Bible and the Talmud, children are examples of foolishness and capriciousness, requiring restraint and firm discipline.

It simply would not have occurred to a Roman or Jewish teacher to hold up a child as a religious example. Yet that's precisely what Jesus does. "Unless you change and become like little children," he says, "you will never enter the kingdom of heaven" (Mt 18:3). Obviously, he is not saying his disciples must literally become children again just like he wasn't telling Nicodemus to go back into his mother's womb (Jn 3:4). Neither is he endorsing a kind of cosplay where we adopt childlike language and habits. Jesus explains his meaning in Matthew 18:4: "Whoever takes the lowly position of this child is the greatest in the kingdom of heaven."

This is so like Jesus, isn't it? Peter, James, John, and the rest are arguing about which of them is going to be the greatest, Jesus' right-hand man in the messianic kingdom, and Jesus responds by undermining the entire line of inquiry. To enter God's kingdom at all, he says, you must change and become like children. Forget right-hand man; you can't even *get in* until you humble yourselves.

And *anyone*—not just the Twelve—who follows the path of the child is the greatest in God's kingdom.

Our instinct here is to spiritualize Jesus' words and make them solely about our hearts. We must change and become internally like a child: humbler, more innocent, more trusting. That's not a bad way to start, but there are a couple problems with a too-spiritualized interpretation. First, it's not particularly representative of real children. Only idealized children are always innocent, trusting, humble, and open. Those who work with real children understand that children can also be shrewd, skeptical, manipulative, and selfish—just like the rest of us. Jesus never romanticizes children, and neither should we. (For the record, we shouldn't demonize children either.)

The other problem with the spiritualized reading is that it doesn't take Jesus' actual words seriously enough. Listen again to Matthew 18:4: *"Whoever takes the lowly position of this child."* Some versions say, "whoever humbles himself" or "whoever becomes humble." Either way, Jesus is describing an intentional, volitional shift, a change of posture, location, or status—not simply a heart change. His disciples understandably wanted honor and esteem. They were the Messiah's first followers, after all. Surely, they deserve a special role for being the first ones! But Jesus shuts that down. Instead, he says, shift your solidarity from the high-status folks to the low-status folks, the well-networked to the no-networked. When you adopt the lowliest position in the world, Jesus says, then you receive the highest place in God's kingdom.

## Children and Vulnerability

Among all the people of the first-century Mediterranean world—from Praetorian guards to peasant farmers—the child was the most powerless, and this is the main reason that Jesus uses children as exemplary disciples. No doubt childhood two thousand years ago was very different from childhood today.[4] Nevertheless, amid all our modern developments, one aspect of childhood remains true across the years: vulnerability. Children are extraordinarily vulnerable because they are weak, needy, and defenseless, and this is one of the major reasons why, even in the twenty-first century, children still occupy the lowest rung of the social ladder.

Of course, all human beings are vulnerable. Clad in fleshy bodies that can be fatigued, struck, and broken, sometimes beyond repair, humans are quite defenseless compared to other creatures. It's not just our bodies, though. Our minds, hearts, and souls are delicate, too, able to withstand much, but also irreparably changed by what we are forced to endure. In truth, humans are perpetually needful. We need things like food and water, protection from the elements, sleep, physical touch, and intimacy with others.

After my oldest child was born, I bought a little sign for his room in a moment of sleep-deprived humor. In curling blue script on a white ceramic background, it read: "Bottomless pit of needs and wants." I hung it over his crib and smiled wryly about it every day, but it's a sign all of us could hang over our beds. Infants aren't the only needy, wanting ones. Whether we like it or not, human beings are born in neediness, live our lives in neediness, and die in neediness.[5] It's just who we are.

At the same time, there are few humans as naturally vulnerable as children. Their needs vary depending on their age and physical, neurological, or psychological makeup. While most will grow in independence over time, children often remain dependent on their families and other institutions well into what is now call emerging adulthood. If children find themselves victims of neglect, mistreatment, or exploitation in one or more of such settings, the consequences can be dire. Even more so if they find themselves living in perilous places too: a country torn apart by war, a region hit by a tsunami, or a school targeted for a mass shooting.

While the treatment of children has generally improved over the centuries, their natural dependency means there is an unavoidable imbalance of power between children and adults. I have a friend whose toddler son used to try to run out the front door when it was bath time. Stark naked and giggling mischievously, Malachi would race down the hall on his tiny legs and pull wildly at the doorknob. Once or twice, when the door was not bolted, he managed to get it open just before my friend caught him. Each time she'd scoop him up laughing and carry him back to the waiting tub. Through his squeals of delight, she would say, "Where do you think you're going? What exactly is your plan?" Malachi was blissfully unaware of the absurdity of his attempted escape or the danger he might be in if he made it out the door. Compared to adults, children are quite defenseless, especially within private homes.[6]

I am haunted by the image of five-year-old Omran Daqneesh of Aleppo that was captured by photographer Mahmoud Raslan in 2016 after a Russian airstrike destroyed his home during the Syrian civil war.[7] Slight in frame, Omran sits in a bright orange ambulance seat wearing a stunned, vacant expression. His hands rest forgotten on his thighs. He seems entirely dissociated from his body, which is covered head-to-toe in thick gray ash. His large black eyes stare blankly into space with one almost swollen shut. A deep red smear of blood runs down the length of his face, and one ear looks torn. His long dark hair, which you can imagine his parents tousling playfully, is a mess and covered with the gray powder of concrete debris.

Omran's home was destroyed, and his life ruptured by a war waged by adults. Adults created the political and socioeconomic conditions that led to the violent conflict. Adults designed, manufactured, distributed, and deployed the weaponry that enabled the war. Adults recruited, signed up for, and served as soldiers to wage and perpetuate the war, and adults launched the missile that annihilated Omran's neighborhood. He has his own personhood and story, which I won't presume to tell, but I think of him now because he illustrates vividly the vulnerability of children whose lives are determined almost entirely by the decisions of people bigger, stronger, and more powerful than they. Omran is one of 2.3 billion children worldwide.[8]

Children are no less vulnerable in the United States. On the one hand, they're talked down to, shushed, and excluded, and their needs are ignored in most settings in modern society. On the other hand, children are so adored and desired that people go to incredible lengths to obtain them. On social media, children are romanticized, accessorized, and turned into royalty. Some children are the center of their communities with everything revolving around their wants. Meanwhile, some children, especially Black, Brown, and Native children, live under the constant shadow of criminality and the school-to-prison pipeline.[9] While helicopter parenting remains a problem for some, millions of others don't even have their basic needs met. Leaders proclaim, "Children are our future!" while childcare centers, schools, and churches fail to compensate fairly those who care for and educate them. Politicians declare, "We must protect our children!" while gun violence surpasses car accidents as the leading cause of death for American children.[10] Amid all this, children seem to be one of the only groups that it remains socially permissible to loathe publicly.

I think Jesus understood children's vulnerability and the multitude of ways families and organizations fail them, which is one reason why he has dire words for those who would hurt children: "If anyone causes one of these little ones—those who believe in me—to stumble, it would be better for them to have a large millstone hung around their neck and to be drowned in the depths of the sea" (Mt 18:6).

But there's more. It's not just that Jesus knows about the vulnerability of the child. Jesus identifies with their vulnerability in a personal, sacramental way: "And whoever welcomes one such child in my name *welcomes me*" (Mt 18:5). When you receive the vulnerable, socially marginal, and politically disempowered child, he says, you also receive me. The only other place Jesus speaks like this is in the parable of the final judgment where he says that those who minister to "the least of these" are, in fact, ministering to him (Mt 25:31-46).

Jesus' identification with children is even more profound in light of the doctrine of the incarnation. Christians confess that the Word, God's eternal wisdom, became a human child.

Conceived by the Holy Spirit and born of the Virgin Mary, Jesus grew up much like every other Jewish peasant child (Lk 2:52). Mary cradled Jesus' neck and swaddled his flailing arms. Joseph cooed and smiled, teaching him to coo and smile back. Toddler Jesus had to learn to eat and talk and walk. Child Jesus had to learn to swing a hammer and memorize his prayers. Eventually, he passed through the crucible of puberty. His home synagogue in Nazareth would have witnessed his deepening voice and watched his face sprout its first pimples and fine, black hairs.

To such normal developmental milestones, Matthew's gospel adds that Jesus and his family were forced to flee a maniacal ruler who threatened him with death. He lived for several years as a refugee, probably among the Jewish Diaspora who had made a place for themselves in Alexandria. Doubtless the child Jesus had his share of skinned knees, runny noses, and tummy aches, but did he also deal with the traumatic stress, cultural confusion, and isolation of other refugee children? Perhaps. We are not told.

The eternal Son of God took upon himself the helplessness, ignorance, and vulnerability of children. Our conduct with children—how we think of them, speak of them, and work with them—must be informed not only by Jesus' teaching, but also by his own life as a child. By joining divinity to humanity in the person of Jesus Christ, God has blessed infancy, childhood, adolescence, and adulthood with their own meaning and dignity. At the very least, Jesus the child helps us to see that children have their own agency and purpose before God.

One of the challenges is that there's profound disparity of power between children and adults, especially within private homes. The child's vulnerability calls for adult protection, but not everyone heeds, or is capable of heeding, that call. And when families are severely stressed, underresourced, or isolated, they can become malignant places.[11]

Still, amid the chaos and confusion, the struggle and hypocrisy, Jesus comes to us, his baffled and bickering disciples, and he comes to us with the child. He places the child in our midst and offers us an invitation. Unless you change and become like children, you won't enter the kingdom. Whoever takes the path of the child is the greatest in the kingdom, and whoever welcomes one such child in Jesus' name welcomes Jesus himself. In fact, as Mark's Gospel says, "the kingdom of God belongs to such as these" (Mk 10:14).

## God's Relationship with Children

If the kingdom of God belongs to children, then we ought to assume from the start that the children in our care are known and loved by God. Indeed, they have a relationship with God from birth. You might object, as many often do, "But infants lack the power of rationality. They can't communicate. They can't possibly know God. And they're sinners too!" Let's take these matters one at a time.

Can an infant know you? Can an infant know you love them? They cannot know you rationally, that is true, but they can know you relationally, and they can know you love them in the very same relational way.

Infants know people through the sound, sight, touch, and smell. This begins when they're still in their mother's wombs, hearing everything from the woosh of her circulation to the muffled timbre of her voice. The first way infants learn they are loved is through their senses: the warmth and compression of swaddling, the contented fullness of their belly, and even the refreshing dryness of a clean bottom. All these are what love feels like to an infant. All these are how an infant comes to know you and your love.

Can an infant talk to you? Not with intelligible words, but they do communicate. When they are thirsty, hungry, tired, or in pain, babies make all sorts of interactive noises: grunts, squeals, howls, wails, and screams. Sometimes caregivers even learn to tell the difference between a baby's various cries: one indicating hunger, one weariness, and so on. Each of these cues represents a tiny child's request for the adults around them to listen, engage, and provide care.

If they "talk" to us in such ways, what makes us think they aren't also communicating with God? Why would we think their cries to us are not simultaneously cries to their Creator who made them, loves them, and knew them from before they were born? If they are in a Christian household, especially, they have access to the truth and power of God's kingdom through their family members and church. Just as infants get to know us over time, so also, they get to know God.[12]

But what about their sin? Like all human beings, children are born into a sinful world and inherit sin from our first parents. They sin because they are sinners along with the rest of us. Without God's grace, they are separated from God and unable to participate in the flourishing life in God for which human beings were created.

We give thanks, therefore, that God's grace goes before them, revealing God's truth through creation, the rites of the church, the preaching and teaching of Scripture, and the love of caregivers. God's Spirit is seeking children from the moment they are born, "not wanting anyone to perish, but everyone to come to repentance" (2 Pet 3:9). As Peter says on the Day of Pentecost, "The promise is for you *and your children* and for all who are far off—for all whom the Lord our God will call" (Acts 2:39).

As caregivers know well, a child's faith commitment, when and if they make one, almost never appears out of nowhere. It grows over time through years of worship, instruction, and immersion in the life of a Christian community. We should do all we can in the church and at home to encourage the growth of children's personal relationship with God, but we do so assuming that they are becoming disciples long before they can articulate a testimony of Christ's saving work on their behalf. They are, in fact, our younger sisters and brothers in God's family, beginning their own journey of faith just a few decades behind us, and we should treat them accordingly.

## Sacramental Signs and Learning Teachers

Because of the unique status Jesus gives them, along with being our fellow disciples, children serve our households and churches in two major ways: as sacramental signs and as learning teachers.

A sacrament is an outward, visible sign of an inward, spiritual grace. They are material things through which God makes present some transcendent reality. The visible immersion of a person in water signifies and, in some mysterious way, mediates the inward cleansing a person receives as they become one with Christ. The bread and wine of the Eucharist signify and, in some mysterious way, mediate the presence of Jesus Christ with whom we have been made one by the Spirit.

Because Jesus says that to welcome children is to welcome him, there's a way in which children, too, have a sacramental function in the church. Children are visible signs of Christ's presence among us: the only begotten child of the Father who chooses to reveal himself through the poor and powerless. If this is the case, then churches ought to consider the way children assist adult disciples in worship simply by virtue of being children. There are both formal and informal ways in which we can be attentive to the sacramental presence of God through the children in our midst.

In the worship service of our former church, they regularly invited the children to come down during the closing song to dance before the Lord. I am told this practice began early in the church's history. Sometimes the children would clutch wand-like sticks with ribbons, flags, or bells fastened to the tips, and then shake or swirl them in the air as they danced. Little girls would twirl their dresses and small groups of friends would hold hands and shuffle in joyful circles. It was the first time I'd seen a ritual like this, and it delighted me week after week. Watching a gaggle of kids from toddlers to ten-year-olds hop, twirl, and waltz in time was an exercise in resurrection hope. Because it always followed Holy Communion, the dancing children were a kingdom sign through their unselfconscious worship.

As I experienced in church, children as sacramental signs can do many things for the adults who are privileged to be in relationship with them. Sacraments impart grace, yes, but they can also do things like instruct, edify, and warn. Among our families, then, children can evoke affection, require intellectual reflection, provoke self-criticism, encourage faith, and even convict and inspire repentance. All these things will happen as we are open to the presence of children among us and treat them as our fellow apprentices.

Alongside their work as sacramental signs, children are also learning teachers. What I mean by this is that children teach us things even as they are learning things. While they are certainly learning things in a more obvious way than we are—whether to tie their shoes or solve algebraic equations—the learning and teaching never go just one direction. Childrearing is always a two-way street of teaching and learning together, which is why from the start I've asked us to think of the goal of families as apprenticeship to love. Again, Coolman has wisdom to offer: "Here is the heart of parenting: to live life immersed in joy, purpose, compassion, and faith—and to share that life with children."[13]

I often tell new parents that 90 percent of discipling children is learning how to disciple ourselves. In other words, most of Christian childrearing involves prayerfully seeking to become the kind of person you want your child to become—to demonstrate the kind of behavior you want to see in your children. As Jesus observed wisely, "The student is not above the teacher, nor a servant above his master" (Mt 10:24). Coolman says the apprenticeship model "is more about parents simply being with their children, doing life together." At the end of the day, the calling of parents and caregivers is to "walk with their children, sharing work, sharing play, sharing *themselves.*"[14] Where do we want our children to end up? Wherever that is, we begin by heading there ourselves. Our children will accompany us on the way.

Just a few months ago, my youngest child requested I return to her room well after I had already said goodnight. Sitting on the edge of her bed, squinting through the dark, I realized she was crying.

"What's wrong, my love?" I asked.

"I think I need to quit gymnastics," she sobbed.

"Okay," I said, "Tell me more."

In the minutes that followed, she walked me through what she was seeing and experiencing in her classes. She shared both her emotions and her observations about her physical abilities and limitations. I asked about alternatives to wholesale quitting, and we talked through those options, but by the end of our conversation, we agreed that it was time to step away from an activity she'd been enjoying for a long time. We hugged for a full minute while she sniffled and calmed herself, and then I said goodnight again.

As I prepared myself for bed afterward, I reflected on just how much I have to learn from my ten-year-old: about physical and emotional self-awareness, about recognizing my needs, about asking for what I want, and about saying no. The truth is we've been trying from early on to help her and her siblings develop healthy boundaries. Sometimes we sound like a broken record: "Respect his no, please." "It sounds like you're not respecting her no." "Please respect each other's no." And even though we want to resolve conflicts without yelling, if someone isn't getting the message and they feel they must yell to get their "no" heard, then we're okay with that. My youngest's ability to say no to gymnastics made me think that maybe our efforts are working. As an older disciple, yes, she is my student, but she is also my teacher. I am her teacher, but I am also her student.

Children, whatever their ages and abilities, will hold our hands as we journey into God's kingdom. Together we'll learn how to choose patience in difficult circumstances, express our anger in healthy ways, choose financial sacrifice over consumption, and welcome hurting people into our home. And along the way, children will be directing our steps just as often as we are directing theirs.

## The Limits of Childrearing

Given all the realities I've named, some caregivers experience serious anxiety. Sometimes we're barely getting through the day. Sometimes a lunchbox gets left behind, your friend's life is a mess, the roof is leaking, and dinner is macaroni and cheese from a box. Sometimes your spouse leaves you, you're in bankruptcy court, your child is suspended, and your depression meds aren't working like they used to. All these things are real and affect how we care for the children in our midst.

My mother-in-law, whose middle son was born with a rare brain disorder, never could have predicted the cost, both personal and financial, of numerous brain surgeries, 24-7 nursing care, and the multiple diseases that eventually took his life. My friend Leanne, who has adopted multiple adolescents out of foster care, could not have predicted all that would be asked of her and her spouse as they seek to live in embodied solidarity with their children. Every aspect of their lives has been affected and will continue to be affected since parenting is a lifelong endeavor. Even so-called normal circumstances of parenting involve countless lost hours of sleep, work, creativity, and rest. Is it worth it? Most parents would say yes, even if they sometimes have their doubts. But, as Stanley Hauerwas says, "The crucial question for us as Christians is what kind of people we need to be to be capable of welcoming children into this world, some of whom may be born disabled and even die. . . . In a world of such terrible misery . . . having children is an extraordinary act of faith and hope."[15]

Hauerwas's point stops me in my tracks. It makes me think of the question I asked tearfully on the way home from the hospital with our firstborn: "Can we really do this?" On the one hand, the answer is no. The task is too big and the factors to numerous for us to raise children well. On the other hand, Jesus is alive and he calls us to follow him. If the tomb is empty, then we have every reason for hope. Through Christ and by his Spirit, we can become the kinds of people who live in solidarity with children. Through Christ and by his Spirit, we can pursue a church and a world in which children are centered by the adults in power, and receive the nurture and protection they require. On our own we can't do this, but in Christ by the Spirit we certainly can. Redemption and transformation are always possible in God's economy, even if we can't see it right away.

God meets us in our real lives where we really are.[16] And God has been pleased to work in and through all kinds of families with all kinds of problems through the whole story of redemption. The goal is not perfection; the goal is faithfulness. Faithfulness means putting all of what we are at God's disposal in our current circumstances and with our current capacities. Sometimes that's a beautiful thing. Sometimes it's a chaotic mess. Sometimes it's excruciatingly painful. But God remains with us and over time, slowly but surely, God can make us more faithful. Thankfully, God's Spirit will continue to work on us and our children into eternity, and we will learn a great deal from each other as we journey toward the coming kingdom together—in our failures as much as in our triumphs.

## Toward a Pattern of Life

In the fourth century, John Chrysostom was archbishop of Constantinople and known throughout the Eastern Church for his eloquent preaching. Chrysostom had a rigorous vision of Christian discipleship, and he upset many people in power with his demands. As a result, Chrysostom was beloved by the common people and generally disliked by wealthy citizens and clergy. You get a sense of his passionate yet down-to-earth approach in his sermons, especially those on marriage and family life.

When he addresses the work of parenting, Chrysostom seems sympathetic to the desire to give our children every possible advantage. Yet he also seeks to move the hearts of parents away from earthly concerns to heavenly ones:

If from the beginning we teach [our children] to love true wisdom, they will have greater wealth and glory than riches can provide. . . . Don't worry about giving [your child] an influential reputation for worldly wisdom, but ponder deeply how you can teach him to think lightly of this life's passing glories; thus he will become truly renowned and glorious. . . . Don't ask how he can enjoy a long life here, but how he can enjoy an infinite and eternal life in the age to come. Give him the great things, not the little things. Don't strive to make him a clever orator but teach him to love true wisdom. He will not suffer if he lacks clever words; but if he lacks wisdom, all the rhetoric in the world can't help him.[17]

Far more important than wealth and social connections, Chrysostom says, is the orientation of children's desires toward God and God's kingdom.

How can parents and caregivers do this? He concludes with this admonition: "A pattern of life is what is needed, not empty speeches; charity, not cleverness; deeds, not words. These things will secure the kingdom and bestow God's blessings."[18] Yes and amen. Far more than ideal models or gender-based roles, we need a pattern of life that seeks to embody God's kingdom among the varied details of our humdrum lives.

Just as there is no ideal family, there is also no pre-set formula for how to parent. It is learned as you go with the help of good resources, wise counselors, supportive networks, and lots of gut checks and prayer. This is how the Holy Spirit invites us and empowers us to discern the times and improvise, and we should seek to do so informed by Scripture, in conversation with Christian tradition, and in community with a safe church. In the chapters that follow, I suggest we center three core practices for our life's pattern: sabbath, baptism, and Eucharist. From these can flow a manner of living in which the focus of each day is this: *How will Jesus by his Spirit teach us to love today?*[19]

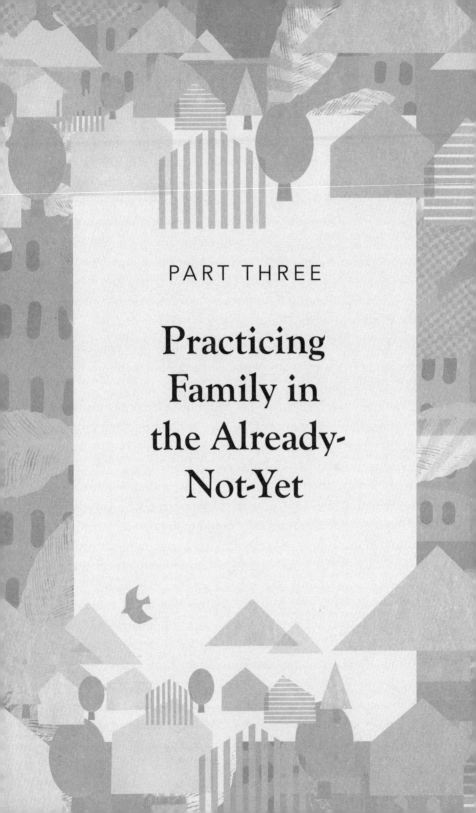

PART THREE

# Practicing Family in the Already-Not-Yet

# 9

# Families and Sabbath

**Saturday mornings are for Dungeons & Dragons.** At least they are in our family.[1] We've been playing together almost every Saturday since the summer of 2020: Ronnie and me, our two oldest children, and our friend, Brandon. I am the Dungeon Master (DM), which means I serve as rule keeper and lead storyteller. I provide the outline of a central plot with planned challenges, but the full story—all the relationships, actions, and choices—is improvised with dice rolls used to determine success or failure. Around the table we've crafted a tale, officially called a campaign, of colorful and unlikely friends in a fantasy world. There's a half-elf sorcerer, a dragon-born barbarian, a high elf Druid, and an air Genasi warlock. Together they have rescued kidnapped children, slain a dragon, subdued a den of fire giants, and turned an abandoned mansion into a successful inn.

At first, the game was just a fun distraction from the upheaval and anxiety of the pandemic, but it's become so much more. We've learned to navigate differences in personality, both for the real-life players and their in-game characters. Cooperating despite these differences has meant learning to communicate well and set boundaries—and then figure out what to do when such attempts fail.

I've watched my oldest children learn to see each other as team-mates instead of rivals. They're teens, so they still have their spats, but every week they come back to the table and re-enlist in a common cause. I've also seen us as parents learn to give them the freedom to take risks and make mistakes. One such instance resulted in the death of my daughter's original character, Navarra, who had been part of the campaign for two years. Her loss was mourned inside the fantasy world and in real life around our kitchen table.

Character death notwithstanding, playing D&D has also been just plain fun. We're doing many different things throughout the week, but our campaign is one enjoyable activity with shared aims to which we keep returning. Almost every Friday night, we check in with each other: "Are we playing tomorrow morning?" And we're all smiles when the answer is yes.

If Christian families are to be apprentices to love, then we want our homes to be places where desires are becoming oriented to God, self, and neighbor, and such orientation takes place, in part, through our habits—practices large and small that help to cultivate virtue within us over time. Research shows that shared time and ritual are also essential for deep relationships and overall satis-faction with one's life.[2] Not everyone will enjoy D&D, of course, and the sequence between practice and virtue is by no means automatic (you don't insert a practice, push a few buttons, and out pops patience). But for our family, the fantasy role-playing game combined with the rest of our life together has helped us become better apprentices of love one Saturday morning at a time.

## Practicing Family with Church Tradition

Still, there are more than a few challenges to talking about household practices. I want to be practical and concrete; abstrac-tions aren't very helpful. But I also want to avoid formulas, one-size-fits-all approaches, or guarantees of success. This and the next couple of chapters are not meant to urge you to try harder. Rather, they are brainstorming with you what family life could look like. Things are going to look different for you and yours depending on things like age, ability, and environment.

We do have agency as individuals and as families within our small realms of influence. God's kingdom is here, and we have supernatural resources available to us by the Spirit. At the same time, individual families (and even churches) can only do so much. Many of the things that might cause a family to flounder are beyond their control: the health of the neighborhood, the quality and cost of healthcare, the quality of schools, the policies of employers, and more. In other words, some things are up to us, but many things are not up to us. Sometimes the best we can do in adverse circumstances is muddle through and survive. And thanks be to God when we do!

We also have reason to be hopeful without being triumphalist. Sometimes there are things that can't change no matter how much we desire it. In that case, there's no use pretending things are different from what they are. God meets you *there*, not where you wish you were. At the same time, Christ's resurrection and the Spirit's power mean there's always hope. Perhaps some change is possible, even if only small and incremental. Perhaps we can find transformation by being present to the lives we already have with renewed vision. So, the next few chapters include a steady back-and-forth between "You can do it!" and "It's okay if you can't do it!" Because that's the already-not-yet tension real Christian families live with.

As we seek to discern and improvise faithfulness, we don't have to reinvent the wheel. Despite the mixed bag that is church history, there are many sustaining practices that the church has handed down to us. I think the most basic ones—those that frame and fuel everything else—are sabbath, baptism, and Eucharist. These three are like the headwaters of a river. Many rivers have headwaters that originate from melted snow or underground aquifers. A river's size and strength are not determined by where it starts, but the features of the headwaters are vital to the health of the water downstream. Things such as sediment, organisms, and chemicals from upstream are inevitably distributed through the river as the water flows toward the sea.[3]

Like mountain headwaters feeding a river in the valley below, sabbath, baptism, and Eucharist are, through the grace of God, the means through which Christian life gains vitality. When acted on, they have the potential to nourish the daily lives of families as apprentices of love. It is good and right, then, to draw on the theological richness of these rituals, whether to implement a new habit or to attend to our already-in-progress life together in a new way.

## Sabbath

Sabbath first emerges at the beginning of the Jewish and Christian stories. Before the birth of Jesus Christ, before the kingdom of Israel, before the exodus, before Adam and Eve, there was, Genesis says, the Sabbath. After making and ordering everything in the heavens and the earth, after blessing it and calling it "very good," God rested on the seventh day. "Then God blessed the seventh day and made it holy, because on it he rested from all the work of creating that he had done" (Gen 2:3). God's rest on the seventh day undergirds the command to rest given to Israel in the law of Moses, which is then expanded on in the Prophets.

Scripture tells us that rest is essential to being creatures, to being human, and to being God's people.[4] To be a creature is to be dependent on God, the only uncreated one, for existence and sustenance. Sabbath is a manifestation of that dependence, a recognition that despite the good and important work we do—whether honeybees crafting a hive, chickadees building a nest, or farmers mending fences—all that we are depends ultimately on our Creator, the source of life. To be a creature is to have limits: finite abilities, finite resources, and a finite lifetime. To rest, to sabbath, is to acknowledge and seek to live within those limits—to happily occupy the category "creature" within God's good creation.

Sabbath is also essential to being human. According to Genesis 2, part of the human calling is to tend and keep the garden.

Tend and keep intentionally calls to mind the work of Aaron and the Levites in the tabernacle. Human beings, God's image on earth, are responsible for tending God's presence in the world. It makes sense, then, that keeping sabbath would be core to our vocation. As God's likeness, we must rest as God rested. In so doing, we communicate to the rest of creation our total dependence on God. Not only that, but the work humans do (and don't do) in the world has profound consequences for the created world. When humans don't rest—when humans don't live within their limits—the world suffers.

Finally, Sabbath is essential to being God's people. We see this vividly in the story of Israel. When the Lord first brought them out of Egypt, he commanded them to observe a day of rest: a day for all—enslaved and free, humans and animals—to cease their labors. Such comprehensive rest would require a great deal of preparation so that true cessation of work was possible. Why was rest so important to their covenant with God? Because their God rescued them from slavery in the Egyptian Empire. Under Pharaoh's regime, the people had to sustain lives of constant production. They were cogs in the Egyptian machine, useful only for the furtherance of Pharaoh's goals. As a result, the people of Israel were anxious and afraid, and their humanity was undermined. Likewise, creation only existed for Pharaoh's production schedule. The land and its resources, just as the people, were something to be exploited.[5]

After hundreds of years under this system, God's people needed drastic reshaping—a re-formation in view of God's true creative purpose for creation, and one of the major ways that reshaping took place was through observing the Sabbath. So, when the Ten Commandments were given and Israel confirmed their covenant with God at Sinai, keeping Sabbath was the fourth command. Anglo-American Bible scholar Walter Brueggemann argues that the Sabbath command is the vital hinge between the commands that pertain to God and the commands that pertain to neighbor. In other words, sabbath rest is the indispensable bridge that joins honoring God as Creator and honoring our fellow humans as God's creation. Rest in God's provision and care, therefore, would lead Israel to honor God and honor each other's humanity. Neither are possible without sabbath.

After centuries of hustling for survival, trusting in their own strength and endurance, how will Israel learn to trust God? After centuries of being treated as commodities for Egypt's enrichment, seeing themselves and others as rungs on Pharaoh's production ladder, how will Israel learn to see themselves and others as God's image? Through the regular cessation of labor. Through trusting God to provide for them. Through expecting God's creation to have what they need. Through the intentional choice to live within their limits and the limits of the created world. Only through regular work stoppage could the people of Israel learn to see God, themselves, and others anew, and learn to treat God, themselves, and others accordingly. Not as means to an end of constant production but ends in themselves.[6]

Now, one might say: That's the people of Israel. What should Christians, especially Gentile Christians, think of the Sabbath? Let's turn once again to Jesus for wisdom.

When Jesus preached his first recorded sermon in Nazareth, he framed his ministry using the sixty-first chapter of Isaiah: "The Spirit of the Lord is on me, because he has anointed me to proclaim good news to the poor. He has sent me to proclaim freedom for the prisoners and recovery of sight for the blind, to set the oppressed free, to proclaim the year of the Lord's favor" (Lk 4:18-19). After reading the text aloud, Jesus sat down and announced to the assembled people, "Today this scripture is fulfilled in your hearing" (Lk 4:21). With this short statement, Jesus claimed to be the embodied fulfillment of the servant spoken of in Isaiah. Jesus is the one sent by the Lord to declare good news, release the captives, restore sight to the blind, and set free the oppressed.

Isaiah calls all of this "the year of the Lord's favor," a reference to the year of Jubilee, a time designated in the law for returning land to its rightful inheritors, freeing the enslaved, and forgiving debts. Jubilee was not a one-off event in the life of Israel but the culmination of a whole covenant calendar structured around observing Sabbath. Every seven days God's people would rest. Every seven years the land would rest. Every fifty years, all people would be relieved of their burdens and begin to rest anew (Lev 25). This sacred rhythm of communal time was the backbone of Israel's life together under God's care.

Therefore, when Jesus says that he is the fulfillment of the year of the Lord's favor, he is associating his good news with the Sabbath. He is linking God's kingdom with the year of Jubilee—a real event in Israel's history. As a result, we are right to conclude that Jesus' mission is not a purely spiritual one. Certainly, he takes on and defeats the "powers and authorities" and "made a public spectacle of them, triumphing over them by the cross" (Col 2:15), but Jesus' gospel proclamation has a worldly, material dimension too. In his preaching at Nazareth, Jesus expresses in Isaiah's words the embodied shape his Father's reign will take: healing, wholeness, and freedom for all.

Families cannot be apprentices to love without sabbath, for the love of God and neighbor requires it. Yet many contemporary Christians have forgotten this, and many Western societies are structured such that cultivating our double love of God and neighbor is grossly inhibited.

With all its conveniences, lifesaving medicine, and technology, modern life is often dehumanizing. I have no desire to go back, mind you. I am grateful for vaccines and emergency rooms, public education and libraries—not to mention the right to vote! But that doesn't change the fact that the general conditions of our daily lives regularly undermine our humanity and undercut neighborliness in diabolical ways.[7] Too many of us have come to see ourselves as little more than productivity machines and other people as either helps or hindrances to our ability to "get ahead."

Sometimes Christians are even more passionate about the produce-or-perish lifestyle. Sometimes they assume that being a "good Christian" means being even more productive than those "in the world." And then there's the added pressure of doing more, being more, and making more *for Jesus*. My institution has an unofficial motto often quoted by weary students: "Where your best hasn't been good enough since 1860." Though said with a wry smile and sardonic laugh, the joke bespeaks a damning truth. Resisting this culture, at my school and in society at large, can feel like trying to escape a powerful rip current.

Those who claim Jesus Christ as Lord should above all be aware of our creatureliness and seek to live within those realities. If our households are going to be apprentices to love within Christ's church and God's kingdom, then we must begin by restoring sabbath to the center of our lives together. What if Christians as a group became the kinds of people known for their sabbath, their care for bodies, minds, and souls, and their resistance to exploitation and dehumanization? It seems too far out of reach even to imagine, but if Jesus is raised from the dead, then maybe even Western Christians can learn to rest. In this chapter I propose four practices for Christian families toward this end: getting enough sleep, observing a designated day of rest, play and wonder, and family prayer.

## Getting Enough Sleep

The most straightforward way sabbath can be embodied in a Christian family is through regular sleep. Maybe this seems like a minor thing, but it's not. To cease activity, lay down, and go to sleep is to show extraordinary trust in God, one's household, and one's neighbors. When we close our eyes and let our brain descend into unconsciousness, we are letting go of all illusions of control. We are admitting our need for rest, and we are defenseless and vulnerable. Perhaps that's why when there is trouble in a marriage a wounded spouse sometimes chooses to sleep elsewhere. It's a form of self-protection. It says, "I don't feel safe with you. I'm uncomfortable with this kind of intimacy right now." When we're dealing with clinical anxiety, depression, and other mental illnesses, we often find our sleep disturbed. Our mind is not at rest so our body resists rest too.

Despite how important sleep is to our overall well-being, sleep deprivation is common. In the United States, more than 30 percent of adults get less than the necessary seven to nine hours of sleep per night. Nearly 40 percent report accidentally falling asleep during the day. Teenagers are the most acutely sleep deprived, with nearly 90 percent not getting enough sleep every night (eight to ten hours are recommended). Sleep deprivation also disproportionately affects racialized minorities in the United States, with Black Americans being the worst off.[8] Not only is chronic lack of sleep linked to a host of health problems such as hypertension, diabetes, and heart disease, but it also seriously undermines mental health.[9]

Given technological advances such as electric lights, televisions, laptops, and smartphones, we are now equipped with a myriad of ways to avoid sleep even when our bodies need it. Sometimes we're lonely and down, so we scroll social media looking for a serotonin boost. Sometimes we're overwhelmed, so we immerse ourselves in online feuds or distract ourselves by bingeing a drama. Sometimes caregivers find themselves staying up later to get precious time alone. I am an acute introvert, but I spend much of my days teaching or in meetings. When I come home at the end of the workday to four very chatty people, I often want to stay up well after bedtime just to enjoy the solitude. I know my body needs the sleep, but my mind whispers persuasively, *it'll feel so good to be alone.* I succumb to the allure of an audiobook or streaming show more times than I care to admit.

Learning to rest is a daily commitment for ourselves and our family members. While "hustle" culture tells us we must earn the right to rest, our Creator has embedded in our bodies the daily necessity of sleep. One of our tasks as kingdom households is to resist the dehumanizing effects of late-modern capitalism with its nonstop advertising, consumption, and entertainment, and the first place to start is with our sleep practices. Making a habit of prioritizing sleep will not only do important work within our souls teaching us to live within our God-given limits but will also have mental and physical benefits too. As a pastor friend once quipped, "Sometimes the most spiritual thing you can do is go to bed."[10] I couldn't agree more.

## Observing a Time of Sabbath

The second way a Christian family can learn to rest is through a designated time to observe sabbath together. Ideally, such a time would encompass an entire day: maybe all of Saturday or all of Sunday. The day should be an intentional time to cease productive activities (things you do for the sake of some profitable end) and consumptive activities (things you do that involve buying or selling). I realize that sometimes this isn't feasible. Single households may need chunks of Saturday and Sunday to do chores and grocery shopping. Households with children might find their Saturday mornings given to soccer games or track practice. Some might have adults or teens who have to work on the weekends. So, creativity will be required to designate a period of rest. But it will have to be intentionally and relentlessly pursued too. Under modern conditions, "interrupting the ceaseless round of striving requires a surprisingly strenuous act of will, one that has to be bolstered by habit as well as social sanction."[11] Nevertheless, if a few hours on Sunday is all you can do right now, then do that with purpose, enthusiasm, and prayer. God can bless and multiply the meager loaves and fishes we have to offer.

Because our family contains two pastors, Sundays are workdays for us. So, we've sought to make Saturdays our day of rest. Making it happen is hard, though. Home repairs, laundry, lawn maintenance, oil changes, grocery shopping, bill paying—all the things that couldn't get done during the work week are staring us in the face on Saturday morning, and that's not including the occasional birthday party, visit from extended family, and other social events. So, making the day (or period) truly *restful* requires advanced planning and a willingness to say no.

When our children were young, we generally decided for them what our sabbath days would look like. As they got older, we solicited their ideas and input, deciding together what we wanted. A few things have been continuous through the years: We limit our individual screen time to a couple hours each. We try to spend the rest of our day reading, walking outside, listening to music, cooking or baking, and other things that are creative, enjoyable, and usually nonelectronic. We try not to do chores on our sabbath day, although we still make and clean up meals, and at the close of the day, our dinner is usually eaten together followed by a family-chosen movie, TV show, or game.

When the kids were small, we'd go to parks or forest preserves for a few hours and enjoy the outdoors or we'd spend the afternoon at our public library, often bringing a lunch to eat there while we read books and play board games. These days we're likely to sit outside and read together if the weather is nice or play games if it's not. This is just what my family does, though. Depending on the age, ability, and interests of household members, your sabbath might look different. The point is not really *what* you do, but that you practice regularly withdrawing from the routines of productivity and consumption.

Keeping up with this practice has become harder as our children have gotten older. Their friendships are more important to them now, and they have made commitments to their own activities. During certain times of the year our oldest has track practice or speech tournaments on Saturdays and our middle has choir competitions. Since Ronnie and I are both bivocational pastors in the early stages of a new church, we often find we must do some church-related things on Saturday to get ready for Sunday. Our plan is for this pattern to be a temporary season, but it's hard in the interim, and we don't have direct control over the length of this interval. I don't like what these disruptions do to our family sabbath, and I can feel the difference when we haven't had our period of rest. But I'm also aware that patterns can be re-established, and time reclaimed when this season passes. As your family grows and changes, so will your observance of rest—and that's okay.

Sabbath can be especially hard for people who come from poor or immigrant families, as well as people who've experienced trauma. From a young age some have been ingrained with a sense of always having to try harder and do more to "make something of yourself." Your parents and relatives were well-meaning, but their commitment to bettering the family sometimes leaves you feeling like you're never good enough. At the same time, hurting people will use busyness to keep themselves distracted from pain. *If I ever stop moving*, you think, *I'll have to feel my feelings and face the consequences of what I've endured.* Given all of this, don't be surprised if your subconscious fights tooth and nail against intentional rest, and don't be discouraged if you need the help of a friend, spouse, doctor, or therapist to support your efforts.

Finally, it's important to know that you will likely never observe a time of sabbath without something looming over your head—a project, a deadline, or a chore. But that's precisely the point. Sabbath ultimately requires the practice of faith: trust in the God who made you, loves you, and holds your family together, even when you are unproductive. What you gain from the habit of rest will far outweigh what is lost through your intentional inactivity: In short, reclaiming your body, mind, and soul from the marketplace, nation, and other entities that claim it for their purposes. The more you practice resting, the easier it will be to let things be while you focus on simply existing as a beloved human being in God's good world.

## Play and Wonder

For households that are used to running themselves ragged and scheduling every moment, simply getting enough sleep and keeping an intentional sabbath might be enough of a challenge to get started, but there's more to consider for those who have the bandwidth. Amid our efforts at rest and restoration, I suggest we pursue some form of play and wonder.

Play is difficult to define, more of an "I know it when I see it" kind of thing, but it is at least an activity of pleasure and joy that engages mind, body, and spirit. Play is also interpersonal, connecting us to others and the world. It fires and drives imagination.[12] Play might not seem particularly spiritual, but like sleep and rest it is rooted in trust: trust in God, trust in each other, trust in the world. Only those who feel some degree of safety and security can play, and taking time to play demonstrates a willingness to accept that unproductive time is good and even sacred in God's kingdom despite our culture's insistence otherwise. As with sabbath keeping, play takes different forms in different families, but the point is to engage in joyful, fun, and unproductive activity that allows mind and body to rest from work and remember God is God.

Shortly after my grandmother died, when I was around twelve years old, my grandfather came to live with my family. My mom took out a loan and remodeled our garage into an apartment for him, and he lived with us for the next ten years until his death. Typically, Grandpa did his own thing in the mornings and afternoons but spent dinner time and evenings with us. Because of his physical limitations, play with Grandpa was limited to things he could do in one of our adjoining spaces. On the weekends we would make chocolate chip cookies or listen to music or I would read to him from books or the newspaper. When my children were young, a lot of our play looked like toy trains and dolls. As they grew in independence, we were able to do more complex things: taking walks through nearby forest preserves, reading together, and playing board or card games. Such times, as small as they seem, are the ways we tell each other, You are a person apart from what you do or produce. You are worthy of life and love. I trust you, you trust me, and we trust God.

Christians in the West don't often think about wonder as a central aspect of discipleship, but in societies where adult life is characterized by horrid metaphors like the rat race, the daily grind, or the hamster cage, perhaps that's not surprising. I've said elsewhere that wonder is "amazement elicited by something unexpected and mysterious." Wonder contains surprise because the cause is often unanticipated. Wonder often gives you the feeling of being drawn in while also being repelled. Novelty can be exciting even as there is fear of the unknown. To wonder is to become conscious of one's finitude and ignorance. For some, simply recognizing our smallness can usher in God's wondrous presence.[13]

If Christian families are apprentices to the love revealed in the Word-made-flesh, then I think wonder is essential to our apprenticeship. Swiss theologian Karl Barth said, "Christ is the infinitely wondrous event which compels a person, so far as he experiences and comprehends this event, to be necessarily, profoundly, wholly, and irrevocably astonished."[14] Even as disciples learn and grow, they do not leave wonder behind; rather, it grows along with their knowledge.[15] In a world that often turns God into a theorem or idea disconnected from embodied life, Christians insist that God is with us in the world and we live in God's kingdom now by the Spirit. This is an astonishing reality that changes the way one sees, experiences, and lives. Wonder is also an experience closely linked to other important virtues, such as humility, patience, and gratitude—all of which are necessary to resist both personal sin and social evil.

Play doesn't always lead to wonder, of course. Honestly, a toddler's made-up games can be terribly boring, and the swing set isn't nearly as enjoyable for the one pushing as the one swinging.

Still, I find that play and wonder are often linked experientially. The mental and physical posture one has while pursuing play often clears the way for wonder to emerge. Being fully present with a two-year-old's make-believe can lead to wonder at existence: Who am I in this vast universe to get to spend time with this precious child? Pushing a swing for fifteen minutes can give you just enough stillness to catch sight of a red-tailed hawk circling nearby trees. What an amazing world we get to live in!

The challenge, though, is that so much of our daily life is evacuated of wonder, especially in the industrialized world. Households must choose to put themselves in positions to experience wonder.[16] The best way to do this is through encounters with beauty, both the natural and manmade kinds. If you have access to safe sidewalks, streets, or paths, walks are an excellent way to expose yourself to beauty of all kinds. During the pandemic lockdown, afternoon walks were a consistent practice that kept our family sane. They were intentionally purposeless, slow, and meandering—exceptionally unproductive. We stopped and looked at bugs on the sidewalk, collected interesting leaves, braided dandelions into crowns, stacked rocks into towers, claimed "walking sticks," and watched Canada geese shepherding their goslings.

Going outdoors isn't the only option. Human-made beauty is another possibility. For our family, that has meant going to see art installations at our public library, listening to recordings of Broadway musicals, visiting museums on free or discounted days, and watching wildlife documentaries such as *Blue Planet*.

Studies show that the combination of play and wonder are good for body and mind, and they certainly benefit the soul. Wonder brings us into contact with our creaturely limits and requires that we face our reliance on God. Also, the cultivation of wonder in and around where we live can impart a sense of shared responsibility for our places—reminding us of our calling to care for God's world (Gen 2:15). One of the terrible legacies of European and American imperialism is the lack of connection between people, the land we live on, and the creatures we live alongside. Cultivating wonder through play is one small, mundane step toward claiming our place in the world, wherever it might be, as truly *ours* under God's creative rule.

## Prayer

Flowing from the practice of sabbath, Christian households are invited to pray together too. Like rest and play, prayer emerges from trust in God: trust that you can, in fact, take time to pray and that God will meet you there, even when you don't feel it. Prayer is also a practice that reinforces trust in God. Of course, prayer isn't something that only happens during times of rest, but households will find they must schedule prayer the same way they must schedule rest and play. Also, prayer shares with sabbath keeping the acknowledgment of total divine dependence. Through our baptisms, we have been initiated into God's kingdom and share in Christ's priesthood. Interceding on behalf of ourselves and the world is part of what that priesthood includes. "The end of all things is near. Therefore, be alert and of sober mind so that you may pray" (1 Pet 4:7). The end is near . . . therefore pray.

How does a household make prayer a regular practice? Again, there is no blueprint, but these days there are plenty of resources to assist you. My family prefers to pray at the beginning and end of our days. When our children were young, we used the "Daily Devotions for Individuals and Families" from the Book of Common Prayer (BCP 1979) every weekday morning. Here's what our liturgy for the mornings looked like:

*From Psalm 51*

Open my lips, O Lord, *
    and my mouth shall proclaim your praise.
Create in me a clean heart, O God, *
    and renew a right spirit within me.

Cast me not away from your presence *
   and take not your holy Spirit from me.
Give me the joy of your saving help again *
   and sustain me with your bountiful Spirit.
Glory to the Father, and to the Son, and to the Holy Spirit: *
   as it was in the beginning, is now, and will be for
      ever. Amen.

*A Reading*

Blessed be the God and Father of our Lord Jesus Christ!

By his great mercy we have been born anew to a living hope
through the resurrection of Jesus Christ from the dead.

*1 Peter 1:3*

*A period of silence may follow.*

*A hymn or canticle may be used; the Apostles' Creed may
be said.*

*Prayers may be offered for ourselves and others.*

*The Lord's Prayer*

*The Collect*

Lord God, almighty and everlasting Father, you have
brought us in safety to this new day: Preserve us with your
mighty power, that we may not fall into sin, nor be overcome
by adversity; and in all we do, direct us to the fulfilling of
your purpose; through Jesus Christ our Lord. Amen.[17]

We would gather at the table during or shortly after breakfast.
Then, taking a page from our church's Godly Play program, we'd
light a candle to represent the light of Christ, recite the printed
Scriptures from the prayer book, read a passage of Scripture
where it says, "A Reading," pray together, say the Lord's Prayer,
and conclude with the "Collect." Now that our children must leave

for school in the morning at three different times, we pray with each of them extemporaneously while they are having breakfast, but our commitment to that abbreviated prayer practice began around our Christ candle when they were still toddlers.

In the evenings, we've done a variety of things through the years. For a time, we did a condensed version of our morning routine, omitting the Scripture reading for brevity and concluding with one of the evening prayers in the BCP's Compline liturgy. My favorite of such concluding prayers is this one:

> Keep watch, dear Lord, with those who work, or watch, or weep this night, and give your angels charge over those who sleep. Tend the sick, Lord Christ; give rest to the weary, bless the dying, soothe the suffering, pity the afflicted, shield the joyous; and all for your love's sake. Amen.[18]

In another period we read from a book that leads you through imaginative prayers, which required extended times of stillness and quiet.[19] They were a good way to wind down together before bed, but at times proved too challenging for our energetic youngest child. Today, because the older children get up so early in the morning, we do brief end-of-day prayers together, simple intercession ending with the Lord's Prayer, before blessing them on their way to bed.

Of course, what our family has done reflects the privilege we have of being present with our children in the mornings and evenings. Not every family has that kind of time together, and there's no use feeling guilt or shame about that. Is it ideal? No. Does it mean that household prayer is completely out of reach? Also, no. The point is not precisely when you pray, how you pray, or what you pray, but *that* you pray. It will certainly require creativity in a household with limited shared time. Maybe the best you can do is a blessing before a common meal or a prayer while driving to tutoring or Taekwondo class. Whatever is necessary for your family, I appreciate resources like the BCP because using them means I don't have to come up with what to say.[20] We can pray those prayers knowing they have been prayed by others throughout history, often drawing deeply on Scripture.

Many who come from an evangelical background find the notion of prewritten prayers uncomfortable. They worry such prayers when used regularly can lead to prayer becoming a rote exercise without meaning or sincerity. Anything done repeatedly can become meaningless, but it doesn't have to. There is significant benefit to our daily prayers becoming etched in our memories. I remember talking to our middle child about the difficulty she had falling asleep one night. I asked her how she helped herself relax, and she replied, "Oh, I just prayed the 'Keep watch, dear Lord' prayer over and over till I finally fell asleep." Because we've prayed that prayer almost every night for several years, I was not surprised that she had it memorized. I'm grateful that our regular practice made an impression on her, even when it seems hit-and-miss in busy weeks or lackluster in execution. In that moment of need, she had an impulse to pray that we had helped cultivate, and she had words at hand with which to do so. Both are things that all disciples of Jesus desperately need.

In a world where "to live is to possess" and "to be is to do," sabbath is an essential corrective. Ceasing work and resting together cultivates intimacy and interdependence—what we might simply call communion—between God, self, neighbor, and creation. Furthermore, other sabbath practices like play and prayer empower God's people to counter anxiety, coercion, exploitation, and violence. In the United States, especially, which is a deeply anxious, exploitative, and violent society, sabbath is a vital means for survival, let alone resisting the status quo and cultivating the virtues necessary to be Jesus' apprentices together.[21]

# 10

# Families and Baptism

**When my children were small,** we bathed them, first in a small baby tub and then in a regular bathtub. These times were sweet, soothing, and fun—and then they learned to splash. My oldest, especially, found splashing exceptionally entertaining. He regularly drenched both me and the bathroom. I'd guess only about half the water remained in the tub once I pulled him into a towel. While I was sometimes annoyed by this regular soaking, more often I was amused. I couldn't help thinking of the renewal of our baptismal vows at church, which is often accompanied by a priest sprinkling the congregation with consecrated water. Of course, my kids weren't yet aware of the link between their sacramental "washing" and their daily washing, but I was. Their delighted splashes brought together the church's sacramental life and our family life in a vivid way. Every bath time became a time to remember my baptism and be thankful, even if I had to change my clothes afterward.

For Christians, baptism is the rite of initiation into the new covenant community. Of course, Christians the world over practice baptism in different ways. Some baptize the infants and children of believers, some baptize only those who make their own profession of faith in Christ, and some baptize only adult members of the community. Baptisms take place in lakes and rivers, bathtubs and pools, as well as in sanctuaries. Sometimes water is poured and sprinkled, other times bodies are entirely immersed. Whatever form it takes, baptism is a foundational practice of Christian faith in imitation of Christ, at his command, and in continuation of the practice of the apostles.

Ritual washing did not start with the church though. Christian baptism is based on Jewish practice, most famously exemplified by Jesus' cousin John the Baptist. As the Gospels and Acts testify, John's baptism was a "baptism of repentance for the forgiveness of sins" (Lk 3:3; Mk 1:4; Acts 19:4). Jesus submitted himself to this baptism and received the Father's anointing as Israel's Messiah, God's beloved Son (Mt 3:13-17; Lk 3:21-22). Jesus also expressed through his baptism an embodied solidarity with the people he came to save. Though Jesus himself had no need to repent, he joined the teeming crowds assembled along the Jordan River and allowed himself to be immersed in the muddy waters with them. He presented himself as a new and greater Moses, leading a new exodus through the depths of chaos, sin, and death and into the promised land of God's kingdom (Gen 1:2; 7:10; Ex 14:22).

As a result, baptism is first and foremost a sign of God's gracious gift. Though we were dead in our trespasses and sins, enslaved to the principalities and powers of this world, because of God's mercy we have been buried with Christ and raised with him to new life. In so doing, God has rescued us from the domain of darkness and brought us into his reign, grafting us into the fellowship of God's people and granting us freedom through the Spirit as a foretaste of future glory. None of this is at our initiative, but by the extraordinary goodness and power of God. So, baptism is a ritual done to us—we don't baptize ourselves. We receive baptism just as we receive God's grace in our redemption.

At the same time, there is no doubt we have a responsibility to act on the gospel's summons. We are invited to repent and trust in Christ every day, surrendering to the Spirit's sanctifying work. We are responsible for keeping in step with Spirit, working out our salvation with fear and trembling (Gal 5:25; Phil 2:12), but it remains God who initiates and brings about his kingdom. Our response is only possible through God's Spirit. So, baptism is only supposed to happen once: "There is one body and one Spirit, just as you were called to one hope when you were called; one Lord, one faith, one baptism; one God and Father of all, who is over all and through all and in all" (Eph 4:4-6).

Those of us who follow Jesus into the baptismal waters also do so in intentional imitation of his vocation. Through it we are made a kingdom of priests, prophets of a new creation, the first fruits of a new humanity in Christ's image. Far from setting us apart from the world as special, separate, and wholly other, baptism weds us even more closely to the world God loves and means to save.[1] United with Christ through the Spirit we become part of God's redemptive mission. Our whole lives are taken up into the reign of God. From the mundane to the extraordinary, all of it falls under Christ's rule, and that means every aspect of our lives, both as individuals and households, has the potential to participate in God's new creation.[2]

What does the core practice of baptism have to do with Christian families? First, it is how every household member is initiated into the church, the family of God. Each of us, young and old, have a share in Christ's priesthood. On that basis we can approach our life together as one of mutual apprenticeship. In my Anglican tradition we have regular times in which we are called to remember our baptism and recite our baptismal vows anew. They remind us that through baptism we have a new identity, new community, new allegiance, new story, and a new way to live. In the United States, especially, with its insistence that we see ourselves primarily as citizens or workers or consumers, remembering our baptism undercuts that narrative. Our king is Jesus, and we are loyal first to him and his kingdom.

Learning what our baptism means for us as individuals, households, and churches is a journey. In fact, I would argue that we are still learning what it means over two thousand years later. But assuming Christian families will be worshiping with a local church of one kind or another, there are other practices that flow from our baptism that facilitate further apprenticeship. I would suggest we focus on three: caring for our bodies, caring for our places, and doing the work of storytelling and timekeeping.

## Caring for Our Bodies

Receiving and giving bodily care is a universal human experience and it often takes place within our homes. Despite this reality, some of us have the habit of denigrating the labor involved in the care of bodies, especially needful, dependent bodies. Of course, small children often require such assistance, but so do people who are sick or injured, as well as elderly people and people with disabilities. Across many cultures it's common to find that jobs associated with dirt, refuse, and bodily processes are viewed as less skilled, less honorable, and less valuable. But humans are ensouled bodies, or bodily souls. We are an inextricable unity of flesh and spirit that cannot be divided. The soul-ish stuff is not more important than the bodily stuff. Yet, one of many malformations of the Western imagination is alienation from and denigration of our bodies.

By contrast, Jesus never denigrated bodily life, nor did he shrink back from interacting with people's bodies through presence and touch. He even washed his disciples' mud-caked and assuredly stinky feet (Jn 13:1-17). He prioritized and promised the kingdom to those who offer aid to bodies in need: the poor, the sick, the hungry, the imprisoned, the stranger, and the naked (Mt 25:35-36). Jesus clearly saw eternal value in such work. Remembering the ritual washing of our baptisms, therefore, has the potential to infuse other mundane washings and other kinds of bodily care with transcendent significance.[3]

Bodies aren't the only things that require regular care, though. We wash our clothes, dishes, and floors. We wash our pets, windows, and carpets. All these activities are aimed at the things with which our bodies regularly interact: the places where we rest, the spaces where we eat, the clothes that protect our skin, the utensils with which we prepare our body's food. Just as baptism integrates us into the body of Christ, joining our lives with the life of God and God's people, so also these household washings are one of the means that joins us as a family. They both reflect and foster our interdependence. They also demonstrate our mutual dignity: We are worthy of care—our bodies, our clothing, our spaces, and our tools. They help us tell a new story about ourselves and others: that we are human, that we need each other, that we belong to each other.

Before the Industrial Revolution, the home was a site of production—a place of work in addition to a place of rest. Rather than romantic soulmates, married couples were coworkers in farming or trade while their children provided labor in support of the household's survival. After the Industrial Revolution, work was largely moved out of the home and into the factories, stores, and offices of emerging cities. The new wage-earning economy transformed relations at home. White middle-class men aspired to earn enough income to permit their wives to remain home. With this shift came a corresponding shift in the imagination: the public realm, especially the cutthroat world of business, is for men, while the private realm, the realm of affection and nurture, is for women and children. As a result, household chores such as cooking, cleaning, and laundry in addition to household-related errands like groceries became "women's work," and because it was work that didn't earn a wage, it was seen as unbecoming of men.

Thankfully, many Christians now realize that this White middle-class ideal is, in a word, balderdash. It also happens to be unsustainable in most industrialized societies today. According to the US Bureau of Labor Statistics, in 66 percent of married-couple families with children, both spouses work for wages outside the home.[4] Some do so because they have to, some because they want to, and some a combination of both. But the fact remains that even though many households have two or more wage-earners, women continue to bear the burden of most household labor. One famous study calls it "the second shift"–the multiple additional hours of housework that go into a woman's day after she returns from her full-time job.[5] Of course, we can't prove how much of this is simply a sexist holdover from a bygone era. Nevertheless, the status quo remains unjust for most women in dual-income homes. Such is not the way of life exemplified by Jesus who did the work of a servant and told us to do likewise (Jn 13:1-17).

Not only is household labor important and honorable, it's also capable of being done by anyone with the physical capability, time, and know how. There is no real reason to allot tasks by gender, as though men are less suited to washing dishes or pulling weeds. Chores are for everyone. Children, especially, will benefit from regular household duties that are appropriate to their stage of development and abilities. It teaches them their inherent dignity and worth, as well as their essential role in the family and broader world.

In daily life, though, some division of labor is often necessary. When I was a seminary student and Ronnie a full-time pastor, I did almost all the cooking and cleaning because I was the one who had the most time and energy to do so. In our current season, our roles are almost completely reversed. Thankfully, our children are old enough now to share the chores, which we divide among them and rotate week to week. We've given our kids regular chores from a young age, both to help us out and to give them a sense of responsibility for our family's space. They've been doing their own laundry since they were around four years old. For the first couple years, we had to supervise them closely, but now they do it without any help at all.

As each of our households go about the bathing, washing, and cleaning rituals of our life together, I hope we can do so with reference to our shared baptism. One possible tool is to post signs over places of washing that say, "Remember your baptism and be thankful." Another is to memorize short, one- or two-line breath prayers for use while washing dishes, showering, doing laundry, or watering plants. Perhaps one of these prayers, based on Scripture, would be suitable:

- [Breathing in] Lord, make me a well-watered garden, [breathing out] a spring whose waters never fail (Is 58:11).
- [Breathing in] Lord, give me your living water [breathing out] so I will not get thirsty (Jn 4:15).
- [Breathing in] Lord may justice roll down like a river, [breathing out] righteousness like a never-failing stream (Amos 5:24).
- [Breathing in] Lord, I thirst for you [breathing out] in a dry and parched land (Ps 63:1).

The laborious tasks involved in caring for our bodies are not going away any time soon. Most of us cannot afford to offload our domestic necessities to others, and the just treatment and remuneration of such laborers are a serious concern for kingdom citizens. So, why not try approaching them as opportunities for virtue cultivation? Such attempts won't make laundry any less arduous or dishes any less time consuming, but they can become small and mundane moments of apprenticeship to love within our regular routines. We can thereby join Brother Lawrence in his prayer-filled labors: "The time of business does not with me differ from the time of prayer; and in the noise and clutter of my kitchen. . . . I possess God in as great tranquility as if I were upon my knees at the Blessed Sacrament."[6]

## Caring for Our Places

Caring for places is another practice that emerges from our baptism. As we are submerged into Christ in our baptism, we are also initiated into his tending of the world (Gen 2:15). Caring for places is precisely what it sounds like: taking care of the sites where we live out our days—our homes, our neighborhoods, and our communities. Again, this may sound strange to folks who are used to thinking of souls and "spiritual lives" as the most important aspects of life, but our so-called spiritual lives are our lives, which includes our bodies and the places where we reside. As we seek to survive and resist the dehumanizing effects of modern society, we must seek remedies for our alienation from the created world, not to mention its exploitation in the name of profit.

Our disconnection from the land has its roots in sin, yes, but more specifically in the impact of European imperialism. As Willie James Jennings says, when European Christians took possession of the New World, they used their power to reconfigure the relationship between people, land, and identity. Whereas many Indigenous peoples understood themselves as deeply interconnected with the land and all its flora and fauna, Europeans saw themselves as "bodies floating through space." The land and its resources were evaluated for their production potential and cordoned off as "inert segments of space"—private property owned by whoever was powerful enough to keep it. "The land no longer spoke of who we are and who we should or could be," Jennings says. "The animals were no longer kindred beings. They became our tools and resources, and we became geographically adrift in the world."[7]

Given this history, therefore, caring for our physical setting is part of being apprentices to love in God's kingdom today. We can begin thinking about this in reference to our homes and then work our way into our neighborhoods and communities. David Matzko McCarthy defines home as "a place where we are deeply connected to others."[8] To make our places into homes is the work of homemaking: setting up and caring for the material conditions in which we live, no matter how humble. Whether a single rented room or a four-bedroom house, we want our spaces to become homes where we can more easily become friends with God and neighbor.

At the same time, a caveat is needed: Christians must be careful not to understand homemaking in the sense of acquiring more stuff and coming up with more artful ways to display our stuff. Certainly, we want our spaces, as much as our situations permit, to reflect beauty, truth, and goodness, but that is not the same as acquisition for the sake of showing off to others or proving to ourselves that we've "made it." Homemaking is not ultimately for the sake of private enjoyment or respite from the world. Rather, we make homes for the sake of connection with God, self, and others. If our aim is apprenticeship to love, then all the work of homemaking, big and small, must be oriented by that goal, starting with the "neighbors" within our home and moving out to include literal neighbors beyond the home.

Is it possible in your space to have one room arranged specifically for the purpose of gathering and sharing? One of the most important homemaking decisions Ronnie and I ever made involved where to place our family's television. In our current house, we are privileged to have two rooms where the TV could suitably go, but we decided to place it in a lower-level room, leaving the first-floor living space screen-free. Then we arranged the furniture such that occupants can see and speak to each other easily in front of the biggest window and the dining room where we eat our meals. When we have more guests than we have seats, we bring in extra chairs from the garage and basement to "widen the circle" and include more. It's not the prettiest setup. All our furniture is used or IKEA, and most bear the signs of wear and tear. But that arrangement of couches, chairs, and beat-up coffee table has become for us a sacred site of kingdom joining.

Our places aren't simply our homes though. Our places also include our neighborhoods and communities. If we want to learn to see the land and its inhabitants as connected to us, then we will need to improvise ways to press toward that goal. I know an Anglo-American family that lives in a part of the Chicago suburbs with many Mexican and Mexican American residents. To become better neighbors, they are learning to speak Spanish as a family. A household of single women I know have made it a point to learn and catalog all the plants and animals in their immediate vicinity. When they choose what to plant in their flower beds, they do so not primarily with a mind to what looks good, but rather what best suits the local ecology, even down to the types of butterflies that frequent the area. There's a couple in our church that regularly serves with the local park district clearing out invasive trees and shrubs that choke out native plants. Our communities also need neighbors who care about things such as fair housing, a just zoning code, and clean waterways. All these things are part of caring for our places, and they constitute a kind of homemaking that extends beyond the walls of our private homes.

## Storytelling and Timekeeping

We are temporal beings, but living in light of time, both its expansiveness and its limited-ness, it not something modern humans are very good at. Alongside displacement and disembodiment, another terrible fruit of European imperialism is alienation from time—past, present, and future. We don't see ourselves as creatures with a past, we don't know how to inhabit the present, and we cannot envision the future—let alone a better future. Without temporal rootedness and some kind of shared story, apprenticeship to love is nearly impossible. As Canadian-American philosopher James K. A. Smith says, "Faithfulness requires knowing when we are in order to discern what we are called to."[9]

So, another essential practice for Christian families is storytelling and timekeeping, which are linked. The core Christian story, of course, is the good news of Jesus Christ: the power of God through which Israel's long-awaited Messiah restores all of creation under God's reign through his death, resurrection, and ascension, through the Holy Spirit's power.[10] In the church, Christians are supposed to learn what it means to have our stories—individual, family, national, and global—understood in and through the gospel story. Families can support this work by speaking the truth to one another as we interact with stories in our daily lives: tales from grandparents, stories reported through news media, or even gossip from workplaces and schools. All these stories are meant to be read through the lens of the gospel and, therefore, judged by the claims of the gospel.

For instance, national stories about events past or present are subject to evaluation by the good news. Instead of allowing the national narrative of, say, American exceptionalism to continue unquestioned as it emerges from schools, political ads, or civic events, Christian households can remind one another that "Christians are bound to the land and neighbors as fellow sojourners. Our unity is in the reign of God."[11] When political ads come on the television or radio, we can reframe what we've heard, pointing out the truth and sifting out the falsehood. When we watch films that speak falsehoods about the world—that violence is redemptive, or wealth buys happiness, or abuse should be tolerated for the sake of love—we can speak the liberating wisdom of the gospel to each other.

Similarly, our extended family members might attempt to narrate family history in ways that are false and harmful. This is especially the case in families with histories of addiction and abuse. The pressure to keep secrets and downplay the impact of such failures can be immense, but under the gospel's scrutiny and the Spirit's guidance, the truth about patterns of abuse or neglect can be named, even when it is painful. "Grandpa chooses to continue hurting people with his hands and his words. So, we won't be able to see him until he acknowledges there is a problem and gets treatment for it." "Cousin John is addicted to a drug that is hurting his body and his loved ones. Aunt Catherine is trying to help him to get sober, so she can't come visit us this summer."

Re-narration is difficult to do in general, let alone in the so-called information age. Despite having the internet at our fingertips, we are often desperately lacking in accurate data about the events happening around us, and though constantly inundated with information, we struggle to know what is true and what is false. And many of us are not practiced in thinking through world events in view of a full-throated gospel vision.

Our family experienced the complexity of renarration as we processed the war of Israel against Hamas following the October

7 terrorist attacks in 2023. Part of our task with our children, then ages fourteen, thirteen, and ten, was to have enough accurate information about the past to be able to help them make sense of the present. We did our best to relay some of the history of anti-Semitism, reminding them of their knowledge of the Holocaust from lessons at school. Then, we explained some of the details of Israel's founding in 1948 and the Nakba (mass dispossession and displacement of Palestinians), the Six-Day War (1967), and subsequent cycles of violence and failed attempts at peace. Eventually, we had to frame things theologically: that Jesus is a Jew and we have been grafted into a faith with Jewish roots, that there is a sizable Palestinian Christian community in Gaza, that God detests death and wants the freedom and flourishing of both Israelis and Palestinians, and that genocide is always and everywhere wicked. Though this was a lengthy conversation, we considered it essential to help them process what they were seeing and hearing. It's by no means certain that we framed the conversation exactly as we ought to, but we felt compelled by the storytelling demands of the gospel to be sure our children were thinking within the framework of both accurate history and God's kingdom in Christ. It was worth the risk of "messing up."

As we think about storytelling in our households, I would suggest we prioritize three emphases. First, we must learn that we are creatures. The stories we tell each other should underline the reality that we are limited and finite beings with their source and goal in God. Second, we must learn that we are Gentiles (at least those of us who are). We are not the original covenant people of God, but outsiders who were invited in. This means the Old Testament is not primarily about us, and we are not the heroes of God's story. We have been grafted into the vine (Rom 11:17-18). Last, we must learn that we are kingdom citizens above all. National narratives are deeply compelling. They draw on common language and a particular version of history to unite people and foster allegiance to the nation's "way of life." Because of their power, therefore, Christian storytelling must subvert national narratives along with all those that defy Christ's lordship over history with Christian stories and symbols.

One practice that has been central for our family's storytelling work is simply reading books together. Studies show reading together is great for children's development, literacy, and lifelong learning, but it's also a relatively easy way to encourage the discussion of the good, the true, and the beautiful. When our children were very small, each child got to pick a book to read before bed. Once they became old enough for chapter books, we would often rotate who got to choose a chapter book to read together. Through that method, we've worked through several fantasy series. Though fictional, these epic tales have become shared narratives, which provide a shared language and imagination through which we can discuss life in the real world. Now that they are teenagers, reading together has ceased to be a regular practice, but we share other things like television shows, movies, podcasts, and music. Ronnie and I have a whole list of films that we are looking forward to sharing with them as they become old enough for the themes and discussions that will surely follow.

For households without children, a book club could be a better option. Housemates can read on their own time and then come together once a month or every two months to discuss the stories encountered. The same setup could work for a streaming series or film or another form of storytelling. My husband and I have occasionally read books to each other during downtime or on long road trips. There's no reason that a group of friends couldn't do the same. Along the way, the question isn't whether the story or message is explicitly Christian, but whether it's true. Does it correspond to what's real? Does it tell the truth about the world? And does it point to what's real under Christ's lordship? Sometimes paying attention to the disjuncture is just as important as noticing the harmony.

Re-narrating our lives is a tall order, and there are no guarantees that our efforts will pay off. As we look back over the church's story, we can see many instances of courageous and inspiring counternarratives to anti-kingdom cultural norms, but we see just as many failures to rightly discern and oppose the same. This truth should instill in us not hopelessness but appropriate humility. We may miss things. We may get it wrong. But in our pursuit of faithfulness to Jesus and his kingdom, it's vital that we try.

We've talked a lot about storytelling. Let's reconnect now with timekeeping. Through most of church history, Christians attuned themselves to sacred time through routine observances like daily prayer, weekly worship, and the rituals of the church calendar. Such observances were oriented to the natural world: the journey of the sun across the sky, the phases of the moon, the position of the constellations, and the agricultural rhythms. Regular Christians did not have access to Scripture for private reading and study. Only since the advent of the printing press has the notion of a personal Bible been thinkable, and only in the past century and a half has purchasing a Bible become affordable enough for regular folks to do so. In the past not only were copies of Scripture rare, but most Christians wouldn't have been able to read them even if they had them. How did Christians in these periods without access to Scripture keep themselves immersed in the story of God? They heard the Bible read in church on Sundays and holy days, they observed the church calendar as a community, and they memorized prayers.

The church calendar has been a central feature of the Roman Catholic and Orthodox traditions throughout its history, but Protestants have been mixed in their reception of the practice. Among low-church Protestants, especially, the church calendar has often been written off as too formal or traditional, so many are unfamiliar with it. Why keep such traditions? The way Christians mark time matters. Just as we should narrate world history with the death and resurrection of Jesus Christ as the turning point, we should also orient our days, weeks, months, and years by the gospel of Jesus Christ.

There are many ways to do this, but the seasons of the church year are one way that does not require inventing something new. It begins with the first Sunday of Advent, around late-November, and runs through the last Sunday of Ordinary Time, often called Christ the King Sunday. The point of the seasons in between is to walk disciples of Jesus through the pivotal events of Christ's life and the life of his church, even as disciples go about their own lives through the same year. The hope is that you begin to see your life and the life of your household and community within the frame of salvation history.

Here's a summary of the progression: Advent begins the church calendar because the church lives in the period between Christ's first and second comings. Kingdom citizens are supposed to be devoted to watching and waiting for our Lord's return. Christmas lasts for twelve days and focuses on Christ's incarnation and birth. Epiphany is several weeks long and devoted to remembering Christ's glorious appearance to the nations. The season of Lent, which lasts for forty days (not counting Sundays), is devoted to practices of repentance in imitation of Christ. Beginning with Palm Sunday, Holy Week walks God's people through Christ's Passion, culminating in his resurrection on Easter Sunday. The season of Easter, which lasts for fifty days, celebrates the new creation brought about through Christ's resurrection. The Feast of Pentecost recalls the coming of the Holy Spirit, giving birth to Christ's church, followed by Trinity Sunday, commemorating the revelation of God as triune. Finally, Ordinary Time stretches from Trinity Sunday through Christ the King Sunday. It's appropriate that it's the longest period of the calendar because it's devoted to the "green growing years" of the church: life together in the kingdom of God.[12]

I know a family that has several single-color table runners that correspond to the colors of the church year. They are not fancy, but by changing them out through the year, they frame their mealtimes within the symbolism of sacred time. Some families have special foods they make for each season or seasonal hymns they sing during times of family worship.[13] I am not a crafty person, but I've known folks to do crafts with their friends for special days such as All Saints, Christmas, and Easter.

If your church follows the lectionary, then you will also rotate through most of the Scriptures within a three-year cycle. But even if your church does not, there's nothing that says your household can't make use of the lectionary on a weekly basis, or the Daily Office from the Book of Common Prayer, or another Bible reading plan written to correspond with the church year. Traditionally, each season has its own symbols, hymns, rituals, and themes, which with some forethought and creativity, can become part of a family's daily or weekly rhythm.[14] Of course, how a family observes the church calendar will vary depending on capacity, ages, and abilities. Thankfully, there are numerous resources today for families who need ideas for what this might look like.

Alongside observing the church calendar, our storytelling and timekeeping should also include the practice of *memento mori* or remembering one's death. Like most, I would prefer to live in denial about the brevity and fragility of my life. Yet, the church has taught for a long time that being mindful of one's future death, however near or far it may be, is essential to living a faithful life before God.[15] One day each of us will die and our lives in the meantime are given both meaning and perspective by keeping that reality before our minds. "To be a creature," Smith says, "is to be passing away, amid things passing away." Furthermore, we're each only one of billions of people who have ever lived on the earth (the Population Research Bureau estimates 117 billion, to be more precise).[16]

In the universal scheme of things, therefore, we don't matter all that much, and yet, at the same time, we matter a whole heck of a lot. Each of us bears the image of our Creator and is invited into covenantal friendship with God. Also, we matter immensely to each other with our lives ever and always intertwined with the lives of others. Thus, I am precious to God and to all with whom I am related. Their flourishing depends on me, and mine on them. But that preciousness does not make our lifespans any longer or our lives any less difficult.

So, it's appropriate for Christian families to make remembering our deaths a habit in ways suitable for members' stages of development. Adults and teenagers might benefit from a *memento mori* app or calendar reminder. During Advent a couple years ago, I downloaded the WeCroak app, which has one purpose: five times per day, it sends you a reminder, "Don't forget, you're going to die." The timing is entirely random, so you can't predict when you will receive the notifications. I have received surprise *memento moris* while impatiently waiting in traffic, sitting in church, struggling with a writing project, and ruminating over a poorly executed class. Each time it breaks me out of whatever mental rut I find myself in and brings my creaturely limitations to the front of my mind once again. Whatever *this* is I'm dealing with, it will eventually pass away just as *I* will eventually pass away. That doesn't mean it's not important, but it does mean its importance is limited.

If your family chooses to observe the church calendar, there are some built-in times to think about death, especially Advent and Lent (Ash Wednesday, in particular), as well as All Saints' Day. Other saints' days are often observed on the days of their deaths and their stories include accounts of their deaths. A household could make it a practice to include short stories of saints at some point during their daily or weekly devotions. For children, especially, there are many books today that address the themes of mortality and death in ways that are age appropriate. A family with children might want to acquire a few of these options or borrow them from the library. Remember, the point of *memento mori* practices is not to inculcate fear. Central to the saving work of Christ is to free us from the fear of death (Heb 2:15). The point, therefore, is to engage in practices that will help us to experience increasing freedom from the fear of death over time.

Remembering our deaths can also be helped along by making it a point to regularly attend funerals or memorial services. Rather than avoiding such events, perhaps we could reframe such gatherings as valuable invitations to collective *memento mori*. We've tried to take our children to as many funerals as possible, whether for family members, friends' family members, or church members. This is not because we're suckers for the morbid, but because in addition to grieving with those who grieve, funerals offer something extraordinarily rare in the Western world: extended time to ponder life's big questions, ones that the daily grind allows us to ignore. What makes a person's life meaningful? What is a good life? What will people remember about us when we die? What happens to us when our earthly lives are over? What are we hoping for in the future?

Baptism is the rite through which God's promises in Christ are made evident and the means through which we demonstrate our allegiance to Christ as Lord. Households of faith can press into the significance of our baptism through some things we're already doing, as well as new things we may decide to implement as time and energy permit. Some might want to pick just one of the many options I've suggested and see whether it's possible to create a new family habit in the realm of caring for our bodies, caring for our places, or storytelling and timekeeping. The hope is that within the context of our ordinary lives, we would begin to see all things under Christ's lordship and all places as sites of God's kingdom growth—including the people, places, and things we call home.

# 11

# Families and Eucharist

**By now it's a cliché,** but it also happens to be the truth: Ronnie used some of his time at home during the 2020 lockdown to perfect his bread making. As he did so, we were treated to classic white, sourdough, and honey wheat in addition to treats such as homemade bagels and calzones. But the bread that rose to the top was a garlic and herb bread, which he makes in a cast iron Dutch oven with olive oil and garlic salt sprinkled on top. The garlic and herb bread became so beloved that once the stay-at-home orders were lifted, Ronnie started making it for our dinner guests. Now it's served for guests so often that the aroma almost inevitably elicits the question: "Are we having people over for dinner?"

I am more than a little delighted that our family associates the smell of baking bread with hospitality. I already think of our household tables as extensions of the church's eucharistic table, but the additional sensual link to our practice of hospitality is especially meaningful. As Jesus welcomes and joins with us over the offering of his body, so we welcome and join with others over the offering of Ronnie's crackly, warm bread. It's not the same thing, of course, but there is a link, however small, that points toward other ways that Christian families might embody the truth and beauty of Eucharist in their daily lives.

# Eucharist

The Eucharist, also called Communion or the Lord's Supper, is the meal Jesus gave to his disciples as the way to remember and commune with him. The first meal took place in conjunction with the Jewish Passover and intentionally drew on and transfigured the elements of that traditional meal. Of course, the original Passover was held in Egypt on the night when God rescued the Hebrews from slavery. The particulars of the Passover are outlined in Exodus 12, where each household is told to choose an unblemished male lamb, sacrifice the lamb, spread the blood of the lamb on their door posts, eat the flesh of the lamb, and then keep the Passover as a day of remembrance for every generation afterward.

In the centuries following the first Passover, Jewish observance of the holy day went through some changes. For one, the lamb was sacrificed in the temple of Jerusalem rather than the home. Thus, it was a ritual sacrifice first and then a meal shared by the family.[1] In the observance of the "remembrance," the Jewish father would speak of the Passover as though he himself had been there. It was not strictly an event of the past being memorialized, but the past event somehow brought into the present reality. Finally, for some Jews at the time of Jesus, the Passover was a sign of God's final and future rescue of God's people, which the exodus from Egypt prefigured.

As a result of these changes in Passover observance, we can see that when Jesus celebrated Passover with his disciples, he wasn't simply replicating the meal but reconstituting it. He was offering a new Passover through which he would bring about God's promised and eternal exodus. Jesus specifically celebrated the Last Supper on Passover night, the night when the sacrificial lambs would be eaten by the people (Mt 26:17-19; Mk 14:12; Lk 22:14-15). Also, they ate the Passover meal in Jerusalem with wine and bread and the singing of a hymn. Unlike traditional Jewish Passovers, Jesus is the leader and host of the meal despite not being the father of any of the disciples. Also, he reorients the meal away from the lamb, which is never mentioned by the Gospels, to his own person—his body and blood—linking it to the new covenant promised by Jeremiah (Jer 31:31-33). Jesus is saying, "I am the new Passover lamb of the new exodus. This is the new Passover of the Messiah, and I am the new sacrifice."[2]

Jesus told his disciples to observe the new Passover meal regularly in remembrance of him, and we know from the New Testament and early church documents that they did so. Paul summarized the tradition of the eucharistic meal in his First Epistle to the Corinthians:

> The Lord Jesus, on the night he was betrayed, took bread, and when he had given thanks, he broke it and said, "This is my body, which is for you; do this in remembrance of me." In the same way, after supper he took the cup, saying, "This cup is the new covenant in my blood; do this, whenever you drink it, in remembrance of me." For whenever you eat this bread and drink this cup, you proclaim the Lord's death until he comes. (1 Cor 11:23-26)

The Eucharist is shared by baptized members of Christ's body and enacts in a ritual way our exodus from sin and death and entrance into sabbath rest. When we are gathered around the table, we participate in fellowship with God and neighbor, the sacrifice of Christ on our behalf, and the presence of Christ among us. Like baptism, Eucharist is a gift from God. That is why in many churches you come forward to receive Communion with empty hands outstretched. There is nothing you can bring to Jesus and yet he gives you all of himself. Unlike baptism, though, Eucharist is meant to be repeated: "For whenever you eat this bread and drink this cup, you proclaim the Lord's death until he comes" (1 Cor 11:26).

Because of the way Jesus links himself to the bread and wine—"This is my body . . . this is my blood"—the Eucharist has become the central ritual of Christian faith. From its rich symbolism flows countless other practices of loving God, loving self, and loving others. It demonstrates human fellowship with God, which is accomplished at God's initiative. We bring God our meager resources, which are themselves gifts from God—"the fruit of the earth and the work of human hands"—and we give them back to God. In God's mercy, he elevates, consecrates, and transforms the gifts into spiritual sustenance. At the table, we are all recipients of grace. At the table, all enmity is done away with, and we are truly one in Christ. At the table, we experience a foretaste of God's kingdom come and creation made new.

Perhaps due to its symbolic centrality, the apostle Paul had a keen interest in correcting sinful behavior around the table. Paul was scandalized that the wealthy members of the Corinthian church were eating and drinking their fill before the poor members even arrived (1 Cor 11:17-22). Why were the poor church members coming late? Because they only had liberty to attend Christian gatherings after finishing a full day of labor while wealthy folks could arrive any time they wished. Paul chastises them strongly, saying that to eat the body of Christ and drink the blood of Christ without discerning "the body" is to "eat and drink judgment" against themselves (1 Cor 11:29). The meal is of such importance to Christian love that he urges them to consider each other: "So then, my brothers and sisters, when you gather to eat, you should all eat together. Anyone who is hungry should eat something at home, so that when you meet together, it may not result in judgment" (1 Cor 11:33-34).

Because it is the sign of our communion in Christ, the eucharistic ritual is linked to practices of forgiveness, restitution, and reconciliation. It provides a new order for human relationships. An order based on what Christ has done for us rather than what we can do for ourselves. An order based on a crucified and raised Messiah who calls us to take up our own crosses and follow him. An order based on love not coercion, which recognizes that no one else needs to die to make the world right.[3] Through the table we express our reconciliation with God and each other and learn how to see one another around the table as fellow recipients of God's new world. How can families of various shapes and sizes observe the Eucharist in their daily life? I have three suggestions: eating meals together, offering hospitality, and practicing reconciliation.

## Eating Meals Together

The most straightforward connection between the Eucharist and Christian family life is the shared meal. Whether home-cooked and served at a dining table or eaten on the sidelines of a baseball game, every shared meal gestures in some small way toward the eucharistic meal. Through the shared table we express our need for sustenance and receive it together. Humans are like other animals in the sense that we become what we consume. What we eat and drink is transformed into fuel for our bodies, building new cells and repairing damaged ones. The act of sharing in the body and blood of Christ, whether conceived of literally or figuratively, draws much of its power from the biological significance of eating and drinking.

Through meals we also express our dependence on one another and ritually enact our shared life. Most homes, whether an efficiency apartment or a two-story house, have a space with a table around which people gather to eat. When I was single and living with two other single friends, we ate most of our meals sitting on the floor around the coffee table in our small living room. Now our family gathers around the deeply scratched and scarred table in our dining area. Wherever it takes place, eating together is something unique to human cultures, a ritual that creates bonds and fosters trust. You don't see Labradors commiserating about their days over bowls of chow nor do hamsters debate politics while they consume their greens. Yet, humans commune through food.

Not every meal does this well, of course. Many family meals are tense and conflict prone precisely because they manifest the problems that are present beyond the meal. Tragically, many a story of disordered eating begins around the table as parents or grandparents criticize, shame, and try to control their children and grandchildren. I have adult friends who find eating with people very difficult for precisely this reason. At the same time, because of the widespread romanticization of home-cooked meals some find meal preparation laborious and stressful. Frankly, if preparing the meal is so overwhelming that communion is inhibited, then it might be best to let the freezer or premade sections of the supermarket provide dinner. The main thing is not what family meals should or shouldn't be. Rather, it is enacting together an echo of the Eucharist. As such every meal can be a small act of defiance to worldly ways of thinking and being.

How many meals and which meals can be shared will vary from family to family. Some might be able to commit to at least one meal together every day. Some might be able to commit to two dinners together per week. Some families might have a designated day for the "family meal" on Friday, Saturday, or Sunday nights. I know a household of single guys who do this and rotate the person in charge of planning and executing the meal. Again, the point is not necessarily how often you get to eat together, but you'll need to discern what is both hopeful and realistic for you and yours.

Something you might consider for these family meals is an easy-to-implement ritual for joining in one another's lives. Many households do some version of "highs and lows," where each person shares the high point and low point of their day. I know a family that has a glass mason jar filled with paper strips with questions printed on them—some silly and some serious. They take turns drawing from the jar as part of their conversation over dinner: If you could visit one time and place in the past, what would it be and why? If you could have one superpower, what would it be and why? The internet contains lots of ideas for these kinds of questions, so you could create a custom-made version for your family. Another option is to ask and discuss an open-ended question that allows you to process your day or week in relation to our shared apprenticeship: How did Jesus teach you to love today? Where did you see God at work today?

Even if the meal must be eaten in the car on the way to practice, it's still possible to connect and tend to one another in the process. When the schedule does permit a longer time of sharing across a real table, it's possible to be intentional about that time together without asking too much of yourself and your family members.

## Hospitality

The second practice that emerges from the Eucharist is hospitality. In God's kingdom, disciples of Jesus have been made one by the Spirit, but living this out is not natural. Practice is required. The ministry of Jesus, not to mention his parables, demonstrates many instances in which the kingdom of God is manifested through the joining of peoples, often in a shared meal. The story of the apostles as well as their letters are filled with proof that welcoming the stranger and being welcomed as the stranger are central to Christian living. Here are just a few instances of exhortation to the practice of hospitality:

- "Keep on loving one another as brothers and sisters. Do not forget to show hospitality to strangers, for by so doing some people have shown hospitality to angels without knowing it." (Heb 13:1-2)

- "Above all, love each other deeply, because love covers over a multitude of sins. Offer hospitality to one another without grumbling. Each of you should use whatever gift you have received to serve others, as faithful stewards of God's grace in its various forms." (1 Pet 4:8-10)

- "Be joyful in hope, patient in affliction, faithful in prayer. Share with the Lord's people who are in need. Practice hospitality." (Rom 12:12-13)

One challenge for those of us in capitalist economies is that our environments assume scarcity and an endless number of perpetually cultivated desires. Because the world is viewed as a zero-sum game, we're taught to live so that material gain is the highest good, which justifies getting as much as possible while giving as little as we can get away with. The kingdom economy, by contrast, assumes there are enough resources for all, and being in communion with God requires that we prefer the needs of others before our own (Phil 2:4). The kingdom economy trusts that the joining of lives results in healing and freedom for all, and God will provide for our needs (Mt 7:32-33). This is, I hasten to add, much easier said than done! But a regular practice of hospitality is one powerful way to survive and resist the malformation of consumer capitalism.

To be clear, hospitality is not the same as entertainment. Hospitality is not a presentation of one's largesse to demonstrate moral superiority. Hospitality is not showing off one's got-it-all-together-ness for the benefit of poor less-fortunates. Christian hospitality is the recognition that we need others and others need us in God's kingdom, so we create space within our lives and places to join with others. Indeed, we will only become more fully ourselves as we know ourselves with others, and they will only become more fully themselves as they know themselves with us. As Potawatomi botanist and author Robin Wall Kimmerer says, "What happens to one happens to us all. We can starve together or feast together. All flourishing is mutual."[4]

Practically speaking, like so many other rituals, hospitality must be planned. In our household, we assume at least two meals per week will include others beyond our family. This means we plan our grocery shopping, meal choices, and extracurriculars around these shared mealtimes. Not every family member is present for every meal. We are well into the years of after-hours choir rehearsals and youth group meetings, and sometimes extenuating circumstances force us to forgo hospitality for some other event, like when my youngest has a band concert. But after several years of weekly hospitality, welcoming people is now central to our life together. Even though we still have to plan ahead, it's a habit that has reshaped our desires and our lives.

It might also be possible to commit to a more long-term form of hospitality. Could an extra room be allotted "the Christ room," as Dorothy Day called it, for others in need of a place to stay? I know a couple who buy houses with at least one extra room for precisely this purpose. They have had a total of seven people stay with them over the years through various seasons and for various lengths of time. While such visitors are sometimes challenging, they are grateful for the ways their family has been shaped by the practice.

If regular meals with others won't work and a room can't be set aside, perhaps there are other things you can do as a household to be prepared to welcome others. I have a friend who always has ingredients on hand for a three-bean chili to be able to whip up a warm, filling meal if someone needs it. I have another friend who has a coffee and tea station always ready for visitors. Not everyone can do everything, and we shouldn't try. But I wonder what is possible in your place to make it more hospitable to those beyond the bounds of your household. There may be other ways to improvise toward this end.

## Practice Reconciliation

Not only does the Eucharist symbolize our oneness with Christ and each other, it also embodies the reconciliation the gospel enacts by the Spirit. As the epistle to the Ephesians says in dramatic form:

> For he himself is our peace, who has made the two groups one and has destroyed the barrier, the dividing wall of hostility, by setting aside in his flesh the law with its commands and regulations. His purpose was to create in himself one new humanity out of the two, thus making peace, and in one body to reconcile both of them to God through the cross, by which he put to death their hostility. (Eph 2:14-17)

Or as Paul says more succinctly in the letter to the Galatians, "There is neither Jew nor Gentile, neither slave nor free, nor is there male and female, for you are all one in Christ Jesus" (Gal 3:28). Our location "in Christ" and our communion in "one new humanity" means practically that we have a new order for our relationships: one that is rooted in love and not coercion, peace and not violence.

Reconciliation, therefore, is a core entailment of the gospel, willed by God and empowered by the Spirit. Yet the way of life that makes for reconciliation is hard and costly. This is the case whether we're talking about families, communities, or nations. Unfortunately, most societies are plagued by the ongoing consequences of oppression and violence, as well as the antagonisms that fester even where overt violence is absent. In the face of massive injustice and inequity, the roots of which go back centuries, it can feel overwhelming for families even to imagine how they might challenge, let alone remedy the situation. But there is something Christian households can do, both for their own members and those beyond the bounds of their home, in the cause of peace: Practice reconciliation.

If all members of a family are apprentices to love, then all members of the family are accountable to God, self, and neighbor to grow in love. Certainly, it is appropriate to account for the limitations posed by age, health, and ability. A three-year-old is not expected to show the same forbearance with her siblings that a thirteen-year-old would be. A thirty-five-year-old with chronic pain and illness is in a different situation from a fifty-year-old in good health. Still, no one gets a pass on seeking to grow in virtues such as self-control, forbearance, and humility, which are required with the Spirit's help to learn to love one another well.

The daily ins and outs of family life are full of opportunities for exercising our apprenticeship to love: late rides, missed meals, broken electronics, unfinished chores, past-due bills, late-night homework emergencies, and more. No matter how understandable it is when stress and finitude combine such that we hurt one another, it is vital that we do what is necessary to make it right.

In short, Christians have an obligation in Christ to confess, repent, and make restitution for our wrongdoing, even within the small confines of our households. On this point, Scripture makes our way plain: "Make sure that nobody pays back wrong for wrong, but always strive to do what is good for each other and for everyone else" (1 Thess 5:15). Also, "Do not repay evil with evil or insult with insult. On the contrary, repay evil with blessing, because to this you were called so that you may inherit a blessing" (1 Pet 3:9).

Furthermore, following in the footsteps of Jesus, those who have the most power in the family must take the lead in the practice of reconciliation: Recognizing when they sin against others, confessing it, repenting of it, and making restitution for it. This is not easy. Many of us never had such behavior modeled for us. Many of us have only ever seen adults deny their sin, gaslight, manipulate, and attack those who attempt to tell the truth. The healing process from such sinful ways of relating to one another is long and arduous, but it can be done, and we can develop new habits of relating. This is especially vital work for families in which children are present. Reconciliation must become a core practice of Christian households.

I remember an incident in my family many years ago. I was making dinner and for a reason I can no longer recall, I yelled at my two young children, then four and three years old. I was angry and loud, and they cowered, wide-eyed and afraid. At family prayer that evening, I remembered my outburst and knew I needed to apologize. So, I got down to their eye level, took both their little hands in mine, and said, "You know how when we were making dinner, mommy got really angry and yelled at you? I lost my patience and scared you, and I should not have done that. I'm very sorry."

Their little eyes looked back at me, sweet and trusting. The youngest smiled and shrugged, "It's okay, Mom," and gave me a hug. But the oldest was not satisfied. He crossed his arms, cocked his head, and scowled. "Mommy, aren't you forgetting something?" Surprised, I said, "Umm . . . what?" He replied, "Please, ff . . . ff . . . ff . . . forgive me?" He was right, of course. I hadn't asked them for forgiveness. Swallowing my pride (again), I said, "Buddy, will you please forgive me?" He smiled broadly and announced, "I forgive you!" And then I did the same with his sister. To this day I am grateful for his instinct for thorough reconciliation.

I have two practical suggestions for how to make reconciliation central to family life. First, convene regular family meetings. The point is to gather the members of the household for regular check-ins about the state of life. It can be once a week, but that might be too much to manage. Once every two to four weeks is probably sufficient with occasional "called meetings" as needed.

Are there any hurts that need to be remedied? Are there patterns of behavior that need to be addressed? Are there victories we need to celebrate? Are there scheduling problems or space-sharing challenges that need attention? Family meetings are a place to do all the above and more. Of course, not everything can or should be settled in a group meeting like this, but many things can. Also, it provides a good opportunity for adults to practice and model to children both healthy communication and the process of confession, repentance, and restitution.

Through regular practice, apologies should become second nature for all family members. Anglo-American author-advocate Wade Mullen has helpfully outlined what is included in a good apology. It might be worth posting these elements in a public place near where your family meetings take place:

1. Surrender—give up the desire to defend ("I owe you an apology").
2. Confession—rightly name each wrong to acknowledge fully what has been done ("I was wrong when I . . .").
3. Ownership—acknowledge the active role you had in the wrongdoing ("I take complete responsibility for . . .").
4. Recognition—specifically state the harm caused by the wrongdoing ("I see how my actions caused you . . .").

5. Empathy—make a true connection with the weight of what has been done ("I am grieved and filled with remorse").[5]

In addition to thorough apologies, a family committed to practices that make for peace is going to eschew violence of all kinds—and that includes with children. We simply cannot be apprentices to love and model the nonviolent way of Jesus while also using violence to teach. Again, this commitment is not easy. Many of us grew up with verbal abuse or physical punishment as the main disciplinary tools of the home. We have never seen adults creatively and empathetically work through conflicts and the big feelings they create to come to nonviolent and person-affirming solutions. But our process of healing and liberation by the Spirit can and must include other ways of relating to those around us, especially children, who are the most vulnerable of the vulnerable among us. Thankfully, there are many resources available today for parents and caregivers who want to pursue childrearing without physical punishment.[6]

If practicing reconciliation means rejecting violence and coercion in our interactions with each other, then we also need to question the violence and coercion that we encounter in media. This is especially important in the case of children who do not necessarily know some behavior is problematic unless adults they trust say so. Christian parents have long been wary of the sexual content in films and TV shows, and the same should be true of coercion and violence. One doesn't have to become an insufferable bore to regularly flag interactions seen on television or films as troublesome. As much as I enjoyed introducing my teens to *Parks and Recreation,* there have also been several instances in which I pause the show to say, "Okay, y'all, that is sexual harassment, and it's illegal," or "Kids, that's assault, and it's wrong." When you start paying attention to coercive, abusive, and violent behavior in entertainment, you'll be amazed how much there really is—even in much-beloved classics. The children in our midst need to be told that Christians don't live that way because it's not the way of Jesus.

But critiquing such behavior isn't enough. We also need to exercise our sanctified imaginations to envision other possibilities. One of the problems with the pervasiveness of violence in contemporary culture is the way that it forecloses other options. We have learned violence is usually the only possibility and that is usually results in a good outcome, neither of which are true. Often, violence begets more violence and narrows the field of vision so much that those involved can't see another way to live.

I remember a conversation that took place after our family finished watching *Hamilton* together. One of our children voiced sadness over the way Hamilton died. She noted how his wife, Eliza, lived for much longer and got to do a lot more for others as a result. I pondered out loud, "I wonder what Hamilton and Burr could have done differently." What followed was a fruitful conversation about relationships, communication, honor, masculinity, and more. We didn't solve anything, but we did imagine other ways the story might have worked out. Envisioning nonviolent options in fictional worlds helps strengthen the imagination muscle for nonviolent options in the real world.

Learning to practice reconciliation is likely to be especially difficult for families in which members have histories with trauma and abuse. In such settings, it's advisable to obtain professional assistance outside the home to support your mental, emotional, and relational health. As someone with a history of mental health challenges, I know just how difficult it can be to find the right people, not to mention the right price for your financial situation. But it is worth the effort—both for your own health and for the health of your family. Remember, sanctification by the Spirit's power includes such healing work.

## Putting It All Together

For the first thirteen years of our family's life with children, we structured our life with many weekday rituals. They were the means through which we told stories about ourselves, God, and the world and made meaning of our days. They were how we accompanied one another through life's vicissitudes. Some of those rituals included:

- Morning worship during breakfast, which included lighting a candle, reading Scripture, and praying before school.
- Family dinner every night, complete with each person sharing their day's highs and lows.
- Reading a family book together every evening, followed by a brief time of prayer and blessings right before bed.
- Friday night pizza and a movie with friends.

Weekends had their own rituals and rhythms too. Often Saturday mornings were spent at the library with a long walk or hike through a forest preserve in the afternoon. During and after the Covid-19 lockdowns, we played Dungeons & Dragons on Saturday mornings for two hours followed by lunch and some kind of outing together. Saturday evenings we attended church together followed by dinner with friends. If we were traveling, these rhythms looked different or had to pause until we returned home, but for the most part these things gave our days and weeks a comforting, manageable structure. They were like trail markers on a hike, or the buckets, crimps, and pinches needed for rock climbing.

Now that our children are in their adolescent years, however, our neatly structured schedule has changed dramatically. It feels like it happened overnight too. We've done our best not to over-schedule. We've limited the kids' extracurricular involvement: no more than one art and one sport each, and only one sport at a time. We prioritize family meals, prayer, and weekly worship even with the new arrangements, but right now we have three children at three different schools, each with their own friends and extracurricular activities. Ronnie and I have our friends and priorities too. This new phase of life with teenagers means that many of our former ways of marking time and touching base have had to go, or at least transform, and we're still working out what that looks like.

Christian families have their origin in love, their goal is love, and the journey to that goal is apprenticeship to love. Apprenticeship to love is another way of saying we are learning together how to be citizens of God's kingdom in Christ by the Spirit. God's kingdom is communion with God, who is love, and communion with self, others, and creation. Communion with the triune God means shalom for all—healing, liberation, and flourishing, beginning now and continuing into eternity. This is, in fact, God's plan for the world. So, when we align ourselves with that purpose, we are aligning ourselves with what God is already doing. We don't need to wonder if we're doing God's will or fulfilling God's calling. We are simply placing ourselves before God in a posture of receptivity and readiness.

The goal of families, therefore, is decidedly *not* to conform to a model drawn from the Bible. Not only does such a blueprint not exist, but neither are we promised success for perfectly emulating the "biblical" design. Families are for a purpose beyond themselves. Family is not a thing Christians are meant to perform or something to manufacture to prove their righteousness or earn trophies in eternity. Rather, families are the settings in which we learn how to live under God's reign with all their flaws and limitations. Amid all the good things we could do together, Christian families must always keep the main thing the main thing. Every day, no matter what the household is facing, the guiding question is this: *How will Jesus by his Spirit teach us to love today?*

In beginning to answer that question, Christian families can return again and again to the rituals of sabbath, baptism, and Eucharist for their imaginative and theological resources. These are the core practices through which the Holy Spirit cares for, nourishes, and trains God's people. It makes sense, then, that these practices and the theology they embody would be foundational for those seeking to improvise faithfulness today. Wherever you live, whatever the specific circumstances of your family, you can, by the Spirit's power, pursue a way of life aimed toward cultivating the virtue needed to survive and resist the evils of our day, and maybe even embody a vision of what God's kingdom looks like however limited and incomplete.

This will not be easy. Given the fallenness of our world, no attempt at faithfulness to Jesus will be. But the ideas I've included in these latter chapters are not a new law meant to guilt trip, shame, or condemn. Our household's calling amid our current season and context is to (1) see and name what is happening and what is needed (discern); then, (2) creatively respond from our abilities and resources based on the teachings of Jesus and tradition of the church (improvise). So, kingdom faithfulness is going to take different forms for different people. We get to learn together what following Jesus means for our people in our place. The point is to enact a family way of life—to become a certain kind of people together.

There's no triumphalism, though. Failure is inevitable. We live in the time between the times, and that time is full of enemies, difficulties, and discouragement. God is always at work, and the resources of his empowering Spirit are offered to us to see God's will be done on earth as it is in heaven. Yet, due to human frailty and finitude, we will only be able to do so much. This does not mean that we should not try. We offer our best attempts to cooperate with God's power as he makes all things new, but we do so in a posture of repentance and humility, ever mindful of how often we muck things up despite the best intentions. Our humble efforts must be viewed in the scope of God's "long game"—the triune God's eternal project of creation. It is within that larger story that our little stories find abiding significance and make an eternal impact.

# Epilogue

**As I write this,** my husband is at work in a warehouse, which occupies most of his time on four out of five workdays. He's working a part-time job because our new little church can't yet afford to pay him a salary, and my salary alone can't support our family in the suburbs of Chicago. Before Ronnie left for work this morning, he exclaimed wryly that he'd be going by the grocery store after work for the third day in a row to obtain yet another essential food item we've run out of.

Preparing to leave for my college office, I see my laundry, which I've been meaning to do for over a week, still sitting in a large pile on our bedroom floor. I wonder to myself whether I'll get to it this afternoon. At the same time, our living room features a miniature mountain of the kids' coats, bags, shoes, books, and other items that we had to move yesterday to access the furniture. As I grab my coffee on the way out the door, I notice the sink is full of dishes and every surface in sight needs a wipe down.

Whatever I imagined family life would look like, it didn't include this. I have learned that there are seasons to life, and not all seasons will be as taxing as this one. I have learned that a clean house doesn't matter much if the people inside aren't loving each other well. I have also learned that the messy particulars of our family's life together are precisely where God meets us every day: on the way to volleyball practice, in the after-dinner chores, in the finishing-homework-at-the-last-minute sprint before bedtime, and in houseguests who keep us up long past our bedtime. God is always present and at work among us, so we expect God to show up even in the less-than-ideal specifics.

I think contemporary Christians need a paradigm shift, especially in the United States. We need a change in how we think about family and how we live as families. A paradigm shift requires a change in our "thought world," which then provides a framework and motivation for changes in our practice.[1] One without the other just won't work. This book is my attempt to jump-start a change in how we think about and practice family.

With Jesus Christ at the center of our family theology and practice, we realize that family is a not an uncomplicated historical and cultural phenomenon. Very often, family has been the excuse to accumulate wealth, amass social and political power, and prop up the unjust status quo. But the kingdom of God will not allow such injustices to stand unopposed. The community of Jesus' disciples lives differently, not allowing the purpose and ends of family to remain as they are in this present evil age. As they await the return of Christ, families are meant to be apprentices together, seeking in their halting ways to imitate Christ and learn how to be faithful kingdom citizens. The church is the ultimate outpost of God's kingdom, but families can function as "domestic churches," a smaller kingdom outpost where we learn to practice new creation.

I think Christian families today are both worse off and better off than you might think. Things are worse off because the challenges facing families are enormous. Each family member carries their own traditions and traumas, which have left their mark on body, mind, and soul. We are infected with sin, too, which affects every part of us, working against our best efforts to love God and our neighbors. We are also seeking to resist centuries of malformation under imperialism, including the evils of sexism, racism, economic exploitation, and violence. To resist such patterns of thinking and acting is also to resist powers and principalities–spiritual forces of darkness–that are actively seeking to keep the corruption going.

At the same time, we are trying to survive in a world that seems increasingly less hospitable to human flourishing. Earth is warming and the consequences for the planet's ecosystems are already proving devastating. Societies worldwide are opting for quasi-fascist populist nationalism while wars declared and undeclared rage across both hemispheres. Millions of families have been displaced in the wake of such disruptions and they're making their way to more "developed" countries for potential relief and safety. Meanwhile, in more affluent countries inflation, stagnant wages, and the broadening gap between the classes means it's harder and harder simply to take care of basic needs. In the face of such global and local crises, what good can our little families do?

Despite how bad things look, things are also better than you might think. In the face of all the previous realities, it's not your family's responsibility to change the world. You couldn't do it if you tried. It's not your family's responsibility to be perfect–to precisely emulate a divine design. Nor is it your family's responsibility to bring about God's kingdom on earth. The future of our community, our nation, and our world does not ultimately rise and fall on our family's performance. Jesus Christ, the Lamb of God, holds the scroll that contains the unfolding future; we do not (Rev 5:5-7). He is worthy to guide and direct the course of global history; we are not.

Does this mean what we do doesn't matter? Should we eat, drink, and be merry because Jesus has it covered? Not at all. The call of Christ to follow him remains, and obedience is our expected response. Thus, we can attend to the small, limited, and

seemingly insignificant aspects of our daily lives with assurance
that God's eternal project with creation is not in question. We
have paradigms to unlearn, wounds to heal, and unhealthy patterns to replace. We have practices to implement, reconciliation
to pursue, and love to share, and we do so while trusting that
God's Spirit continues to hover over the chaos of creation, renewing the face of the earth.

So, no matter what your family looks like—big or small, biological or chosen, with children or without, homeschooling or
public-schooling, multiple incomes or one or none—I hope you
will begin to ask the following together every morning: *How will
Jesus by his Spirit teach us to love today?* More than likely, you
can ask and answer this question within the life you currently
have. If you're seeking to discern the times and improvise faithfully, the Spirit will likely call you into new places, relationships,
and practices. But it doesn't have to be heroic to be obedient.
It doesn't have to be Instagram- or TikTok-worthy to be faithful.

As I finish writing this epilogue now, the sun has set and another day is past. My family is at home awaiting my arrival so
we can eat dinner and begin our end-of-day routines. Given the
fragility of human life, I am aware of just how privileged I am to
have a family to go home to—and one I look forward to seeing
again. Even that is not guaranteed. All could be lost in a moment,
as families in war zones can testify.

Yet the gospel of Jesus Christ proclaims that despite the per-
sisting woundedness of ourselves and our world, God is making
all things new. We do not trust in family blueprints to save us. We
trust in Christ in whom God's kingdom has been inaugurated
and will one day be fully established over the whole earth. Until
that day, we muddle through as best we can together, accom-
panying one another on the narrow way of Jesus, and trusting
his Spirit to take our meager efforts, even our failures, and bless
them and multiply them for our good and the good of the world.

# Acknowledgments

**I have many people to thank for** their help and support with this book, but I am only allowed so many words. So, I offer my sincere gratitude to:

- Everyone on the InterVarsity Press editorial team, especially Cindy Bunch, Al Hsu, and Ethan McCarthy, who first approached me about this book.

- My InterVarsity Press writing group, Tim Gaines, Tara Edelschick, Michael Jordan, and Kathy Tuan-MacLean, who listened and provided comments on my earliest chapter drafts.

- My dean at Wheaton College, David Lauber, and department chair, Keith Johnson, for their backing, especially in acquiring time for research.

- Wheaton College for their G. W. Aldeen Faculty Development Grants, which helped fund this project, as well as the resources provided through the Leland Ryken Award for Teaching Excellence in the Humanities.

- My extraordinary colleagues and friends, especially Aubrey Buster, Amy Peeler, Jennifer Powell McNutt, Danielle Corple, Nathan Luis Cartagena, Christin Fort, Beth Felker Jones, Julie Newberry Douce, and Allison Dick.

- My teaching assistant, Isis Toldson, who read over early drafts and offered critical feedback.

- The twenty-eight intrepid students in my first-ever Marriage, Sex, and Family course.

- My beloved siblings at Christ Our Advocate, especially Andrew and Audrey, Aaron and Whitney, Nathan and Angela, Bonita, Michelle, and Kristin.
- Our friends who are now family, including Gabby, Regina, Brad, Brandon, and Connor.
- My mom, Wendy, and my siblings, Leah and Ian.
- My husband, Ronnie, for whom there are no adequate words, and my children, William, Emmelia, and Althea, to whom this book is dedicated.

# Questions for Reflection and Discussion

**Part 1: Rediscovering Family as Household of God**

1. In chapter one, McGowin describes the family blueprint she received from her church. What family blueprint did you receive from your family of origin or community? Have you ever had reason to question the blueprint? To the extent that you feel comfortable, explain what you've questioned and why.

2. What stands out to you from the survey of "biblical families" in chapter one? Do you agree with McGowin that there is no family blueprint found in Scripture? Why or why not? If you think there *is* a family blueprint, what would it look like and why?

3. In chapter one, McGowin suggests that, lacking clear maps or blueprints, the Christian life is largely one of *discernment* and *improvisation*. How does this correspond to your experience? In what ways have you had to discern and improvise in your personal life? In your family's life together? Based on your understanding of Scripture, what do you think should be the standards we use for determining what faithful discernment and improvisation look like?

4. In chapter two, McGowin provides an overview of Jesus' teaching on family. Do you think it makes a difference to begin with Jesus and his teaching rather than, say, Genesis 1–2 or Ephesians 5:22-33 (or the like)? Is there any

aspect of Jesus' teaching on family that you find especially challenging? Explain to the extent you can.

5. At the end of chapter two, McGowin discusses how Jesus interprets Genesis 1-2 with respect to God's purposes for marriage. Do any aspects of her discussion challenge your sense of the "biblical family" or family blueprint? Why or why not?

6. McGowin opens chapter three with the story of Perpetua and her companions, who chose loyalty to God's kingdom and God's household over loyalty to blood relatives. What kind of community would your church need to become for that story to be possible in your own context? In other words, what kind of changes would have to take place for your church to be the kind of community that cultivates such loyalty? Does the thought of that kind of loyalty cause you any anxiety? Why or why not?

7. According to chapter three, the gospel of the kingdom includes the creation of God's household, the church, which is made up of Jews and Gentiles. What kinds of "joining" amid difference have you experienced in your church(es)? How does your experience of church compare to the "mutual love, healing, and liberation" that's supposed to be manifested in God's household?

8. In chapter four, McGowin contrasts the "launchability" paradigm with the "apprenticeship to love" paradigm? What are the strengths and weaknesses of both paradigms? How do they correspond (or not) with your own experience of family? What difference do you think it would make to your household if apprenticeship to love was your primary paradigm? What are you doing now that already contributes toward that goal? What do you think might need to change?

9. In chapter four, McGowin defines love as "will[ing] the good of the other." Also, "Love extends oneself for the purpose of nurturing the growth and well-being of the other." Is this how you understand love? Why or why not? Do you think the question, "How will Jesus by his Spirit teach us to love today?" is a suitable focus for Christian families? Why or why not?

10. In chapter four, McGowin argues that self-sacrificing love is not the end goal of communion in the family. Rather, the end goal is mutual love or equal regard. When have you experienced self-sacrificing love? When have you experienced mutual or equal regard love? Do you think McGowin is right in her prioritization of the latter over the former? Why or why not? What might have to change in your household dynamics to make equal regard love the priority?

## Part 2: Signs of the Kingdom in an Evil Age

1. In chapter five, McGowin says that every family has its own tradition and trauma. To the degree that you are comfortable, discuss some aspects of your family's tradition and trauma. What did your family of origin hand on to you that you hope to retain and replicate? What did your family of origin hand on to you that you hope *not* to retain and replicate? Who do you have in your life that is helping you sift through the tradition and trauma and then discern and improvise a faithful path forward?

2. Every family is impacted by sin "inside" and sin "outside." To the degree that you are comfortable, discuss the kinds of sin that most impacts your family and prevents you from being the household of faith you're meant to be within the household of God. Be sure to discuss things "inside" and "outside" the home, including the systemic issues McGowin references in chapter five.

3. In chapter six, McGowin describes the way transformation
   happens within individuals and families as they seek the
   Spirit's renovation of their desires and habits. Can you think
   of examples of virtue formation in your life or your family's
   life together? Where have you seen desires change and
   habits shift to be more aligned with God's kingdom? If you
   can't think of something, then, to the degree that you are
   comfortable, share a place where you want to see transformation take place.

4. In chapter six, McGowin outlines the challenges families
   face in the impact of imperialism, sexism, racism, and consumer capitalism. These are big concepts that can feel abstract, but what are the tangible ways you see their impact
   in your household today? Discuss where you've seen
   any or all of them affecting your family's life together. (If
   you can't think of anything specific, perhaps others with
   whom you're in relationship can help you to discern their
   influence.) What things are you already doing to mitigate
   the impact of these challenges on your household?

5. In chapter six, drawing on the work of Willie James Jennings, McGowin asks us to consider the impact of the
   merchant, the soldier, and the missionary on our families, especially as they led to the deep-seated desire for
   "possession, mastery, and control." Where do you see
   that desire operating in your family's life? Where do you
   see that desire operating in your church or your neighborhood? Where do you see that desire operating in your
   school or workplace?

6. In chapter seven, McGowin demonstrates that singleness
   was the preferred state for the apostle Paul and the privileged vocation for the first several centuries of church
   history. What do you think of the fact that early Christians
   saw the church as the means to escape the pressure to

marry and reproduce? How does this compare to your per-spective on singleness or the perspective on singleness communicated by your church(es)?

7. In chapter seven, McGowin argues that both singleness and marriage are vital, sacramental vocations in God's household: "Both are complementary gifts to Christ's church, both image God's covenantal love, and both ways of life have mutuality or equal regard as their goal." Is this how you're used to thinking about singleness and marriage? What might need to change in your family or church practice in order to honor both states of life as worthy of dignity?

8. In chapter seven, McGowin shows that Christian views of marriage through the centuries have been significantly in-fluenced by faulty understandings of women. What have been your experiences with these realities? How have they impacted your personal experience and relationship with others? McGowin concludes, "Instead of patriarchy and gender-based roles, Jesus and his disciples follow a tra-jectory of freedom in view of God's kingdom." What dif-ference does this make for your paradigm and practice of marriage?

9. In chapter eight, McGowin reminds us that "children are persons, not products." If you have children or help care for children, have you ever been tempted to treat them as products rather than persons? To the degree that you are comfortable, share the things that have helped you to change your approach. Do you think she's right that there's no "precise formula for raising children"? While there might not be a precise formula, certainly there are some basic el-ements. What do you think would need to be included in that list of elements?

10. McGowin argues in chapter eight that God already has a nascent relationship with our children. Do you agree with

her assessment? Why or why not? How might your family or church's approach to children need to change in order to approach children as fellow disciples, sacramental signs, and learning teachers?

## Part 3: Practicing Family in the Already-Not-Yet

1. In chapter nine, McGowin describes the centrality of the Sabbath for Jewish life with God and how essential rest is for the love of God, self, and neighbor. In your experience of family or church, has sabbath (or rest) been similarly prioritized? If so, how? If not, can you describe the signs or symptoms of a lack of rest? Can you imagine a life in which sabbath is considered essential and prioritized as such?

2. Choose one or two of the household practices based on sabbath that McGowin suggests implementing in chapter nine. Does one stand out to you as especially inviting? Does one seem especially daunting or challenging? Are there any that you're already doing? Can you think of others that you might suggest instead? What kind of support do you think you might need in order to implement one or two of the sabbath practices in your family?

3. In chapter nine, McGowin argues that sleep, rest, and prayer arise from trust in God and reinforce trust in God. Have you ever found sleep, rest, or prayer difficult? Do you think she's right to link these things to trust in God? Why or why not? How might regular sleep, rest, or prayer (or all the above) cultivate trust in God and God's provision?

4. Baptism is the central practice of chapter ten. If you have been baptized, what was your baptism like? To the degree that you can recall, how does your experience of baptism compare to McGowin's account? Is remembering your baptism meaningful for you today? Why or why not? To the degree that you are comfortable, share your baptism story and how you understand that event in your life of faith.

5. Choose one or two of the household practices based on baptism that McGowin suggests implementing in chapter ten. Does one of these stand out to you as especially inviting? Does one seem especially daunting or challenging? Are there any that you're already doing? Can you think of others that you might suggest instead? What kind of support do you think you might need in order to implement one or two of the baptism practices in your family?

6. In chapter ten, McGowin links storytelling and timekeeping as Christian practices arising from our baptism. What are the primary ways your household practices storytelling? What are the primary ways your household practices timekeeping? What difference do you think it would make to approach these practices through an explicitly kingdom-oriented lens?

7. The Eucharist (or Holy Communion) is the central practice of chapter eleven. What is your experience with Eucharist in your church(es) and how does it compare to McGowin's account? Has the practice been important to you? Why or why not? To the degree that you are comfortable, share a specific or general experience with the Eucharist and how you understand that practice in your life of faith.

8. Choose one or two of the household practices based on Eucharist that McGowin suggests implementing in chapter eleven. Does one of these stand out to you as especially inviting? Does one seem especially daunting or challenging? Are there any that you're already doing? Can you think of others that you might suggest instead? What kind of support do you think you might need in order to implement one or two of the Eucharist practices in your family?

9. In chapter eleven, McGowin emphasizes reconciliation as a central Christian practice, especially within families. To the extent that you are comfortable, discuss how reconciliation

was modeled (or not) in your family of origin. Are there aspects of the reconciliation process that you find yourself or your family struggling with today? What are ways that your family could prioritize reconciliation on a regular basis?

10. In the epilogue, McGowin concludes by suggesting that Christian families are both worse off and better off than we might think. She also cautions Christians against overestimating the impact of individual families on the world. Why do you think Christians are prone to overestimate one family's impact on the world? Do you think McGowin is right to caution against this? Why or why not? Finally, what is at least one point from the book that you will carry with you and seek to implement?

# Further Reading

Jane Marguerite Bennett. *Water Is Thicker than Blood: An Augustinian Theology of Marriage and Singleness*. Oxford: Oxford University Press, 2008.

Todd Billings. *The End of the Christian Life: How Embracing Our Mortality Frees Us to Truly Live*. Grand Rapids, MI: Brazos, 2020.

Rodney Clapp. *Families at the Crossroads: Beyond Traditional and Modern Options*. Downers Grove, IL: InterVarsity Press, 1993.

Holly Taylor Coolman. *Parenting: The Complex and Beautiful Vocation of Raising Children*. Grand Rapids, MI: Baker Academic, 2024.

Stephanie Coontz. *The Way We Never Were: American Families and the Nostalgia Trap*. Revised and updated ed. New York: Basic Books, 2016.

Andy Crouch. *The Tech-Wise Family: Everyday Steps for Putting Technology in Its Proper Place*. Grand Rapids, MI: Baker Books, 2017.

Judith L. Herman. *Trauma and Recovery*. New York: Basic Books, 2015.

Prentis Hemphill. *What It Takes to Heal: How Transforming Ourselves Can Change the World*. New York: Random House, 2024.

bell hooks. *All About Love: New Visions*. New York: HarperCollins, 2001.

Beth Felker Jones. *Faithful: A Theology of Sex*. Grand Rapids, MI: Zondervan, 2015.

David Matzko McCarthy. *The Good Life: Genuine Christianity for the Middle Class*. Eugene, OR: Cascade / Wipf & Stock, 2004.

Bonnie Miller-McLemore. *In the Midst of Chaos: Caring for Children as Spiritual Practice*. San Francisco: Jossey-Bass, 2007.

C. René Padilla. *Mission Between the Times*. Revised and updated. Carlisle, UK: Langham Monographs, 2013.

James K. A. Smith. *How to Inhabit Time: Understanding the Past, Facing the Future, Living Faithfully Now*. Grand Rapids, MI: Brazos, 2022.

Ben Sternke and Matt Tebbe. *Having the Mind of Christ: Eight Axioms to Cultivate a Robust Faith*. Downers Grove, IL: InterVarsity Press, 2022.

Danielle Treweek. *The Meaning of Singleness: Retrieving an Eschatological Vision for the Contemporary Church*. Downers Grove, IL: IVP Academic, 2023.

Bessel van der Kolk. *The Body Keeps the Score: Brain, Mind, and Body in the Healing of Trauma*. New York: Penguin, 2014.

# Notes

### Introduction

[1]Here and throughout, I have chosen to capitalize *White* along with *Black*, *Brown*, and *Indigenous* to acknowledge the symbiotic construction of such racial categories and their persistence. This is one of a few approaches in contemporary race discourse, but I have been persuaded by Imani Perry's succinct explanation: "These are identity categories that were made by law, custom, policies, protest, economic relations, and perhaps most potently, culture. Politeness, grammar rules, and political pieties aside, this strikes me as a simple truth that ought to be acknowledged. I didn't make the rules. I am trying to tell them to you." See Imani Perry, *South to America: A Journey Below the Mason-Dixon Line* (New York: Ecco/HarperCollins, 2022), xi. Thanks to Nathan Luis Cartagena for bringing her work to my attention.

[2]Oliver Burkeman, *Four Thousand Weeks: Time Management for Mortals* (New York: Farrar, Straus, and Giroux, 2021), 205-8.

[3]Rodney Clapp, *Families at the Crossroads: Beyond Traditional and Modern Options* (Downers Grove, IL: InterVarsity Press, 1993), 18-19. Here and throughout, I have chosen, wherever possible, to provide information about the racial and/or ethnic identities of authors I cite so as to acknowledge the significance of such particulars.

[4]James Baldwin, *The Cross of Redemption: Uncollected Writings,* ed. and introduced by Randall Kenan (New York: Pantheon, 2010), 154.

[5]In this claim, I think I am in fundamental agreement with Stanley Hauerwas, who has written extensively about family, marriage, singleness, and children in relation to the church. See, for example, "The Radical Hope in the Annunciation: Why Both Single and Married Christians Welcome Children," in *The Hauerwas Reader*, ed. John Berkman and Michael Cartwright (Durham, NC: Duke University Press, 2001), 505-18.

[6]This is not to say that there isn't an important place for studying and sharing the best data available on things like which family forms seem to result in the best economic outcomes for children or better health outcomes for parents and grandparents. Such research is good and valuable and can be consulted by Christians as they order their lives, but that is not the focus of this book. My aim here is to help equip Christian families *as they currently exist.*

[7]I owe a big debt of thanks to my friend Holly Taylor Coolman for the paradigm of apprenticeship, which I encountered in her book, *Parenting: The Complex and Beautiful Vocation of Raising Children* (Grand Rapids, MI: Baker Academic, 2024), 33-41.

## 1—Searching for the Biblical Family

[1]Don S. Browning et al., *From Culture Wars to Common Ground: Religion and the American Family Debate*, 2nd ed. (Louisville, KY: Westminster John Knox, 2000), 88.

[2]See, for example, Stephanie Coontz, *Marriage, a History: How Love Conquered Marriage* (New York: Penguin Books, 2005) and *The Way We Never Were: American Families and the Nostalgia Trap*, rev. and updated ed. (New York: Basic Books, 2016).

[3]For each of the four examples cited, see the following: Ramon Gutiérrez, *When Jesus Came, the Corn Mothers Went Away: Marriage, Sexuality, and Power in New Mexico, 1694-1875* (Palo Alto, CA: Stanford University Press, 1991), 15-17; Elizabeth Fox-Genovese, *Within the Plantation Household* (Chapel Hill: University of North Carolina Press, 1988), 31-32; Herbert Gutman, *The Black Family in Slavery and Freedom* (New York: Pantheon Books, 1976), xxii-xxiii, 9; and Colleen McDannell, *The Christian Home in Victorian America, 1840-1900* (Bloomington: Indiana University Press, 1986).

[4]Leo G. Perdue, "The Israelite and Early Jewish Family: Summary and Conclusions," in Leo G. Perdue et al., *Families in Ancient Israel*, Family, Religion, and Culture Series (Louisville, KY: Westminster John Knox, 1997), 167.

[5]For more on each of these elements of ancient Israelite family, see Sandra L. Richter, *The Epic of Eden: A Christian Entry into the Old Testament* (Downers Grove, IL: IVP Academic, 2008), 21-46.

[6]Lisa Sowle Cahill, *Family: A Christian Social Perspective* (Minneapolis: Fortress, 2000), 23.

[7]Ephesians, Colossians, and the pastoral epistles are part of the contested letters of Paul and considered deutero-Pauline by most biblical scholars (that is, written by a later interpreter of Paul). I am not going to wade into the details of that argument here, but for the sake of simplicity I have chosen to write as though Paul is the author of all the books traditionally attributed to him.

[8]James K. A. Smith, *How to Inhabit Time: Understanding the Past, Facing the Future, Living Faithfully Now* (Grand Rapids, MI: Brazos, 2022), 43-44.

[9]I am indebted to Frederick Christian Bauerschmidt for his explanation of improvisation in "The Trinity," in *Gathered for the Journey: Moral Theology in Catholic Perspective*, ed. David Matzko McCarthy and M. Therese Lysaught (Grand Rapids, MI: Eerdmans, 2007), 82-86.

## 2—Beginning with Jesus

[1]Lisa Sowle Cahill, *Family: A Christian Social Perspective* (Minneapolis: Fortress, 2000), 29.

[2]Fleming Rutledge, *The Undoing of Death: Sermons for Holy Week and Easter* (Grand Rapids, MI: Eerdmans, 2002), 32-33.

[3]I owe this language for speaking about Jesus' consciousness to the teaching of Bishop Todd Hunter. I recommend his book *What Jesus Intended: Finding True Faith in the Rubble of Religion* (Downers Grove, IL: InterVarsity Press, 2023) for more.

[4]For more on this point, see Dorothy L. Sayers, *Are Women Human?*, new ed. (Grand Rapids, MI: Eerdmans, 2005).

[5]For more, see John H. Walton, *The Lost World of Genesis One* (Downers Grove, IL: IVP Academic, 2009), 66-70.

[6]For more, see John H. Walton, *The Lost World of Adam and Eve* (Downers Grove, IL: IVP Academic, 2015), 104-15.

[7]Ludwig Koehler and Walter Baumgartner, *The Hebrew and Aramaic Lexicon of the Old Testament* (Leiden, NL: Brill, 1994-2000), 1030, electronic ed.

[8]The language of "ontological equal" comes from Walton, *Lost World of Adam and Eve*, 109.

[9]Thanks to my colleague Aubrey Buster for helping me understand the grammatical, historical, and cultural context of Genesis 1-2 and its implications for interpretation.

### 3—God's Kingdom and God's Family

[1]Perpetua's diary and visions were collected, and the rest of her story recorded for posterity. What became known as *The Martyrdom of Perpetua and Felicity* was distributed in the early Christian community as an example of courage and source of encouragement. See "The Martyrdom of Perpetua and Felicitas," in *The Acts of the Christian Martyrs*, vol. 2, trans. Herbert A. Musurillo (Oxford: Oxford University Press, 2000).

[2]Here I am drawing on Albert M. Wolters and Michael Goheen in *Creation Regained: Biblical Basics for a Reformational Worldview*, 2nd ed. (Grand Rapids, MI: Eerdmans, 2005), 120-21.

[3]See Mt 4:19; 8:22; 9:9; 10:38; 16:24; 19:21, 28; Mk 1:17, 20; 2:14; 8:34; 10:21; 14:13; Lk 5:27; 9:23, 59; 14:27; 18:22; Jn 1:43; 8:12; 10:27; 12:26; 21:19, 22.

[4]See further C. René Padilla, *Mission Between the Times* (Carlisle, UK: Langham Monographs, 2013); George Eldon Ladd, *The Gospel of the Kingdom: Scriptural Studies in the Kingdom of God* (Grand Rapids, MI: Eerdmans, 1959); and Scot McKnight, *Kingdom Conspiracy: Returning to the Radical Mission of the Local Church* (Grand Rapids, MI: Brazos, 2014).

[5]I'm grateful to Willie James Jennings for the language of "joining." See *The Christian Imagination: Christian Theology and the Origins of Race* (New Haven, CT: Yale University Press, 2010).

[6]Jennings, *Christian Imagination*, 161.

[7]There was so much freedom for some that Paul himself felt the need to caution against going too far and impeding gospel proclamation among a culture deeply committed to such divisions.

[8]"The Holy Eucharist: Rite II," in *Book of Common Prayer* (New York: The Church Hymnal Corporation, 1979), 363.

234NOTES TO PAGES 59-71

9Willie James Jennings, *Acts*, Belief: A Theological Commentary on the Bible (Louisville, KY: Westminster John Knox, 2017), 39-40, 57-61.

10Amanda Martinez-Beck, *More of You* (Minneapolis: Broadleaf Books, 2022), 3.

11This point was inspired by a sermon from the Rev. Malcolm Foley that I can no longer locate online.

12Malcolm Foley, "Ought We Kiss the Hand That Smites Us?: Why Racial Violence Matters in Church History" (lecture, Mark A. Noll Annual Lecture in History of Christianity, Wheaton College, March 1, 2022).

13David E. Fitch, *Faithful Presence: Seven Disciplines That Shape the Church for Mission* (Downers Grove, IL: InterVarsity Press, 2016).

## 4—Family as Apprenticeship to Love

1The essential dignity of work for humanity is a cornerstone of Catholic social teaching, which has had a major impact on the way I think about family. See, for example, Pope John Paul II, *Laborem Exercens*, no. 9, and Pope Francis, *Laudato Si'*, nos. 127-28.

2Kathy Ferguson, *The Man Question: Visions of Subjectivity in Feminist Theory* (Berkeley: University of California Press, 1993), 7.

3On this point, Stanley Hauerwas is right again when he says, "For the church to be a community capable of sustaining the having and care of children, we must also be a people who are not bent on controlling our economic destinies." See "The Radical Hope in the Annunciation: Why Both Single and Married Christians Welcome Children," in *The Hauerwas Reader*, ed. John Berkman and Michael Cartwright (Durham, NC: Duke University Press, 2001), 517.

4Thomas Merton, *Love and Living*, ed. Naomi Burton Stone and Brother Patrick Hart (Orlando, FL: Harvest/HBJ Books, 1979), 27.

5M. Scott Peck, *The Road Less Traveled* (New York: Simon & Schuster, 1978), 81-84.

6George Hickenlooper, director, *Factory Girl* (Los Angeles: Lift Productions, 2006). The film's depiction of Andy Warhol is disappointing, but Sienna Miller's performance is brilliant.

7William G. Witt, *Icons of Christ: A Biblical and Systematic Theology for Women's Ordination* (Waco, TX: Baylor University Press, 2020), 11-37.

8One of the problems of looking backward, assuming all good things came before us, is that it stifles hope in the work of God today. Also, it usually requires the justification or whitewashing of evils from previous eras. As historian and theologian Justo González says, we must embrace "non-innocent" readings of history and face squarely where our ancestors failed to keep faith with Jesus Christ. This is not a graceless "canceling" but judicious *sifting*, as a friend likes to say: sifting out the sin and keeping the gold, silver, and precious stones. In every generation we can be assured that there's a good mixture of both, just like today.

9Dorothy Day, *The Duty of Delight: The Diaries of Dorothy Day*, abridged ed., ed. Robert Ellsberg (New York: Image Books, 2008), 530.

[10]David Wheeler-Reed, *Regulating Sex in the Roman Empire: Ideology, the Bible, and the Early Christians* (New Haven, CT: Yale University Press, 2017), 84-92.

[11]Wheeler-Reed, *Regulating Sex in the Roman Empire*, 98-101.

[12]Lisa Sowle Cahill, *Family: A Christian Social Perspective* (Minneapolis: Fortress, 2000), x-xi.

[13]See, for example: Bernard I. Murstein, *Love, Sex, and Marriage Through the Ages* (New York: Springer, 1974); Martin Daly and Margo Wilson, *Sex, Evolution, and Behavior* (Belmont, CA: Wadsworth, 1978); Pierre Van den Berghe, *Human Family Systems* (New York: Elsevier, 1979); Donald Symons, *The Evolution of Human Sexuality* (Oxford: Oxford University Press, 1979); and David Buss, *The Evolution of Desire: Strategies of Human Mating* (New York: Basic Books, 1994).

[14]I thought the phrase "eternal relationship of mutual inter-existence" came from Beth Felker Jones, *Practicing Christian Doctrine: An Introduction to Thinking and Living Theologically*, 2nd ed. (Grand Rapids, MI: Baker Academic, 2023), but I have been unable to locate the original source. Nevertheless, Jones offers a great introduction to orthodox trinitarianism.

[15]Peck, *Road Less Traveled*, 83.

[16]Willie James Jennings, *The Christian Imagination: Christian Theology and the Origins of Race* (New Haven, CT: Yale University Press, 2010), 161.

[17]bell hooks, *All About Love: New Visions* (New York: William Morrow, 2001), 54.

[18]Herbert Anderson and Susan B. W. Johnson, *Regarding Children: A New Respect for Childhood and Families*, Family Living in Pastoral Perspective (Louisville, KY: Westminster John Knox, 1994), 49-50.

[19]Anderson and Johnson, *Regarding Children*, 62-64.

[20]Anderson and Johnson, *Regarding Children*, 51-57.

[21]N. T. Wright, "What Is God's Future for the World?" (lecture, Fuller Forum at Fuller Theological Seminary, 2014).

[22]Don S. Browning et al., *From Culture Wars to Common Ground: Religion and the American Family Debate*, 2nd ed. (Louisville, KY: Westminster John Knox, 2000), 274. I first heard this point made by my friend Christin Fort in an unpublished lecture at Wheaton College.

[23]Sophia Tolstoy, *The Diaries of Sophia Tolstoy*, trans. Cathy Porter, ed. O. A. Golinenko et al. (New York: Random House, 1985), 441-42 (emphasis in original).

### 5—Families, Sin, and the Unjust Status Quo

[1]There is much to say about family tradition and how households might recognize, preserve, and draw on tradition in their life together. But the contours and content of such discussions will vary based on ethnicity, racialization, language, and socio-cultural setting. As a result, in this chapter I have chosen to focus primarily on the question of family trauma and its impact.

[2]Judith L. Herman, *Trauma and Recovery*, 4th ed. (New York: Basic Books, 2022), 48.

[3]Andrew Billingsley, *Climbing Jacob's Ladder: The Enduring Legacy of African-American Families* (New York: Simon & Schuster, 1992), 393.

[4]Jaime Inclan and Ernesto Ferran Jr., "Poverty, Politics, and Family Therapy: A Role for Systems Theory," in *The Social and Political Contexts of Family Therapy*, ed. Marsha Pravder Mirkin (Needham Heights, MA: Allyn & Bacon, 1990), 193-213.

[5]Cornelius Plantinga, *Not the Way It's Supposed to Be: A Breviary of Sin* (Grand Rapids, MI: Eerdmans, 1995), 10.

[6]C. René Padilla, *Mission Between the Times: Essays on the Kingdom*, rev. and updated ed. (Carlisle, UK: Langham Monographs, 2013), 31.

[7]For more on this problem, see my book *Quivering Families: The Quiverfull Movement and Evangelical Theology of the Family* (Minneapolis: Fortress, 2018), 209-20.

[8]Pope John Paul II, *Familiaris Consortio*, no. 21.

[9]Don S. Browning et al., *From Culture Wars to Common Ground: Religion and the American Family Debate*, 2nd ed. (Louisville, KY: Westminster John Knox, 2000), 70.

[10]Adrian Thatcher, *Theology and Families*, Challenges in Contemporary Theology (Oxford: Wiley-Blackwell, 2007), 166.

[11]Judith L. Herman, *Trauma and Recovery*, 4th ed. (New York: Basic Books, 2015), 33.

[12]Bessel van der Kolk, *The Body Keeps the Score: Brain, Mind, and Body in the Healing of Trauma* (New York: Penguin, 2014), 21.

[13]I am especially thankful to my friend Angela Cartagena for helping me to understand this and modeling how to proceed.

[14]Brian J. Miller and David B. Malone, "Race, Town, and Gown: A White Christian College and a White Suburb Address Race," *Journal of the Illinois State Historical Society* 112, no. 3 (Fall 2019): 293-316.

[15]Beryl Rawson, *The Family in Ancient Rome: New Perspectives* (Ithaca, NY: Cornell University Press, 1986), 8; Joyce E. Salisbury, *Perpetua's Passion: The Death and Memory of a Young Roman Woman* (New York: Routledge, 1997), 15.

[16]Thanks to my colleagues Nathan Luis Cartagena and Jordan Ryan for naming these realities and providing sources for better understanding the Spanish-American War and its impact.

### 6—Apprenticeship to Love in a Fallen World

[1]"Solitary, but Not Alone," *Denver Catholic*, March 28, 2016, https://denver catholic.org/franz-jagerstatter-solitary-but-not-alone/.

[2]See further Gordon Zahn, *In Solitary Witness: The Life and Death of Franz Jägerstätter*, rev. ed. (Springfield, IL: Templegate, 1986); Robert Anthony Krieg, trans., *Franz Jägerstätter: Letters and Writings from Prison* (Maryknoll, NY: Orbis Books, 2009). I also recommend *A Hidden Life* (2019), the stunningly beautiful film based on Jägerstätter's life, written and directed by Terrence Malick.

[3]Emmanuel M. Katongole, "Threatened with Resurrection: Martyrdom and Reconciliation in the World Church," in *Witness of the Body: The Past,*

*Present, and Future of Christian Martyrdom,* ed. Michael L. Budde and Karen Scott (Grand Rapids, MI: Eerdmans, 2011), 190-203.

4Augustine, *Confessions* 1.1.1.

5Dallas Willard has shared this axiom in many contexts. See, for instance, "Live Life to the Full," *Christian Herald* (UK), April 14, 2001, https://dwillard .org/resources/articles/live-life-to-the-full/. For more, see *The Great Omission: Reclaiming Jesus's Essential Teachings on Discipleship* (New York: HarperOne, 2006).

6David Matzko McCarthy, *The Good Life: Genuine Christianity for the Middle Class* (Eugene, OR: Cascade/Wipf & Stock, 2004), 84.

7C. René Padilla, *Mission Between the Times: Essays on the Kingdom* (Carlisle, UK: Langham Monographs, 2013), 69.

8Padilla, *Mission Between the Times,* 70.

9Rodney Clapp, *Families at the Crossroads: Beyond Traditional and Modern Options* (Downers Grove, IL: InterVarsity Press, 1993), 52.

10Padilla, *Mission Between the Times,* 69-70.

11Martin Luther King Jr., "The Three Evils of Society" (speech, National Conference for New Politics, Chicago, August 31, 1967). Thanks to Malcolm Foley for the language "demonic cycle of self-interest." For more, see Jonathan Tran's *Asian Americans and the Spirit of Racial Capitalism* (Oxford: Oxford University Press, 2021). Tran demonstrates that antiracist efforts predicated on racial identity alone without reference to the political economy of racial capitalism and "aftermarket exploitation" cannot bear fruit.

12Willie James Jennings, "Disfigurations in Christian Identity: Performing Identity as Theological Method," in *Lived Theology: New Perspectives on Method, Style, and Pedagogy,* ed. Charles Marsh et al. (Oxford: Oxford University Press, 2017), 67-85.

13See, for instance, *The Cape Town Commitment: A Confession of Faith and a Call to Action,* produced by the Third Lausanne Congress, 2010.

14Michael P. Guano, "Native Americans, Law, and Religion in America," *Oxford Research Encyclopedia,* November 20, 2017, https://doi.org/10.1093 /acrefore/9780199340378.013.140.

15Willie James Jennings, *After Whiteness: An Education in Belonging* (Grand Rapids, MI: Eerdmans, 2020), 6-10.

16Amy Laura Hall, *Conceiving Parenthood: American Protestantism and the Spirit of Reproduction* (Grand Rapids, MI: Eerdmans, 2008).

17One reason why it's so easy for families to get absorbed into the demonic system I've described is the created goods that families are meant to provide: protection, sustenance, progeny, and more. These are good things, but they too easily become excuses for exploitation of and violence against our fellow human beings. Jesus, the most brilliant human to ever live, knew all this well, which is why he warned against and subverted kinship loyalties, reorienting family around himself and his community of disciples. Jesus knew that God's kingdom requires a revolution in both mindset and practices surrounding family, and he knew just how difficult it would be to follow through because he did it himself—and he was tortured and executed for it.

## 7—Singleness and Marriage

[1] Leo Tolstoy's *Anna Karenina* famously begins, "All happy families are alike; each unhappy family is unhappy in its own way."

[2] Rob Reiner, director; William Goldman, screenplay, *The Princess Bride* (Santa Monica, CA: MGM Home Entertainment, 2000).

[3] Thanks to Al Hsu for bringing this point to my attention.

[4] Barry Danylak, *Singleness in God's Redemptive Story* (Altona, MB: Friesen, 2022).

[5] Pope John Paul II, *Familiaris Consortio*, no. 15; quoted by Al Hsu, *Singles at the Crossroads: A Fresh Perspective on Christian Singleness* (Downers Grove, IL: InterVarsity Press, 1997), 42.

[6] Hsu, *Singles at the Crossroads*, 38.

[7] Danielle Treweek, *The Meaning of Singleness: Retrieving an Eschatological Vision for the Contemporary Church* (Downers Grove, IL: IVP Academic, 2023), 43-62.

[8] There were notable exceptions, of course, such as Clement of Alexandria and Augustine. For more detail, see David G. Hunter, ed., *Marriage and Sexuality in Early Christianity*, Ad Fontes Early Christian Sources (Minneapolis: Fortress, 2018).

[9] My colleague George Kalantzis notes that an additional part of the problem is that Augustine understood the moment of (male) climax as an *ecstasis*, a loss of control and the faculties of will, which is also how sin operates in the human person (shared in private email correspondence, April 23, 2024).

[10] Scot McKnight, *The Blue Parakeet: Rethinking How You Read the Bible*, 2nd ed. (Grand Rapids, MI: Zondervan, 2018), 13.

[11] On this interpretive point, I find some precedence in African American Pauline hermeneutics, which is explored powerfully by Lisa M. Bowens in *African American Readings of Paul: Reception, Resistance & Transformation* (Grand Rapids, MI: Eerdmans, 2020).

[12] See, for instance, the story told by Stephanie Coontz in *Marriage, a History: How Love Conquered Marriage* (New York: Penguin Books, 2006).

[13] One of my favorite books to help toward such ends is John M. Gottman and Nan Silver, *Seven Principles for Making Marriage Work* (New York: Harmony Books, 2015).

[14] Thomas Aquinas, *Summa Theologiae*, Suppl. q. 45 a. 1.

[15] Stanley Hauerwas has repeated this maxim in many contexts, but the first published location might be "Sex and Politics: Bertrand Russell and 'Human Sexuality,'" *Christian Century*, April 19, 1978: 417-22.

[16] Don S. Browning et al., *From Culture Wars to Common Ground: Religion and the American Family Debate*, 2nd ed. (Louisville, KY: Westminster John Knox, 2000), 273-76.

## 8—Children and Childrearing

[1]W. H. Auden, "Mundus et Infans," *Commonweal*, October 30, 1942.

[2]Holly Taylor Coolman, *Parenting: The Complex and Beautiful Vocation of Raising Children* (Grand Rapids, MI: Baker Academic, 2023), 36-37 (emphasis mine).

[3]Haddon Wilmer and Keith J. White, *Entry Point: Towards Child Theology with Matthew 18* (South Woodford, UK: WTL, 2013), 71.

[4]In truth, even the concept of childhood is a social and cultural development that varies across the world.

[5]Arthur C. McGill, *Death and Life: An American Theology* (Minneapolis: Fortress, 1987), 83. My thinking about children and vulnerability first began to take shape in *Quivering Families: The Quiverfull Movement and Evangelical Theology of Family* (Minneapolis: Fortress, 2018), 125-67.

[6]For this reason, I am supportive of R. L. Stollar's project in *The Kingdom of Children: A Liberation Theology* (Grand Rapids, MI: Eerdmans, 2023).

[7]The photo was ubiquitous online in 2016, but you can see it in one location here: https://theworld.org/stories/2016-08-19/photographer-who-took-omrans-picture-aleppo-i-hope-all-photos-children-and.

[8]"Population Under Age 18," UNICEF, accessed January 17, 2023, https://data.unicef.org/how-many/how-many-children-are-in-the-world/.

[9]The school-to-prison pipeline is researched and discussed in many disciplines, including sociology, psychology, education, law, criminal justice, and public health. For an accessible introduction, see William Ayers et al., *Zero Tolerance: Resisting the Drive for Punishment in Our Schools* (New York: New Press, 2001), and more recently, Christopher A. Mallett, *The School-to-Prison Pipeline: A Comprehensive Assessment* (New York: Springer, 2015).

[10]Robert Gebeloff et al., "Childhood's Greatest Danger: The Data on Kids and Gun Violence," *New York Times*, December 14, 2022, www.nytimes.com/interactive/2022/12/14/magazine/gun-violence-children-data-statistics.html.

[11]Adrian Thatcher, *Theology and Families* (Oxford: Wiley-Blackwell, 2007), 166.

[12]This section is inspired by a conversation with my friend Aubrey Spears.

[13]Coolman, *Parenting*, 40.

[14]Coolman, *Parenting*, 37.

[15]Stanley Hauerwas, "Abortion, Theologically Understood," in *The Hauerwas Reader*, ed. John Berkman and Michael Cartwright (Durham, NC: Duke University Press, 2001), 619.

[16]Ben Sternke and Matt Tebbe, *Having the Mind of Christ: Eight Axioms to Cultivate a Robust Faith* (Downers Grove, IL: InterVarsity Press, 2021), 68-85.

[17]Saint John Chrysostom, "Homily 21: On Ephesians 6:1-4," in *On Marriage and Family Life*, trans. Catherine P. Roth and David Anderson, Popular Patristics Series (Crestwood, NY: St. Vladimir's Seminary Press, 2003), 68-69.

[18]Chrysostom, "Homily 21," 69.

[19]If I recall correctly, this question emerged as a wise focus for Christian families in conversation with our friends Nathan Luis and Angela Cartagena.

## 9—Families and Sabbath

[1]You can read more about this in Emily McGowin, "Surviving the Pandemic with Dungeons & Dragons," *The Week*, April 26, 2022, https://theweek.com/covid-19/1012946/surviving-the-pandemic-with-dungeons-dragons.

[2]Oliver Burkeman, *Four Thousand Weeks: Time Management for Mortals* (New York: Farrar, Straus, and Giroux, 2021), 185-201.

[3]"Headwaters," Water Education Foundation, accessed June 21, 2024, www.watereducation.org/aquapedia-background/headwaters.

[4]Walter Brueggemann, *Sabbath as Resistance: Saying No to the Culture of Now* (Louisville, KY: Westminster John Knox, 2014), 1-19.

[5]Brueggemann, *Sabbath as Resistance,* 34-45.

[6]Brueggemann, *Sabbath as Resistance,* 20-33.

[7]I'm grateful to my friend Nathan Luis Cartagena for helping me recognize this reality and put words to it.

[8]Marc Ramirez, "Americans Don't Sleep Enough. The Long-Term Effects Are Dire, Especially for Black People," *USA Today*, January 29, 2024, www.usatoday.com/story/news/nation/2024/01/29/poor-sleep-black-people-health-issues-racism/71480690007/.

[9]"Sleep Deprivation Makes Us Less Happy, More Anxious," *American Psychological Association*, December 21, 2023, www.apa.org/news/press/releases/2023/12/sleep-deprivation-anxious; Luke Andrews, "How Sleep-Deprived Is Your State?," *Daily Mail*, February 8, 2023, www.dailymail.co.uk/health/article-11724873/Sleep-deprived-America-laid-bare-Interactive-maps-40-Hawaiins-7hrs-night.html.

[10]Thanks, Mack Roller.

[11]Judith Shulevitz, "Bring Back the Sabbath," *New York Times Magazine,* March 2, 2003, www.nytimes.com/2003/03/02/magazine/bring-back-the-sabbath.html.

[12]Bonnie Miller-McLemore, *In the Midst of Chaos: Caring for Children as Spiritual Practice* (San Francisco: Jossey-Bass, 2007), 141.

[13]Emily Hunter McGowin, "Wonder and Theology," in *God and Wonder: Theology, Imagination, and the Arts*, ed. Emily Hunter McGowin and Jeffrey W. Barbeau (Eugene, OR: Cascade/Wipf & Stock, 2022), 3-8.

[14]Karl Barth, *Evangelical Theology: An Introduction*, trans. Grover Foley (New York: Holt, Rinehart and Winston, 1963), 71.

[15]Abraham Heschel, discussing the Hebrew prophets, says wonder "does not come to an end when knowledge is acquired; it is an attitude that never ceases," in *God in Search of Man: A Philosophy of Judaism* (New York: Farrar, Straus, and Giroux, 1983), 46.

[16]I talk more about this in my contribution to Kristen Page's delightful book *The Wonders of Creation: Learning Stewardship from Narnia and Middle-Earth* (Downers Grove, IL: IVP Academic, 2022), 116-24.

[17]*Book of Common Prayer* (New York: The Church Hymnal Corporation, 1979), 137.

[18]*Book of Common Prayer*, 124.

[19]Jared Patrick Boyd, *Imaginative Prayer: A Yearlong Guide for Your Child's Spiritual Formation* (Downers Grove, IL: InterVarsity Press, 2017).

[20]Another good resource is Douglas Kaine McKelvey's *Every Moment Holy: New Liturgies for Daily Life*, vol. 1 (Nashville: Rabbit Room, 2017).

[21]Brueggemann, *Sabbath as Resistance*, 1-19.

### 10—Families and Baptism

[1]Rowan Williams, *Being Christian: Baptism, Bible, Eucharist, Prayer* (Grand Rapids, MI: Eerdmans, 2014), 1-19.

[2]Some families participate in infant baptism while others are committed to believer's baptism. While both forms of baptism bear witness to the realities I've described, the time when baptism is administered does make a difference in practice. Those baptized as infants are included in the new covenant community based on their parents' and the church's profession of faith. Baptism, then, marks the beginning of their life of discipleship before they are even conscious of it. When they reach a more mature age, they will be given the chance to continue as Jesus' apprentice or not. Those baptized later when they can make their own profession of faith are included in the new covenant community through their personal testimony. The church then bears witness to their changed life and agrees to join with them in the discipleship journey. Baptism marks the conclusion of their conversion and begins their life as a formal member of the church, even if they may have been participating in the community for some time.

[3]Those of us who have ready access to clean running water may find it harder to recognize the significance of household washing and cleaning. Counterintuitively, the familiarity and ease of accessing water can make you unaware of the gift that water is. When water must be sought at a well in the mornings or evenings, when water must be rationed for drinking and only occasionally used for bathing, and when water must be boiled to eliminate contamination, you're suddenly more mindful of the practices of cleaning and bathing—their costliness and their value.

[4]U.S. Bureau of Labor Statistics, "Employment Characteristics of Families—2022," April 19, 2023, www.bls.gov/news.release/pdf/famee.pdf.

[5]Arlie Hochschild with Anne Machung, *The Second Shift: Working Parents and the Revolution at Home* (New York: Viking, 1989).

[6]Brother Lawrence, *The Practice of the Presence of God* (London: Epworth, n.d.), 9.

[7]Willie James Jennings, "Overcoming Racial Faith," *Divinity Magazine* (Spring 2015): 7-8.

[8]David Matzko McCarthy, *The Good Life: Genuine Christianity for the Middle Class* (Eugene, OR: Cascade/Wipf & Stock, 2004), 74.

[9]James K. A. Smith, *How to Inhabit Time: Understanding the Past, Facing the Future, Living Faithfully Now* (Grand Rapids, MI: Brazos, 2022), 19.

[10]Here I am drawing on Albert M. Wolters and Michael Goheen in *Creation Regained: Biblical Basics for a Reformational Worldview*, 2nd ed. (Grand Rapids, MI: Eerdmans, 2005), 121.

[11]McCarthy, *Good Life*, 89.

[12]The language "green growing years" comes from the Godly Play curriculum on the church year written by Jerome Berryman.

[13]Britta K. Wallbaum and Lindsey E. Goetz, *The Gospel Story Hymnal* (Aurora, IL: Word & Wonder Creative, 2024), is an excellent resource for this. Learn more at https://wordandwonder.org/about/hymnal/.

[14]InterVarsity Press has a lovely series, Fullness of Time, that walks through the major seasons of the year. Each volume is short and accessible, and I was happy to contribute the volume on Christmas. See Emily Hunter McGowin, *Christmas: The Season of Life and Light* (Downers Grove, IL: InterVarsity Press, 2023).

[15]Of course, Christians aren't the only ones who see remembering one's death as an important part of living well. Stoicism, for example, encourages *memento mori* toward a similar end. See the *Meditations* of Marcus Aurelius for more.

[16]Toshiko Kaneda and Carl Haub, "How Many People Have Ever Lived on Earth?," Population Reference Bureau, December 15, 2022, www.prb.org/articles/how-many-people-have-ever-lived-on-earth/.

### 11—Families and Eucharist

[1]Brant Pitre, *Jesus and the Jewish Roots of the Eucharist* (New York: Doubleday, 2016), 61.

[2]Pitre, *Jesus and the Jewish Roots of the Eucharist*, 72.

[3]Thanks to Fr. Kenneth Tanner for this insight.

[4]Robin Wall Kimmerer, *Braiding Sweetgrass: Indigenous Wisdom, Scientific Knowledge, and the Teachings of Plants* (Minneapolis: Milkweed Editions, 2013), 15.

[5]Wade Mullen, *Something's Not Right: Decoding the Hidden Tactics of Abuse and Freeing Yourself* (Carol Stream, IL: Tyndale Momentum, 2020), 142-47.

[6]Ronnie and I especially benefited from Jane Nelson's classic, *Positive Discipline*, revised and updated ed. (New York: Ballantine Books, 2011).

### Epilogue

[1]Ben Sternke and Matt Tebbe, *Having the Mind of Christ: Eight Axioms to Cultivate a Robust Faith* (Downers Grove, IL: InterVarsity Press, 2022), 3-7.

# General Index

abuse, 2, 8, 68-69, 91-95, 190, 210, 211
Adam and Eve, 14, 32, 45-48
apology (or apologizing), 209-10
apprenticeship (to love), 9, 76-84, 88,
    102-4, 105-9, 109-17, 120, 137-38,
    164, 167-68, 213-14, 231
    and baptism, 182-83, 241
    and children, 140-43, 153-55
    and church, 63-64
    and Eucharist, 199-202
    and the future, 217-18
    and healing, 94-95
    and homemaking, 183-89
    and hospitality, 204-6
    and marriage, 129, 134-36, 137-38
    and meals, 202-4
    and prayer, 176-79
    and reconciliation, 206-11
    and sabbath, 166-68, 168-72
    and singleness, 124-28, 137-38
    and storytelling, 189-93
    and timekeeping, 193-97
    and wonder, 173-76
Augustine, 105, 129-33, 238
baptism, 135, 176, 180-83, 185-86, 197
Bible. See Scripture
blueprint (or blueprints), 3, 6-7, 9-10,
    14-20, 24, 27-28, 29-31, 47, 82, 83,
    138, 176, 213-14
bodies (or body), 7, 18, 56, 57, 75, 77,
    78, 80, 111, 122, 126, 130-32, 147
    and healing, 93-95
    caring for, 68, 168-72, 183-86,
        186-87, 202
    as living sacrifice, 60-62
    of women, 78, 130-32
Book of Common Prayer (BCP), 76, 178,
    195, 233, 240
capitalism, 5, 101, 112-13, 116-17,
    126-27, 205, 237

children
    and abuse, 91-93, 94
    and church, 140-41, 149,
        152-55, 157
    and God, 151-52
    and Jesus, 143-46, 149-50
    as learning-teachers, 154-55
    as sacraments, 153-54
    and vulnerability, 146-51
childhood, 8, 75-76, 82-83, 93-95,
    146-47, 150, 235, 239
chores, 137-38, 184-86
church, 40-41, 51-52, 54-56, 126-27,
    135-36, 137, 234
    and children, 140-42, 152-55
    failures of, 3, 31, 63-64, 69-70, 72-73,
        98-100, 114, 149, 193
    formation in, 51, 104, 112, 141-42, 152
    Jews and Gentiles in, 55-57, 61-62,
        74, 191
    and the kingdom of God, 6-7, 10,
        53-55, 76, 216
    practices of, 56-60, 79-80, 117,
        127-28, 138, 158, 162-64, 168,
        180-82, 193-97, 199-202
    purpose of, 62, 63-64, 76, 216
church calendar, 193-97
colonialism, 2, 96
communion, 55, 67-68, 76-77, 82, 104,
    179, 203, 205, 207, 213
confession, 208-10
consumption (or consumerism), 17,
    67, 105, 112-13, 116-17, 120, 170-72,
    182, 205
Covid-19, 3, 31, 118-19, 212
creation, 4-5, 67, 90, 152, 164-66,
    179, 213
    care for, 175-76, 186-89, 213
    creatures in, 104, 113, 164, 168,
        175-76, 191, 195-96
    story of, 42-48, 134-35

# Scripture Index